# The Scottish National Covenant in its British Context

edited by
John Morrill

EDINBURGH UNIVERSITY PRESS

© Edinburgh University Press 1990
22 George Square, Edinburgh

Distributed in North America
by Columbia University Press
New York

Set in Alphacomp Garamond by
Pioneer Associates Ltd, Perthshire,
and printed in Great Britain by
Page Bros Ltd, Norwich

British Library Cataloguing
  in Publication Data
The National Covenant in
  its British context, 1638-51.
1. Scotland, history
I. Morrill, J. S. (John Stephen) *1946-*
941.106

ISBN 0 7486 0203 8

# CONTENTS

|  |  | |
|---|---|---|
|  | *Preface* | iv |
|  | *Acknowledgements* | v |
|  | *Contributors* | vi |
| One. | The National Covenant in its British Context<br>John Morrill | 1 |
| Two. | The 'Politick Christian': the theological background to the National Covenant<br>Margaret Steele | 31 |
| Three. | The Making of the National Covenant<br>Edward J. Cowan | 68 |
| Four. | The Scottish National Covenant and British Politics, 1638–1640<br>Peter Donald | 90 |
| Five. | The Scottish Constitution, 1638–1651. The Rise and Fall of Oligarchic Centralism<br>Allan J. Macinnes | 106 |
| Six. | Scotland turned Sweden: The Scottish Covenanters and the Military Revolution, 1638–1651<br>Edward M. Furgol | 134 |
| Seven. | Courtiers and Cavaliers: Service, Anglicization and Loyalty among the Royalist Nobility<br>Keith M. Brown | 155 |
| Eight. | Ireland and Scotland 1638–1648<br>M. Perceval-Maxwell | 193 |
|  | *Index* | 212 |

# PREFACE

This book celebrates the three hundred and fiftieth anniversary of the signing of the National Covenant in 1638, and originates from a conference held at the University of Edinburgh on 17 and 18 September 1988. Five of the papers given on that occasion are included here as Chapters 3, 4, 5, 6 and 8. Ill health prevented one of the essays deriving from the conference from being completed and the pressure of other commitments prevented another of the envisaged contributions from being included. I am grateful to Margaret Steele and Keith Brown for agreeing to write especially for this volume. They produced the excellent essays published here with exemplary dispatch. My own contribution has also been added to those given at the conference. All concerned hope that this volume, with three of its eight authors non-Scots and five of the eight teaching outside Scotland, should help to confirm that both Scottish history and the history of the British Isles as an entity – with all of the tensions and ambiguities inherent in that concept – are the proper concern of all those involved in the study of Western civilisation. The National Covenant came into being because Scots were confronted by a very specific set of challenges to their laws and to their religion. But many of the intellectual movements that shaped it had their origin and development outside Scotland; and its impact was to change the course of British history. This book should make us all more aware of its wider significance.

Selwyn College, Cambridge                                JOHN MORRILL

# ACKNOWLEDGEMENTS

I am grateful to Dr Michael Lynch for encouraging and persuading me to undertake the task of editing this book, and to Edinburgh University Press for their confidence in and efficient support of an author more diffident than is usual about the task in hand. (I am very well aware that a spell teaching at a Scottish university and a few years at an English university teaching a course entitled *England, Ireland, Scotland c.1534 – c.1707*, does not make me an honorary Scot. I have been associated throughout in planning and bringing this volume to press by the authors, three of whom have kindly discussed my own essay with me. I am also grateful to Jenny Wormald of St Hilda's College, Oxford and to David Smith and John Scally of Selwyn College, Cambridge for their help and comments.

# CONTRIBUTORS

Keith Brown is in the Department of Scottish History at the University of St Andrews.

E J Cowan is Professor of History at the University of Guelph, Ontario.

Peter Donald has followed a doctorate from Cambridge (1987) with a B.D. from New College, University of Edinburgh (1990).

Edward Furgol is the Curator of Naval History at the Navy Museum, Washington DC.

Allan Macinnes is Lecturer in the Department of Scottish History at the University of Glasgow.

John Morrill is Fellow and Senior Tutor of Selwyn College, University of Cambridge.

Michael Perceval-Maxwell is Professor of History at McGill University, Montreal.

Margaret Steele is Faculty Lecturer in the Department of History at McGill University, Montreal.

# One

## THE NATIONAL COVENANT IN ITS BRITISH CONTEXT

John Morrill

I

The signing of the National Covenant in February 1638 has always and rightly been recognised as an event of great importance in the history of Scotland. Like so many of the great 'constitutional documents' that shape the cultural identity of particular peoples, its ultimate importance lies as much in subsequent misrepresentations as in the retrievable historical reality of the purposes and aspirations of those who made it.[1] That said, no one seriously doubts that the National Covenant, of itself and in the bitter wars that were fought in the twenty years after its formulation to uphold and to export it, crystallised out a set of beliefs and practices that have determined the ecclesiastical and religious if not necessarily the political history of Scotland over the past three hundred and fifty years. But the Scottish National Covenant has been less well studied as a critical document in *British* history. English historians have noticed it in so far as it caused Charles I to lose control of his metropolitan kingdom but have seen it principally as an exogenous factor, a contingent and unpredictable happenstance that gave his critics a chance to halt his Personal Rule. Scottish historians have certainly noted its importance as an expression of national alarm at the effective subordination of Scotland to England through the Union of the Crowns. But the extent to which it went beyond being a little-Scotlander reflex to anglicisation (and angli*cani*sation) into representing a considered answer to the problems of multiple kingdoms in the early modern period remains much less fully considered. I would suggest that Scottish historians have considered the *English* context of the Covenant, but not the *British* context. This volume takes up that issue. It looks at the impact of the early covenanting movement on the whole of what John Pocock has called the Atlantic archipelago in the years during which the Covenant itself became established deep in the Scottish psyche. In this introductory chapter, I will seek to suggest that both the nature and the consequences of the Scottish National Covenant need a British context.

The central point I want to make can be neatly encapsulated in a study of the dramatically different Scottish coronations of Charles I and Charles II. The coronation of Charles I in the abbey church adjacent to Holyroodhouse in 1633 shows why the Scots needed a National Covenant; the coronation of his son at Scone in 1651 shows why the National Covenant failed. This essay will be framed by consideration of those two events.

II

Fifteenth- and sixteenth-century England was afflicted by an uncertain succession law which enabled the enthronement of a series of monarchs whose titles were open to challenge. In these circumstances, the importance of coronation and anointing took on particular significance. Fifteenth- and sixteenth-century Scotland saw few challenges to the house of Stewart. Each monarch left an heir of his or her body (and, almost as importantly, did not leave too many heirs); but one after another, the Stewarts died leaving the throne to a child. The result was that Scottish coronations, especially in the sixteenth century, were invariably rushed and improvised affairs through which a given faction sought to legitimise its kidnapping of an infant monarch. Charles I was crowned in the coronation robes of James IV[2] because he was the first Scottish monarch for one hundred and fifty years to ascend the throne as an adult.

The lack of any collective memory of how Scottish coronations were conducted may have made the way Charles chose to be crowned a shade less offensive to the Scottish nation. But only a shade. It represented the epitome of his indifference to Scottish sensibilities. It took place not at one of the two places where Scottish coronations normally had taken place (Scone or, more recently, Stirling) but in the abbey kirk of Holyrood.[3] Worse, the abbey kirk had been reordered for the occasion with the erection of a stage twenty-four foot square and 'railled aboute', at the east end of which, reached by a further flight of stairs, was a communion table.[4] One observer tells us:

> it is to be marked that there was a four-nooked taffil in manner of an *altar*, standing within the kirk, having standing thereupon

## The Covenant in its British Context

two books . . . with two chandlers and two wax candles, whilk were on light . . . . [A]t the back of the altar . . . there was a rich tapestry wherein the crucifix was curiously wrought, and as thir bishops who were in service past the crucifix, they were seen to bow their knee and beck.[5]

In iconophobic Scotland this was provocation indeed, and it is not surprising to find John Spalding commenting that it 'bred great fear of inbringing of popery.'[6] The Scottish bishops were all present at the coronation (if only to swear fealty) but they were in two distinct groups. John Spottiswoode, the archbishop of St Andrews, David Lindsay of Brechin, Adam Bellenden of Dunblane, Alexander Lindsay of Dunkeld, John Guthrie of Moray and John Maxwell of Ross all appeared on the dais 'with white rockets [rochets] and white sleeves and loops [?coops = copes] of gold, having blue silk to their foot'.[7] The other bishops, including Archbishop Lindsay of Glasgow, sat in the body of the kirk in their black gowns. (Did some or all of them refuse to wear the popish rags? Was the Scottish episcopate visibly split? It seems a question worth further investigation.)[8] If the physical spectacle which the Scottish elite encountered as it entered the kirk were not bad enough, the service could only confirm their worst fears. The coronation took place within the context of the Holy Communion service according to the rite of the English Prayer Book and appears to have been modelled closely on the English coronation of 1625,[9] while the coronation oath taken by Charles, although based on that prescribed by the Act of Parliament of 1567, added significantly to it. Charles swore to uphold 'the trew religions of Christe, nou preached and professed within this realme'; to rule 'according to the lawes and constitutions receaued within this realme'; and 'to preserve and keipe inviolated the preuilidges, rights and rents of the croune of Scotland, and not to transfer and alienat the same in aney sorte'. All these promises derive from the Act of 1567 and echo its precise wording. But Charles then added a fourth promise: 'to grant and preserue wnto ws of the clergie, and to the churches committed to our charge, all canonicall prewilidges; . . . and that you vill . . . defend [the] Bischopes, and the churches vnder ther governiment.' It is noticeable that this final and additional oath met a fuller and more emphatic response from the king.[10] In calling upon him to accept the abolition of episcopacy in 1639, the Covenanters sought not only to set aside a body of statute; they sought to make the king violate his coronation oath.[11]

At least he was crowned king of Scotland. Despite the presence of the eight English heralds and two English earls (Suffolk and Holland, in their capacities as Captains of the Gentlemen Pensioners and of the Yeomen of the Guard) in the coronation procession, and despite Laud's presence on the coronation dais (as Dean of the English Chapel Royal), this was an essentially Scottish event. Charles had not sought to be crowned as king of Britain back in 1625/6; his crowning in 1633 was exclusively as king of Scotland, and the gold and silver coins showered upon the commons as they stood around the entrance to the kirk at the king's exit bore the legend 'Carolus Dei Gratia, Scotia, Angl:, Fran: et Hyb: Rex'.[12] (This is significant, for since 1604 all coins in both kingdoms bore the legend 'Jacobus/Carolus DG Mag. Brit. Fra. et Hib. Rex'.) But it was small consolation. The Scottish elite were confronted by a king who cared nothing for their traditions, customs, values, even laws. In part this was an anglicised coronation; but, as we shall see, it is never possible to describe Charles's government straightforwardly as anglicisation, as colonial, as Unionist. There was a naked authoritarianism and a disregard for tradition which transcended or only partially involved an assertion of Englishness.

### III

In order to establish the British context of the National Covenant we must look back to the Union of the Crowns and to the trajectories of change that had become established in the generation before 1638. It was typical of James that he recognised the challenge and the opportunity to make more of the whole of Dual Monarchy than a sum of its parts. But it was also the story of his government of England that he let things drift and achieved little.

It is, however, difficult to establish the precise nature of that commitment to the Union of the kingdoms. Bruce Galloway and Brian Levack have recently and separately argued that James was more gradualistic than used to be thought, that he wished to proceed through a 'union of hearts and minds' and through a melding of peoples and cultures towards an eventual integration of the institutions.[13] But there is no reason to doubt that he was telling Robert Cecil the truth in a private letter of November 1604 in relation to the commission of the two Parliaments established to promote greater union. In it he expressed the hope that once a small start was made to 'this great work' by the commission, the two peoples, 'more ruled with shadows than substances' would come to see 'that the Union is already made', and that the commissioners had made such a pretty reference for the full accomplishment of all other points which fault of leisure could not now permit you to end as it may appear that working in this errand shall never be left off till it be fully accomplished. I mean specially by the uniting of both laws and parliaments of both the nations.[14]

This seems emphatic enough; and James had no reason to dissimulate to Cecil at that stage. If he was as clear about his target as this, he was all too quickly and totally dispirited by the hostility of the English Parliament in 1606/7 to the limited proposals relating to trade, nationality and the Borders. I suspect he had not adjusted to the very different conditions in his kingdoms. James, whose technique in Scotland was to put legislation onto the statute book and then frequently to delay enforcement until an opportune time, was too quickly discouraged at falling at what in Scotland would have been the lowest hurdle. He never recognised that in England monarchs had to work hard to get Acts passed, but then found that these Acts often enforced themselves. Dispirited by the setback in 1607, James permitted twenty years of drift.

Certainly James's ambitions shrank after 1607; but equally clearly the bitter memory of the small-mindedness of English M.P.s and the hankerings after a great uniting of his peoples remained with him to the end. The Star Chamber speech of 1616[15] and the Rubens ceiling for the Banqueting House[16] represent the negative and positive aspects of that lingering passion. There was, then, no move towards 'perfect Union' (a full integration of the institutions and laws respectful of the traditions and interests of both kingdoms); no move towards federal Union (the greater co-ordination of sovereign Parliaments, Councils etc); perhaps a creeping incorporative Union as the Scottish Council lost its deliberative function, becoming an ill-consulted executive body, and as more and more decisions affecting Scotland were made at the English court by a mixture of anglicised Scots and non-scottified Englishmen.[17] Indeed the most *British* thing to emerge by the 1630s was an Anglo-Scottish, *British* nobility, with English wives, English-educated sons and estates and offices on both sides of the Border. Keith Brown describes them vividly in Chapter 7. Edward Cowan has drawn attention to the fact that this group – in attesting the Cross Petition – actually described themselves as 'we British subjects', and sought a strengthening of the civil Union.[18]

There is no need to credit Charles with any Unionist vision. His father's fine words about the sum of his kingdoms being greater than the parts, about the ways each could learn from the other, about the merits of 'a perfect Union'[19] meant as little to him as did his father's recognition that politics was the art of the possible. Charles I may have had some policies that were common to all his kingdoms (the most obvious being the re-endowment of the Churches with sufficient of the lands plundered from them at the Reformation to allow them to plan their evangelisms free from lay control, and – concurrently – a determination to ensure that the laity lost all ability to interfere in ecclesiastical government),[20] but they were not a *British* policy. What is striking about Charles's policies towards Scotland is not anglicisation but a naked authoritarianism. Charles was an unimaginative man, who governed Scotland with a greater indifference to its laws, customs and traditions because he failed to study and to understand what those might be. The years, even decades, of drift did not, as far as I can determine, produce much systematic thinking and planning behind the scenes. One thing which is clear about Charles's government in the 1630s is that it was not based (as, arguably, English policy in Ireland regularly was) upon a clear sense of the relationship between the kingdoms, or upon any developed plan to alter that relationship.[21] Equally, the National Covenant, however much made necessary by absentee kingship, did not provide any remedy that took cognisance of the need to develop a Unionist (presumably federal Unionist) strategy for the future. The Covenanters seem to have considered that a king of Scotland, faced by the bonding of by far the greater part of their nobility and lairds, would have no capacity within Scotland to impose his will.[22] They seem not to have considered that Charles might use English and Irish resources to impose his will on the Scots. Only in 1639–41 did the covenanting leaders work out a British solution to their problem: extensive and feasible proposals for federal Union. Once worked out, these remained the essence of Scottish constitutionalism for the remainder of the century (and beyond). But the English never showed the slightest interest in federal Union. The Scots should have learnt their lesson in 1641 as the Long Parliament put the proposals for *conservatores pacis* on a back burner and turned off the heat.[23] At no point, even in 1639–40 while he still had reason to believe that he commanded events, does Charles I appear to have seen the solution to his Scottish problems to lie in an incorporative Union. He wanted a separate Scotland with weak institutions which he could control. It was left to the Rump of the Long Parliament and to Cromwell to articulate and to effect a ruthless subjugation and incorporation of Scotland. If the National Covenant is, then, to some extent a response to problems created by the Union of the Crowns, it did not, of itself, suggest a remedy to those problems.

IV

The National Covenant unquestionably arose from a whole series of challenges Charles had delivered to Scots religion, law and property.[24] But its *occasion* was the series of innovations Charles attempted in the government, discipline and practice of the Kirk. We need to look particularly at the ecclesiastical dimensions of Dual Monarchy.

It is odd that James's letter to Cecil in November 1604 should contain no reference to the Union of the Churches.[25] This is significant because after the failure of the limited Union legislation in 1607, the area in which James might be thought most effectively to have continued to work towards Union was in relation to the Churches (for example, in the English consecration of Scottish bishops in 1611 and in the Five Articles of Perth).[26]

James was quite capable of clumsily ignoring the right procedures and of permitting an apparent subordination of Scotland to England, as in issuing the mandate for the consecration of three Scottish bishops by four English diocesans under the Great Seal of England;[27] or as in instructing Archbishop Abbott to release Huntly from the excommunication declared by his kirk session when the earl had settled in London.[28] But these represented slipshodness, not calculation. In the case of Huntly, for example, the aim was not to override the authority of the Kirk, still less to allow the earl – a stubborn recusant – to take Holy Communion in the Church of England, but to protect him from the secular penalties of excommunication in English law so long as he resided south of the Border.[29] At heart, James remained a Scot and proud of it, telling the Scottish Council in 1617 of the 'salmonlyke instinct' that had drawn him back to where he had been spawned.[30] If he admired the reverence and richness of developed Anglican liturgy, he admired (as much as Elizabeth disparaged) preaching and sought to make good sermonising as ubiquitous in England as it was in (at any rate Lowland) Scotland. James's preoccupation was with developing mutual respect amongst his peoples, and in relation to religion this meant principally establishing the full catholicity of the two Churches. He sought to provide for each of his national Churches all those marks which their respective leaders believed to be necessary marks of all branches of the True and Visible Church. The English Church had been defective in its preaching; the Scottish Church was defective in that it lacked an apostolic succession. It was this desire to raise the status of the Scottish Church, not any attempt to subordinate it to the English Church, that surely explains the consecrations of 1611 (and the manner in which they were carried out).[31] This, too, may form part of the explanation of James's determined actions to restore the Scottish episcopate in the years 1596–1612. But that restoration cannot be seen principally as a prelude to Union of the Churches, either in the sense of their integration or of their federation. Scottish bishops remained very different from English ones. There is no evidence of any intention to move beyond episcopacy-in-presbytery. The bishops were to monitor and to supervise (but not to supplant) the authority of kirk session and presbytery as constant moderators, not as autocratic prelates with intrinsic power.[32] The restoration of Bishops probably had three primary purposes for James: first, to strengthen his control of Parliament;[33] secondly, to deliver a grievous blow to Melvillian political theory (when James said at the Hampton Court Conference 'no bishop, no king' he clearly did not mean no bishop, no monarchy, but no bishop, no effective secular ruler – the king being a royal eunuch waiting upon the orders of churchmen?);[34] thirdly, to give the Crown, through personally-appointed bishops, that very inspectorate without which his ignorance and impotence with regard to what was happening in the Scottish regions would be even greater. These were reasons enough why Scottish kings would always prefer a centralising episcopate to any kind of presbyterian ecclesiastical structure. Anglicisation need not be invoked as the primary reason for James's policies.[35]

In trying to find a term to describe James's policy towards the two Churches, I have struggled to capture some of these ambiguities. It is necessary to abandon notions of Union and uniformity; but also to recognise that James's knowledge of both Churches did inform his policy towards each of them. The best term I can come up with is *congruity*. James was concerned to make the two Churches more congruous, to remove, as it were, all 'hostile laws' from their relations, but not to plan either a merger of them or a takeover of the Northern Church by the Southern.

It is possible that Charles's policies might also be incorporated within this concept of congruity. Charles was a man concerned above all with *order*. In England and in Ireland, Laud's aim was less to impose new ceremonies and innovations than to compel all men to conformity with (an admittedly narrow) reading of the established liturgy, and where there were defects in ecclesiastical discipline to supply remedies through new canons. What mattered most to Charles in relation to Scotland was not to anglicanise its discipline and liturgy but to provide clear rules and to insist on uniformity of practice.[36] If Charles's method of introducing the Prayer Book represented foolhardy authoritarianism, it was based upon an inability to think in terms of Scottish law and custom, not upon a determination to subordinate Scotland to English ways. It showed a sheer lack of imagination and empathy. If he had tried to impose a new prayer book on *England* without consulting Parliament, Convocation, the Privy Council or (to quote John Row) 'even a conventicle of bishops and doctors', William Laud would have been amongst the first to shriek out at the violation of the rights of the Church.[37]

The Scottish canons[38] show a lack of concern with a narrow uniformity but a preoccupation with order: they may well have maintained an ominous silence about presbyteries and enjoined placing communion tables 'at the upper end of the chancel',[39] but they also laid down rules for ordination much more respectful of Scottish traditions than of English ones, and were clearly not based in any significant way on English models.[40] In their defence, Walter Balcanquhal (not without a certain disingenuousness) wrote that:

> because there was no booke extant containing any rules of such governement, so that neither the clergie nor laity had any certaine rule either of the one's power, or of the other's practice and obedience, and considering that the Acts of their General Assemblies were but written, and not printed, and so large and voluminous . . . we had them reduced to . . . such a paucitie of canons and those published.[41]

Well, yes and no. At least this suggests that there were good reasons for a king obsessed with order to impose canons. But his aim was to improve royal control and not English control of the Scottish Church.

In Charles's view, sinful man could best be brought to an inner obedience to the will of God by learning an outer conformity. As William Laud put it:

> It is true, the inward worship of the heart is the great service of God, and no service acceptable without it; but the external worship of God in His Church is the great witness to the world, that our heart stands right in that service of God . . . . Now, no external action in the world can be uniform without some ceremonies; and those in religion, the ancienter they be the better.[42]

These are sentiments shared in large part by several of the Scottish bishops, including Spottiswoode, who stated that

> In things indifferent we must always esteeme to be best and most seemly which seemeth so in the eyes of publike authority; neither is it for private men to control public judgments.[43]

And later that

> for matters of rite and government, my judgment is and hath been, that the most simple, decent, and humble rites should be chused, such as is the bowing of the knee in resaving the holy sacrament, and otheres of that kinde, prophanenesse being as dangerouse to religion as superstition.[44]

The Scottish Church certainly lacked the ordered liturgy that Charles craved. The Book of Common Order lacked statutory force; rather than prescribing a set form, it gave instruction on how to construct a liturgy and was admired by contemporary Scottish ministers precisely because, as Calderwood put it, 'none are tyed to the prayers of that book; but the prayers are set down as samplers.'[45]

Charles's explanation of his Scottish Prayer Book was both unambiguous and convincing. The Preface recalls the words of the Lords of the Congregation in 1559:

> Religion was not then placed in rites and gestures, nor men taken with the fancy of extemporary prayers. Sure, the Public Worship of God, being the most solemn action of us his poor creatures here below, ought to be performed by a Liturgy advisedly set and framed, and not according to the sudden and various fancies of men.[46]

Order, not uniformity with England, was intended. Walter Balcanquhal recalled James's growing concern at 'that diversitie, nay deformitie which was used in Scotland, where no set or publike forme of prayer was used' which had led him to start the process that led to the 1637 Liturgy. But Charles had taken special care to ensure such differences from the English Prayer Book

> as we had reason to thinke would best comply with the mindes and dispositions of our subjects of that Kingdome: for we supposing that they might have taken some offence, if we should have tendered them the English service book *totidem verbis*, and that some factious spirits would have endevoured to have misconstrued it as a badge of dependance of that church upon this of England.[47]

The Liturgy was based on the English one, 'so that the Roman party might not upbraid us with any weightie or materiall differences in our Liturgies.'[48]

I see no reason to doubt this description of Charles's *intentions*. For him, a want of order in worship and a lack of clear authority emanating from the Crown and exercised through the bishops cast doubts upon the catholicity of the Scottish Church in the same way that the lack of an apostolic priesthood in the Scottish Church or the want of a full preaching ministry in England had troubled his father. Once again, a concern with congruity might better account for Charles's policy than a concern with uniformity or anglicanisation.[49]

V

The National Covenant was at once a very precise and an infuriatingly imprecise document.[50] Although tedious, it is easy to understand; but it is horrifically difficult to interpret. It begins by recalling the 1581 Confession of Faith ('Negative Confession') subscribed by the king, his council and household, and 'by persons of all ranks', and resubscribed in 1590 'with a general band for the maintenance of the true religion and the King's person.' Half of the document is then taken up with the Negative Confession and with a list of all those Acts of Parliament which established true religion in Scotland and drove out popery, and the bulk of the rest with describing a 'general band to be made and subscribed by his Majesty's subjects, of all ranks, for two causes: one was, for defending the true religion [as defined above].... The other cause was for maintaining the King's Majesty, His Person and Estate.' Signatories would 'labour by all meanes lawfull to recover the purity and Liberty, as it was stablished and professed before ... the Innovations and evils contained in our Supplications, Complaints and Protestations.' In the meantime, they would forbear all 'novations, already introduced in the matters of the worship of God, or approbation of the corruptions of the publicke Government of the Kirk, or civil places and power of Kirkmen, till they be tryed & allowed in *free assemblies*, and in Parliaments.'[51] In relation to the king's power, 'we shall, to the uttermost of our power ... stand to the defence of our dread Soveraigne, the Kings majesty, his Person, and Authority, in the defence and preservation of the foresaid true Religion, Liberties and Lawes of the Kingdome.'

This Covenant represents a very specific and clear commitment to a particular form of evangelical Protestantism; if it only cross-refers to those royal ecclesiastical policies which constituted innovation, no one at the English court or anywhere in Scotland in 1637 can have been left in any doubt as to what was meant; and it is unambiguous on how those who subscribed it intended to render the king's will ineffective – by a campaign of corporate passive disobedience. The Covenant is infuriatingly unspecific about the fate of the bishops: was the office itself antithetical to the Negative Confession?[52] There is a menacing ambiguity by the reference to 'free' General Assemblies, implying that there had been unfree ones whose acts might be declared void. Indeed, predicating itself on the assumption that everything which could be construed as a violation of the Negative Confession of 1581 was null and void, it brought into question many Acts of both the General Assembly and of Parliament throughout the reigns of James VI and Charles I. This willingness to deny the force of the positive law of Scotland can be traced back to even earlier than 1581: at the General Assembly held in 1567, early in the civil war, the noble subscribers of the so-called 'Edinburgh Covenant' bound themselves to obstruct parliamentary legislation until 'the faithfull Kirk of Jesus Chryst profest within this realm salbe put in full libertie of the patrimonie of the Kirk... the matters of the Kirk forsaid be first considerit, approvit and establishit.'[53] This is echoed in the National Covenant and, while there is no reason to doubt that it was a yearning for presbyterian forms that lay behind these claims, it demonstrates a willingness to use arguments shocking in their implications for secular rulers. While it may demonstrate the immaturity of parliamentary institutions in Scotland, it also represents a willingness to challenge positive law which was not to be found in England until the Levellers. There is also silence in the Covenant over the civil grievances that most of those who subscribed the Covenant undoubtedly harboured. Perhaps above all there was silence about where their allegiance would lie if they had to choose between their 'dread Soveraigne' and 'the true Religion, Liberties and Lawes of the Kingdome.' Were they simply trying to avoid alienating their more timid supporters, avoiding giving the king an easy opportunity to call them traitors, or were they unable to recognise that they might have to choose? Similar problems of interpretation have flummoxed historians of the first eighteen months of the English Long Parliament.[54] My suggestion is that in the period between the attempted introduction of the Prayer Book and the signing of the Covenant, the leaders did not contemplate that choice. They had come up with a traditional Scottish remedy against a king pursuing an unpopular policy.[55] What the proponents of the National Covenant most obviously ignored was the possibility that Charles would use traditional *English* methods for dealing with a recalcitrant Scotland: if Henry VIII believed in Rough Wooing, then Charles I believed in Wife-Beating.

## VI

In this volume of essays, Margaret Steele, Edward Cowan, Peter Donald and Allan Macinnes all have important things to say on the issues I have raised in the preceding section. I just want to add a few more general points about the Covenant from the viewpoint of someone who has spent many years pondering the collapse of Charles's government in England.

When the Long Parliament met in 1640, it was the abuses of power by a particular monarch, not the whole system of government, that came under attack. The Grand Remonstrance was a critique of Charles's reign alone.[56] The National Covenant, by contrast, is a critique of a system of government. The drift towards popery and tyranny is specifically dated back to the reign of James VI, and even to Parliaments and General Assemblies which predated James's move to England.

The Covenant is no Grand Remonstrance in a second sense: its obsessive concern with religious issues. This has not stopped many commentators from arguing strongly and effectively that the covenanting *movement* was not primarily religious in character or purpose. This case rests, for me, less in a study of the document itself and in the apologias for it (as far as I can determine, almost all the apologias produced by the Covenanters[57] dwelt on the religious crusade; constitutional issues, if dealt with at all, were seen as a means to the end of securing true religion) than in the canards of opponents. (Canards are not always based on falsehood). Typically, when the Covenanters presented their articles of complaint against Laud to the Long Parliament, they categorically stated that 'novations in religion . . . are universally acknowledged to be the main cause of commotions in kingdoms and states, and are known to be the true cause of our present troubles.' Laud, in response, equally firmly ascribed 'the present troubles . . . [to] temporal discontents, and several ambitions of the great men, which have been long a-working.'[58] Someone closer to home, John Spalding, from his eyrie in Aberdeen, could observe that 'here you may see they began at religion as the ground of their quarrel, whereas their intention was only bent against the King's majesty and his royal prerogative.'[59]

It may be. And yet the *passivity* of the Scots prior to 1637; the rapidity with which revolt grew once the Prayer Book appeared; the clarity with which the threats to the Reformed Religion were articulated within the Covenant and the lack of clarity over threats to property and civil liberties; the absence throughout the succeeding period of any Scottish equivalent to the Grand Remonstrance; the lack of any large-scale campaign to prevent anything like the Act of Revocation or the Commission on Teinds for the future; all these things suggest that religion did matter most and was the ameliorating bond bringing together different groups, different interests. Behind the Covenant, of course, lay the Supplication and Complaint of October 1637, attested by 400 nobles and lairds, the representatives of 21 burghs and 120 ministers, the core of the future covenanting movement. *Its* content was exclusively concerned with the Prayer Book and the canons, which 'sowen the seeds of divers superstitions, idolatrie and false doctrine' and which 'ar imposed contrair to order or law appointed in this realme for establishing of maters ecclesiastick'. It ends with a more explicit challenge to the authority of those 'prelats, who have so farr abused ther credite with so gude a King as thus to insnare his subjects, rent our Kirk, undermynde religion.'[60]

If, as seems probable, those who organised the Supplication and then the Covenant had *assumed* that the King would have to give way to a people bonded and banded against him, then the self-sufficiency of the religious concessions demanded in the Supplication is striking. As I have already suggested, there is nothing in the Covenant which would lead to a redefinition of the Union, so that even if the Covenanting lords had gained control of the Scottish Council it would avail them little so long as Scottish policy was made elsewhere.[61] The Scots, unlike the English, could not expect to be able to promote remedial legislation in any parliament which might be called. There seems little reason to me to doubt that what they asked for was what they wanted.

VII

The sum total of what I have argued above is that the Scots had not yet seen their problem fully in British terms. A National Covenant, a bonding together of the Scottish nation, was an effective way of dealing with a Scottish king but not with a king of Britain.

The extent to which it *was* a 'National Covenant' in that sense can, of course be doubted: Keith Brown, in Chapter 7 of this volume, points out the amazing loyalty to Charles of the Scots who dwelt at the royal court; the Aberdeen region had to be coerced into acceptance;[62] John Spalding's account (albeit from the standpoint of one living in Aberdeen) was of the widespread use of intimidation needed to impose the Covenant in a much wider region.[63] Even if one does not believe that the Covenant was a self-consciously fudged compromise between those determined to be rid of bishops and those who wanted an end to innovation but who could see the benefits of a Jacobean ecclesiastical polity, one has to accept that by 1640 the unity of those who had subscribed in 1638 was severely eroded. No fewer than nineteen peers resident in Scotland signed the Cumbernauld Bond in August 1640, for example.[64] While the problem of collating attested copies of the Covenant is enormous[65] it is surprising that no attempt has been made to calculate precisely what proportion of the Scottish peerage and how many other men in certain defined groups failed to subscribe. (Given how much they owed to the monarchy in the past, and the extent to which recent policies had been directed at them, the Lords of Erection would be one obvious group; how many known to have served for the shires and burghs in past parliaments, how many ministers, *failed* to take the Covenant?)[66] There exist lists in the Hamilton Papers[67] and elsewhere of nobles '*pro Rege & contra Regem*' which divide them almost equally in half. One especially interesting list, transcribed into the Nalson Manuscripts, has 1 duke, 2 marquises, 23 earls, 5 viscounts, 11 barons (a total of 42 peers) *pro rege*, 22 earls, 1 viscount and 16 barons (a total of 39) *contra regem*. Even though a third of the loyalists were the court group discussed in this volume by Keith Brown, these are striking figures.[68] The pressure on all to subscribe (at least in the Lowlands) must have been enormous.[69] The appeals of the Aberdeen doctors to the acts of James VI against banding without royal licence, the self-contradictions they discovered in the formularies of the Covenant, the allegation that the Covenant made a 'perpetuall law concerning the externall rites of the Church' struck against the self-interest of most Scotsmen: but this does not mean that many of them did not stop and think.[70]

Nonetheless, we must conclude that the Covenant was, in aspiration and in effect, a document of the Scottish nation.[71] Most men took it and few resisted it. But was it a document *only* for and of the people of Scotland? Peter Donald argues in this volume and elsewhere that the English critics of Charles I's government took a keen interest in the Covenant and in the covenanting movement from early on. By the summer of 1639 we can uncover traces of quite close, furtive links between members of groups seeking to change the direction of English fiscal, ecclesiastical and foreign policies and the Covenanters, links which also had an Irish dimension.[72] By 1640, the Scots had clearly committed themselves to exporting the Covenant: to cleansing the Augean stables by diverting the waters of presbytery through the accumulated filth of

English prelacy. They now preached – as they had not done in 1637 and the first half of 1638[73] – that there could be no security for the Kirk so long as prelacy prospered in England or Ireland; and no security for the constitutional guarantees exacted in 1639 unless the king was bound by similar restraints in those other kingdoms. All this is well established.[74] Did this dawn on the Covenanters only with time? Everything we have seen so far would suggest as much. But there are some tantalising glimpses that suggest that secret contacts between the Scots and disaffected Englishmen might have predated the Covenant. William Laud, writing from the Tower once things had fallen apart, commenting on reactions to the Scottish Prayer Book, wrote:

> Then they grew up into a formal mutiny; and the Scottish subjects began to petition with arms, in their mouths first, and soon in their hands. His Majesty was often told, that *these northern commotions had their root in England* ... which was most true of a powerful faction in both.[75]

I cannot think of any strong reason why Laud would have needed to invent such an allegation. Although he offers no evidence, what he alleged is independently confirmed by John Spalding who wrote, *of pre-covenanting days* (after a discussion of the Balmerino affair, threats to the Lordships of Erection and to lay interest in teinds):

> whereupon followed a clandestine band drawn up, and subscribed secretly betwixt the malcontents, or rather malignants, of Scotland and England; that each one should concur and assist others while they got their wills both in church and policy, and so bring both kingdoms under one reformed religion, and to that effect to root out the bishops of both kingdoms, whereby His Majesty should loose one of his three estates, and likewise that they should draw the king to dispense with divers points of his royal prerogative, in such degree as he should not have arbitrary government, as all his predecessors ever had [and] conform to the established laws of both kingdoms.[76]

Although none of the English members of this 'clandestine band' are named, nine Scots are listed. The presence of Traquair and Lorne along with Rothes, Cassilis, Glencairn, Loudoun, Lindsay, Balmerino, and Cowper does not inspire confidence. Nor does the statement that the group was 'not without advice from the Marquis of Hamilton'. The list precedes a discussion of the offensive policies and is not necessarily a list of the 'clandestine band.' In a subsequent passage,[77] also about a period prior to the introduction of the Prayer Book, Spalding again speaks specifically of a 'privy meeting' convened by

Lorne and drawn from the same group 'and others, of whom the marquis of Hamilton was one, together with a menzie of miscontented persons' including (as ringleaders amongst the clergy) Alexander Henderson, David Dickson and Andrew Cant). This is a combination of highly plausible and highly implausible names and is worrying. It has led some historians to dismiss the whole story out of hand.[78] But can so firm and detailed an account constitute smoke without fire? I am troubled rather than convinced by these accounts. On the one hand, there clearly *were* clandestine contacts amongst members of the group Spalding names from 1634 on (as Rutherford's correspondence shows); the speed with which the Covenant was drawn up, disseminated and promoted is striking, as is the evidence of close collusion amongst most of those Spalding named in the course of 1638; above all, there is the evidence that Eleazor Borthwick was acting as an agent in England for leading Scottish malcontents even before the Covenant was signed.[79] Yet three things point another way. The first, which we have already examined, is the failure of the Covenant itself to propose solutions to the crisis in *British* terms; the second is that covenanting propaganda took so long to address an English audience on the need for reform in England; the third is that it was palpably Charles I himself who first treated his Scottish crisis as a British problem – indeed, the Covenanters can be seen scrambling in response to *his* broadening of the issues. Thus, within weeks of hearing about the Covenant, Charles was laying down contingency plans for a military invasion of Scotland by English and Irish troops;[80] the Scots did not begin to consider military preparations until they became aware of Charles's plans.[81] Similarly, it was Charles who saw the challenge to episcopacy in Scotland as undermining the authority of the Bishops (as an Estate in Parliament and as a separate order within the Church).[82]

Early Scots propaganda played down both English responsibility both for their plight and denied that the Covenant had implications for England. The 1637 *Petition of the Noblemen, Barons, Ministers, Burgesses and Commons* against the canons and Prayer Book not only found in the latter

> the seeds of divers superstitions, Idolatrie, and false doctrine . . . but also the Service Booke of England is abused, especially in the matter of communion, by additions, subtractions, interchanging of words . . . to the disadvantage of Reformation as the Romish Masse is, in the more substantial points, made up therein . . . for reversing the gracious intention of the blessed reformers of Religion in England.[83]

Thus there was no need to intervene in English affairs. The Covenanters' *Answer to the Profession and Declaration Made by James, Marquis of Hamilton*, issued as late as December 1638, contained the following assurance:

> We doe not meddle with the Kirks of England or Ireland . . . all our argument and proceedings being for the Kirk of Scotland, where, from the time of her more pure Reformation than of her sister kirks, Episcopacie heth been ever abolished, till the latter time of corruption . . . .[84]

Not only was the Covenant non-exportable, but the problem was perceived in Scottish terms. It was the fault of the prelatical cuckoos in the presbyterian nest; it was their reintrusion via packed and improperly-constituted General Assemblies that had created the problem. As Andrew Cant and his colleagues toured Scotland in 1638 explaining and justifying the Covenant, the account they gave of the coming of the Troubles was an internal history of Scotland since 1596. Not once, in his sermons at St Andrews, Inverness, Glasgow or Edinburgh, did Cant blame the English.[85] The nearest he came was at Glasgow, where he appealed to his congregation to think on the sufferings of the poor Scots in Ireland, under the lash of 'the proud prelates' there.[86] More typical is his narration at Inverness of how God had singled out Scotland, 'a dark, obscure island, inferior to many' and 'planted a vineyard there' so that other nations 'had more of antichrist than she, she more of Christ than they'. Recently, however, 'Satan envied our happiness, brake our ranks, poisoned our fountains, muddied and defiled our streams; and while the watchmen slept, the wicked one sowed his tares.'[87]

Even the angriest and fiercest of the apologists for the Covenant in 1637, George Gillespie, while he scorned Hooker and other 'English formalists' for their errors, did not see the problem of Scotland in 1637 in British terms. The nearest he comes is in this passage:

> It is not this day feared, but felt, that the rotten dreggs of poperie, which were never purged away from England and Ireland, and having once been spewed out with detestation, are licked up again in Scotland, prove to be the unhappy occasions of a woeful recidivation . . . What doleful and disastrous mutation . . . hath happened to the Church and spouse of Christ in these dominions? Her comely countenance is miscoloured with the fading lustre of the mother of harlotts; her shamefaced forehead hath received the mark of the Beast; her lovely-locks are frizled with the crisping pins of antichristian fashions; her chaste ears

are made to listen to the friends of the great Whore, who bring
the bewitching doctrine of enchanting traditions; her dove eyes
looke pleasantly upon the well-attired harlot; her sweet voice is
mumming and muttering some missall and magical liturgies;
her fair necke beareth the halter-like tokens of her former
captivity, even a burdensome chain of superfluous and
superstitious ceremonies . . . Oh transformed virgin![88]

The blame for the many innovations – those 'best wares which the big hulk of conformity, favoured by the prosperous gale of mighty authority, hath imported upon us' – is very indirect.[89]

As late as February 1639, the Scots could deny anglicisation as the root of their problem. Rather than claiming that an anglicised worship was being rammed down their throats, they claimed that Scotland was being used as a laboratory for experimental liturgies:

The churchmen of greatest power in England . . . sent down to
their associats the pretended Arch-bishops and Bishops of this
Kingdome, to bee printed and pressed upon the whole Church
here, without order or consent as the only forme of divine
worship and government of the Church, to make us a leading
case to England.[90]

But this document does represent a first shift: it was Englishmen (specifically and exclusively Churchmen) who were to blame for the Scottish Troubles. A strengthening sense of the antichristian nature of the episcopal office (one can see this strengthening and clarifying in the minds of writers like Baillie), which clearly had implications for Scottish attitudes to those national churches which retained bishops, combined with an ever greater recognition that the Scottish bishops were but the tools and instruments of the English hierarchy. These are features of the propaganda in late 1639 and 1640. There is no language before April 1640 to match the fury of Robert Baillie's *The Canterburian's Self-Conviction*, in which he alleged that Laud and his 'dependencies' intended to substitute the Mass for the Bible, the laws of Castile for Magna Carta, and to send nobility and gentry to the chain-gangs of Peru or the galleys of the Mediterranean.[91] And, in comparison with the examples cited above from 1638, the blame is squarely removed to England, 'to the Prelacy in England, the fountaine whence all the Babylonish streams issued unto us'. The Scots had come to realise that they needed to trace the streams of corruption back to their source south of the Border.[92] From then on, as Peter Donald, Conrad Russell, David Stevenson and others have amply shown, the Scots determined both to seize the military initiative from Charles and to ensure that antichristian bishops were removed and godly order and discipline established throughout the king's dominions.[93]

### VIII

In the event, of course, as this volume amply demonstrates, the struggle for the Covenant led inexorably on to the War of Three Kingdoms, in which the affairs of each became inextricably bound up with the affairs of the others. English and Irish troops were called upon to impose the king's will in Scotland;[94] the defeat of those armies brought a Scots invasion of England and direct intervention by the Scots in the settlement of England in 1641;[95] the Irish Rebellion in November of that year speedily brought Scottish as well as English armies into Ulster and Leinster;[96] the Scots invaded England again in 1643, provoked in large part by the king's machinations in Ireland;[97] and a crucial dimension of the campaigns of Montrose in 1644-5 was the renewed interest of Ulster Macdonnells in their ancestral lands in the west of Scotland.[98] Scottish disaffection with their English allies, culminating in the Engagement, was inflamed by the latter's betrayal of the interests of the Scots in Ulster. By 1648, most of those involved in public affairs in Scotland recognised that there could be no security for Scotland unless a federal constitution and a uniformity of religion had been achieved in all three kingdoms.[99] In 1641, in the Solemn League and Covenant of 1643, in the peace negotiations at Uxbridge and Newcastle, Scots proposals for ecclesiastical unity and mechanisms for co-ordinating the governments at least of England and Scotland were at the fore. But as, north of the Border, the conditions for constitutional cohabitation became clearer and clearer, so in England, indifference to a formal arrangement turned to hostility. The Long Parliament deferred discussion of the Eighth article of the Treaty of London,[100] dragged its feet over the appointment of *conservatores pacis* in 1643-5, unilaterally shut down the Committee of Both Kingdoms, tampered with the ecclesiastical proposals produced by the (Anglo-Scottish) Westminster Assembly without consulting their partners,[101] and, under pressure from the army, paved the way for religious toleration in 1647.[102] This was indifference more than malice. When the Scots Engagers invaded England in 1648, Cromwell chased them out and moved north to Edinburgh in the aftermath of the battle of Preston. But neither Parliament nor the generals had any stomach for an occupation or conquest of Scotland. Cromwell was delighted when a putsch by Argyll restored power to the anti-Engagers, and was happy to leave them in charge.[103] The English had still to work out a British policy. But while the Scots might agree on the necessity of federal Union, they were split about how best to achieve it. By the spring of 1648, the covenanting movement, which, despite the Monstrose schism, was still substantially intact, was sundered. Over the next three years it disintegrated into fragments as disaster followed disaster and as unpalatable solutions to intractable difficulties presented themselves: Engagers, Whiggamores, Resolutioners, Remonstrants, Protesters – so many possible responses to events in England.[104]

## IX

The coronation of Charles II at Scone on 1 January 1651 brings home the transformations of the years since 1637.[105] After the grim harangue from the Moderator of the General Assembly, during which Charles was both reminded of the public shortcomings and private vices of his predecessors, and given a lecture in political thought that Buchanan would have been proud of, Charles took the Covenants, was acclaimed, took the coronation oath, and was crowned.[106] Two aspects of the ceremony sum up my argument. The first is that Charles was being crowned as head of a faction, not a nation: in no way could anyone delude themselves that the nation was united behind the imposition of the Covenants on this manifestly unworthy and unbelieving king. The second is that those who imposed the National Covenant and the Solemn League and Covenant upon him no longer believed that this was or could be simply a Scottish monarch. The words with which Charles took the Covenants are revealing indeed:

> I Charles, King of Great Britain, France and Ireland, do assure and declare, by my solemn Oath, in the presence of Almighty God, the searcher of hearts, my allowance and approbation of the Nationall Covenant and of the Solemn League and Covenant above written, and faithfully obliege myself, to prosecute the ends thereof . . . and that I shall give my royal assent to acts and ordinances of parliament passed, or to be passed, enjoining the same in my other dominions.[107]

This was no less than sticking by the commitment to British monarchy demonstrated in the solemn proclamation of Charles II as king of Great Britain, France and Ireland by Chancellor Loudoun on behalf of the Scottish government on 5 February 1649, the day news of Charles I's execution reached Edinburgh.[108] While the English had not consulted the Scots over the trial and execution of Charles I, the

Rump's Ordinance abolishing monarchy had referred to England and Ireland, but had pointedly avoided any reference to Scotland.[109] The decision in Edinburgh to declare Charles king not only of Scotland but of Britain was provocation indeed.[110]

Thus, if the coronation of Charles I taught the Scots the need to covenant together against an authoritarian, unfeeling, foreign king, the coronation of Charles II showed that the price to be paid for the struggle against that king was a double denial of the National Covenant: no longer a covenant of all the nation, neither was it a document exclusively for that nation.

NOTES

I am grateful to Peter Donald, John Scally and David Smith for their comments on and criticisms of drafts of this article.

1. See D. Stevenson, *The Covenanters: the National Covenant in Scotland* (Saltire Society, 1988), pp.70–84 for a cool evaluation of its legacy; J. C. Johnson, *Treasury of the Scottish Covenant* (1887) for a cross-section of the myths.
2. J. Haig, ed., *The Historical Works of Sir James Balfour* (4 vols, Edinburgh, 1825), IV, 396; C. Rogers, ed., *The Earl of Stirling's register of Royal Letters . . . 1615–1635* (2 vols., Edinburgh, 1885), I, 660.
3. Charles seems to have been wilfully ignorant on this point. He could write in 1626 to the Scottish Council, ordering the repair of the abbey kirk, and describing it as 'the buriall place of some of our royall antecessours, and the usuall place for the solemnitie of coronatiouns. (*Stirling's register*, I, 96–7). Four years later he asked the Council to choose between St Giles and the abbey kirk (*ibid.*, II, 416–17). I am grateful to John Scally for these references.
4. *Works of Balfour*, IV, 384.
5. J. Spalding, *History of the Troubles and Memorable Transactions in Scotland from the years 1624 to 1645* (2 vols., Aberdeen, 1792), I, 23. The reasons why this was such an affront can be found by comparing this extract with the discussion in G. B. Burnett, *The Holy Communion in the Reformed Church of Scotland* (Edinburgh, 1960), esp. pp.25–43, 64–87. See also W. Forbes-Leith, *Memoirs of the Scottish Catholics* (2 vols, 1909), I, 162–4.
6. Spalding, *History of Troubles*, I, 23.
7. *Ibid.*
8. A later anecdote, quoted by John Rushworth, points in the same direction, though its authenticity must be suspect. Rushworth

has Laud sneer at Archbishop Lindsay of Glasgow as he attended the king, 'are you a churchman and wants the coat of your order?' (cited in J. K. Hewison, *The Covenanters* (2 vols, Edinburgh, 1908), I, 219.
9. For the English coronation of 1625, see Sir William Sanderson, *The Compleat History of the Life and Raigne of King Charles* ... (1658), pp.25–7.
10. The wording of this additional clause closely echoes that of Charles's addition to his *English* coronation oath: Sanderson, *Compleat History*, p.27.
11. The text of the coronation oath is printed in *Works of Balfour* IV, 392–3. The 1567 Act is in *The Acts of the Parliament of Scotland*, (12 vols, 1814) III, 23–4. This oath was created by Act *following* James's coronation at Stirling. For an interesting account of that coronation, see Hewison, *Covenanters*, I, 66–7.
12. *Historical Works of Balfour*, IV, 405.
13. B. Galloway, *The Union of England and Scotland, 1603–1608* (Edinburgh, 1986), esp. pp. 15–16, 165–6; B. P. Levack, *The Formation of the British State* (Oxford, 1987), esp. pp.7–8.
14. *HMC Salisbury* XVI, 362–4.
15. C. H. McIlwain, ed., *The Political Works of James I* (Cambridge, Mass., 1918), pp.329–32.
16. G. Parry, *The Golden Age Restored* (Manchester, 1981), pp.32–7.
17. But, contrary to a common misapprehension, there was no formal Scottish Committee of the English Privy Council until 1638.
18. Edward J. Cowan, 'The Union of the Crowns and the Crisis of the constitution in 17th century Scotland', in S. Dyrvik, K. Myklund, J. Oldervoll, eds, *The Satellite State in the 17th and 18th centuries* (Oslo, 1980), p.131.
19. As in the opening speech to his first Parliament, McIlwain, *Political Works*, pp.269–80.
20. For the Laudian programme in England, Ireland and Scotland on these issues, see W. Scott and J. Bliss, eds, *The Works of William Laud* (7 vols, 1847–60), III, 253; IV, 176–7, 299–304; and numerous letters in VI and VII. See the encomium of English secretary of state Coke on Laud at the latter's installation as Chancellor of Oxford University: 'this worthy prelate maketh it his chief work to recover to the church for the furtherance of God's service what may be restored ... under his majesty's great and powerful order, not [in] England alone, but Scotland and Ireland', V, 128. See also [W. Balcanquhal], *A Large Declaration* (1639), esp. pp.8, 424. For England, see C. Hill, *The Economic Problems of the Church* (Oxford, 1956), esp. pp.307–36; for Ireland, see H. F. Kearney, *Strafford in Ireland* (Manchester, 1959), pp.122–9. For Scotland, M. Lee, *The Road to Revolution:*

*Scotland Under Charles I, 1625-1637* (Urbana, 1985), pp.44-62 is the clearest account we have until Allan Macinnes's major study of the effects of the Revocation fracas is published.

21. For Wentworth's determined plans to anglicise Scotland, cold-shouldered by Charles, see T. Knowler, *The Earl of Strafford's Letters and Despatches* (2 vols, Dublin, 1740), ii, 190-2.
22. For the history and significance of Bonding in Stewart History, see J. Wormald, *Lands and Men in Scotland: Bonds of Manrent, 1442-1603* (Edinburgh, 1985); K. M. Brown, *Bloodfeud in Scotland, 1583-1625* (Edinburgh, 1986). For the theological background, see the present volume, Chapter 2.
23. P. Donald, 'The King and the Scottish Troubles, 1637-1641', University of Cambridge Ph.D. thesis (1988), ch. 6; C. L. Hamilton, 'The Anglo-Scottish Negotiations', 1640-1', *Sc.H.R.*, xli (1962), 84-96.
24. For some introductions to this vast topic, see M. Lee, *The Road to Revolution: Scotland Under Charles I, 1625-37* (Urbana and Chicago, 1985), pp.43-249; D. Stevenson, *The Scottish Revolution 1637-1644: the Triumph of the Covenanters* (Newton Abbott, 1973), pp.29-55.
25. *HMC Salisbury*, XVI, 363-4.
26. J. Spottiswoode, *History of the Church of Scotland* (1655), pp.528-40 gives the core texts; M. Lee, *Government By Pen: Scotland Under King James VI and I* (Urbana, 1980), pp.170-189 offers a clear account; and D. G. Mullan, *Episcopacy in Scotland: The History of an Idea, 1560-1637* (Edinburgh, 1986), pp.152-62 is an interesting gloss; I. A. Dunlop, 'The Polity of the Scottish Church 1600-1637', *Rec.Sc.Ch.Hist.Soc.*, XII (1958), 162-182; I. B. Cowan, 'The Five Articles of Perth', in D. Shaw, ed., *Reformation and Revolution* (Edinburgh, 1967), pp.160-77; P. H. R. Mackay, 'The Reception Given to the Five Articles of Perth', *Rec.Sc.Ch.Hist.Soc.*, XIX (1973), 185-201.
27. A. I. Dunlop, 'John Spottiswoode, 1565-1639' in R. S. Wright, ed., *Fathers of the Kirk* (Oxford, 1960), p.53. It is ironic that James should casually proceed by English letters patent after he had taken such pains to ensure that no claim to jurisdiction was implied: neither archbishop and no bishop of the Northern Province – which had historically laid claim to jurisdiction over Scotland – was permitted to attend, let alone take part in, the consecration. For James's reasons for these consecrations, see below, pp.8-9.
28. Spottiswoode, *History*, pp.525-8. The emollient letter of explanation from Abbott to Spottiswoode contained in this account makes clear that no jurisdiction within Scotland was implied: the order merely released Huntly from the penalties of excommunication in England so long as he resided there. But it was a tactless act by James, nonetheless.

## The Covenant in its British Context

29. Spottiswoode, *History*, pp.525-8.
30. *Register of the Privy Council of Scotland*, 2nd ser., X, 685.
31. For a discussion of notions of catholicity and visibility in the early Stuart Church, see A. Milton, 'The Laudians and the Church of Rome', University of Cambridge Ph.D. thesis (1989) esp. chs 2 and 6.
32. For an emphasis on continuity rather than discontinuity in the early seventeenth century, see W. R. Foster, *The Church before the Covenant* (Edinburgh, 1975) and 'The Operation of the Presbyteries in Scotland, 1600-1638' in *Rec.Sc.Ch.Hist.Soc.*, (1964), 21-33.
33. James restored their parliamentary titles in 1596 before attempting anything else.
34. For James's remark, see D. H. Willson, *King James VI and I* (London, 1956), p.207 for a full transcript of James's speech which gives the context for James's remark.
35. This extends the discussion in Mullan, *Episcopacy in Scotland*, pp.98-103, 122-3.
36. G. Donaldson, *The Making of the Scottish Prayer Book of 1637* (Edinburgh, 1954) remains the best account, superceding and incorporating all others. Lee, *Road to Revolution*, pp.184-222 is a useful summary.
37. Lee, *Road to Revolution*, pp.201-4 is the most forthright writer on the inanity of Charles's methods. For John Row's comment, see his *History of the Kirk of Scotland from 1558 to 1637*, ed. D. Laing (Wodrow Society, 1842), p.394. Charles did of course consult what he (disingenuously) referred to as the 'representative body of the church', i.e. *some* of the bishops; but he did so individually and not (Row's point) in conclave; and not all of them.
38. The canons are in *Works of William Laud*, V, 583-607.
39. Curiously this went further than in England where the placing of the communion table in each church was left to the discretion of the ordinary (which led in many cases, even in Laud's diocese, to an order placing it elsewhere than at the east end); see Julian Davies, *The Caroline Captivity of the Church* (Oxford, forthcoming), ch. 4. But note that the Scottish canon did not insist on (or mention) the railing-in of the Holy Table, something Laud was more insistent on in England.
40. The canons (and the Prayer Book) are discussed at much greater length in my paper 'Ecclesiastical Imperialism under the early Stuarts', forthcoming.
41. *A Large Declaration*, pp.44-5.
42. *The Works of William Laud*, II, xvi (from the Epistle Dedicatory to *A Relation of the Conference ... with Mr Fisher the Jesuit*, and cited in W. H. Hutton, *Archbishop Laud* [1900], pp.69-70.)
43. Quoted in G. Gillespie, *A Dispute Against the English Popish Ceremonies Obtruded on the Church of Scotland* (1637), p.2.

44. Quoted in M. Ash, 'Dairsie and Archbishop Spottiswoode', *Rec.Sc.Ch.Hist.Soc.* XIX (1976), 131. This article also describes the crucifixes, east-end altar with kneelers, and chancel screen which Spottiswoode installed in the church he built in his home parish.
45. See the excellent discussion in Hewison, *Covenanters*, I, 43-5.
46. G. Donaldson, *The Making of the Scottish Prayer Book of 1637* (Edinburgh, 1954), p.102.
47. *A Large Declaration*, p.18.
48. *Ibid.*; Donaldson, *Making*, p.102.
49. If space permitted, I would argue that the history of the High Commission and of the Scottish Ordinal make the same point. See Morrill, 'Ecclesiastical Imperialism', forthcoming. See also G. I. R. McMahon, 'The Scottish Court of High Commission, 1610-38' *Rec.Sc.Ch.Hist.Soc.*, XV (1966), pp.195-209.
50. I have relied upon the text in G. Donaldson and W. C. Dickenson, *A Source Book of Scottish History* (3 vols), III, 95-104, which derives its text from *The Acts of the Parliament of Scotland*, V, 272-6. For an especially helpful discussion of the bibliography of the Covenant see Stevenson, *The Covenanters, passim*. There are especially stimulating commentaries in W. Makey, *The Church of the Covenant* (Edinburgh, 1979), pp.26-31; D. Stevenson, 'The Early Covenanters and the Federal Union of Britain' in R. Mason, ed., *Scotland and England* (Edinburgh, 1987), pp.163-81; and A. Williamson, *Scottish National Consciousness in the Reign of James VI* (Edinburgh, 1979), ch. 7. For a fuller analysis of the Covenant, especially in its theological context, see this volume, Chapter 2.
51. Emphasis added, see this volume, pp.48-53.
52. This needs far fuller treatment than it can receive here or than it receives elsewhere in the book. Many of the conundrums are solved in Peter Donald, 'King and the Troubles'; ch. 2 admirably sums up thus: 'The protest movement, of which the convinced presbyterians were only a part, came instead fairly quickly to attack the bishops, because they were seen to represent an ill-liked manner of government in church and state, and furthermore because the true religion was threatened through them' (p.79).
53. J. K. Hewison, *The Covenanters* (2 vols, Glasgow, 1908), I, 68.
54. Morrill, 'Charles I, Tyranny and the Origins of the English Civil War' in ed. W. Lamont, *Religion, Resistance and Civil War* (Proc. of the Folger Institute Center of the History of British Political Thought, 6 vols., 1990) III, pp.95-114.
55. For comments on the traditions behind the Covenant and a conservative reading of what was intended, see Stevenson, *Covenanters*, pp.28-42.

56. I have argued this case in 'The Religious Context of the English Civil War', *T.R.H.S.*, 5th ser., vol. 34 (1984); and in 'Charles I, Tyranny', forthcoming.
57. In preparing this paper I read fifty-two pamphlets and tracts listed either (a) in the bibliography of Peter Donald, 'The King and the Scottish Troubles', University of Cambridge Ph.D. thesis (1987) or (b) under 'Scotland, Covenant' in *The Short Title Catalogue . . . 1485-1641*; I supplemented this with a check of the author index for all authors identified in (a) or (b).
58. *Works of Laud*, III, 298.
59. J. Spalding, *The History of the Troubles* (2 vols., Aberdeen, 1792), I, 58.
60. D. H. Fleming, ed., *Scotland's Supplication and Complaint* (1927), pp.60-6; D. H. Ogilvie, 'The National Petition to the Scottish Privy Council', *S.H.R.* xxii (1925), 241-8.
61. For the powerlessness of the Scottish Council, see e.g. Stevenson, *Scottish Revolution*, pp.29-33.
62. Stevenson, *Scottish Revolution*, pp.101-2, 138-48.
63. *History of Troubles*, pp.100-121.
64. Hewison, *Covenanters*, I, 357.
65. A task made simpler by the appearance of D. Stevenson, 'The National Covenant, a list of known copies', *Recs.Sc.Ch.Hist.Soc.* (1989).
66. For a range of comment on the social implications of the Covenant, see the arguments of Allan Macinnes (this volume, Chapter 5); W. Makey, *The Church of the Covenant, 1637-1651* (Edinburgh, 1983), pp.1-25; and Stevenson, *Covenanters*, pp.36-42.
67. Discussed by Peter Donald, 'King and the Troubles', p.118 and n.138.
68. Bodl. Lib., MS Dep.c.172, fo.11. (I am grateful to Ian Atherton for preparing a transcript for me). This list, with some variant spellings, was printed in Zachary Grey, *An Impartial Examination of the Third Volume of Daniel Neal's History of the Puritans* (London, 1737), pp.110-12. Both Conrad Russell and Peter Donald, who have studied this document believe it is an authentic copy of a list drawn up in mid-1638; but its purpose and reliability are uncertain. While it is probably less accurate than the list in the Hamilton Papers, the latter only contains a list of those seen as supporters of the Crown. (It consists of 1 duke, 3 marquises, 28 earls and 12 lords.) It may, however, have been the wishful thinking of someone in Hamilton's entourage rather than an accurate statement of opinion. I am grateful to Peter Donald for detailed comment on this point.
69. Stevenson, *Scottish Revolution*, pp.83-7; Donald, 'King and the Troubles', pp.58-80. As for the Highlands, I cannot improve upon Ian Cowan's cautionary note against *assuming* that the

Covenant failed there (I. B. Cowan, 'The Covenanters: a Revision Article', *S.H.R.*, xlvii (1968), p.39 and n.7).
70. *The Generall Demands Concerning the Late Covenant Propounded by the Ministers and Professors of Divinity in Aberdeene* . . . (1638), giving the grounds of their dissent deserves further study. Meanwhile see G. D. Henderson, 'The Aberdeen Doctors' in his collection of essays, *The Burning Bush* (Edinburgh, 1957), pp.75-93.
71. For a good account of the circulation and subscription of the Covenant, see Stevenson, *Scottish Revolution*, pp.83-7.
72. Donald, 'King and the Troubles', pp.179-82; P. Donald, 'New Light on the Anglo-Scottish Contacts of 1640', *Historical Research* LXII (1989), 221-9. I am also grateful to John Adamson for discussions on this point. See also this volume pp.95-101.
73. See this volume, pp.18-20.
74. Stevenson, *Scottish Revolution*, ch. 7; Donald, 'King and the Troubles', chs. 4-6; C. Russell, 'The British Problem and the English Civil War', *History* (1987), pp.395-415.
75. *Works of William Laud*, III, 279.
76. *History of Troubles*, pp.55-6.
77. *History of Troubles*, p.56.
78. Stevenson, *Scottish Revolution*, p.56.
79. H. Guthry, *Memoirs* (2nd edn, Glasgow, 1747), p.15. (See also Stevenson, *Scottish Revolution*, p.57.)
80. See this volume, pp.97-100.
81. See this volume, pp.138-48.
82. M. Mendle, *Dangerous Positions* (Alabama, 1985), pp.115-27. For a similar conclusion, that the Scots were not initially anti-English, see W. Ferguson, *England's Relations with Scotland to 1707* (Edinburgh, 1977), p.116.
83. *A Large Declaration*, p.42.
84. Printed in *A Large Declaration* at p.348.
85. His sermons are printed in *Covenants and Covenanters*, pp. 54-128.
86. *Covenants and Covenanters*, p.97.
87. *Covenants and Covenanters*, pp.78-9.
88. G. Gillespie, *A Dispute Against the English Popish Ceremonies* [sig.A 3].
89. *Ibid*.
90. *An Information to All Good Christians within the Kingdome of England, from the Noblemen, Barrons, Borrows, Ministers and Commons of the Kingdome of Scotland, for vindicating their intentions and actions* . . . (Edinburgh, 1639), pp.6-7.
91. [R. Baillie], *The Canterburian's Self-Conviction* (Edinburgh, 1640), preface [sig.A 4].

92. *The Lawfullness of Our expedition into England Manifested* (1640), p.4.
93. See above, n.63.
94. Donald, 'King and the Troubles', esp. pp.194-215; D. Stevenson, *Scottish Covenanters and Irish Confederates* (Belfast, 1981), pp.1-42. And see the comments of M. Perceval-Maxwell, 'Ireland and the Monarchy', *Historical Journal* (forthcoming, 1990); M. Fissel, *'Bellum Episcopale:* The Bishops' Wars and the end of the "Personal Rule" in England, 1638-1640', University of Berkeley Ph.D. thesis (1983).
95. Stevenson, *Scottish Revolution*, pp.214-42; Donald, 'King and the Troubles', ch. 6; Hamilton, 'Negotiation', 84-96; C. L. Hamilton, 'The basis of Scottish efforts to create a Reformed Church of England, 1640-1', *Church History*, xxx (1961), 171-7.
96. Stevenson, *Covenanters and Confederates*, pp.103-61.
97. Stevenson, *Covenanters and Confederates*, pp.137-50.
98. D. Stevenson, *Alisdair MacColla and the Highland Problem in the Seventeenth Century* (Edinburgh, 1980), passim; Stevenson, *Covenanters and Confederates*, pp.137-50.
99. D. Stevenson, *Revolution and Counter-Revolution in Scotland, 1644-1651* (1977), pp.82-122; Stevenson, *Covenanters and Confederates*, pp.253-84.
100. Donald, 'King and the Troubles', ch. 6.
101. Most fully discussed in L. Kaplan, *Politics and Religion during the English Revolution: The Scots and the Long Parliament, 1643-1645* (New York, 1976). The best discussion of the Westminster Assembly and of the Scots' part in it is now R. Paul, *The Assembly of the Lord* (1985).
102. Stevenson, *Counter-Revolution*, pp.82-94.
103. D. Stevenson, 'Cromwell, Scotland and Ireland', in J. S. Morrill, ed., *Oliver Cromwell and the English Revolution* (Harlow, 1990), pp.153-5.
104. Stevenson, *Counter-Revolution*, pp.115-129.
105. *The Forme and Coronation of Charles the Second, King of Scotland, England, France and Ireland* (Aberdeen, 1651). I have used an original copy. There is an accessible and generally reliable transcript in Kerr, ed., *Covenants and Covenanters*, pp.349-99, based on a 1741 edition of this account.
106. The order is of course highly significant: the acclamation (election by and contract with his people) *followed* his taking of the Covenants (and his election was thus made conditional upon the Covenants), whereas the taking of the coronation oath *followed* the acclamation and was not a condition of election. (For the sequence, see ed. Kerr, *Covenants and Covenanters*, pp.386-9.

107. *Ibid.*, p.386. It is curious, in view of this form of words, that the title of the pamphlet should describe him as King of Scotland, England, France and Ireland (the form used at the coronation of James in Westminster Abbey in 1603 – for which see Ferguson, *Scotland's relations with England*, p.97). The difference did, of course, matter.
108. *Acts of the Parliament of Scotland*, VI:ii, 156–7; Stevenson, *Counter-Revolution*, pp.131–3.
109. S. R. Gardiner, *Constitutional Documents of the Puritan Revolution* (3rd edn, 1906), pp.384–7.
110. Stevenson, *Counter-Revolution*, pp.129–134.

# *Two*

## THE 'POLITICK CHRISTIAN':
## THE THEOLOGICAL BACKGROUND TO
## THE NATIONAL COVENANT

### Margaret Steele

In March of 1638, a nation-wide fast day was held to publicise the mass subscription campaign for the National Covenant. In conducting the commemorative service, the minister of the Currie parish church in Lothian, John Chairtres, spent some time explaining the National Covenant's significance and contents to the congregation before requesting that the parishioners give their support to it *en masse*. Whether Chairtres delivered this lecture in a calm and quiet manner or whether he adopted a more impassioned and provocative style of rhetoric is not known. What is clear, however, is that when the congregation was asked to indicate their commitment by a show of hands, the atmosphere in the church dramatically changed; the orderly, attentive gathering suddenly erupted into an emotionally-charged, evangelical revival meeting:

> at thair standing up and lifting up thair hands, in the twinkling of ane eye thair fell sutch an extraordinarie influence of Gods Spirit upon the whol congregation, mellting thair frozen hearts, waltering thair dry checks, chainging thair verry countenances, as it was a wonder to seie so visible, sensible, momentaneal a chainge upon al, man and woman, lasse and ladde, pastor and people that Mr. Jhon, being suffacat almost with his awin tears, and astonisched at the motion of the whol people, sat downe in the pulpit in ane amazement, bot presently rose againe quhen he saw al the people falling doune on thair knees to mourne and pray, and he and thay for ane quarter of ane houre prayed verry sensibly, with many sobs, tears, promises and voues to be thankful and fruitful in tym-coming.[1]

Expressions of communal religious hysteria occurred elsewhere that day at services throughout the country; indeed, this was probably the most memorable feature of the Scottish people's first encounter with the National Covenant. The episode is particularly noteworthy, however, because the depth of emotion affecting the participants provides the key to understanding why the National Covenant captured the popular imagination in the short term so effectively and why, in the long term, appeals of the 'church in danger' were successfully invoked to challenge royal authority for much of the seventeenth century. Like the popular, religious fanaticism of Islam which fuelled the Iranian Revolution and reverberated throughout much of the Moslem world in the 1980s, evangelical prebyterianism was the covenanting movement's greatest asset in winning public support, motivating adherents, and inspiring revolutionary impulses in early modern Scotland. Yet, what was it about the National Covenant that could trigger such an emotional catharsis among the Scottish people?

Certainly, on the face of it, the formulation of this national petition owed little to populist, fundamentalist sentiment. The origins of the National Covenant lay not in popular agitation but in a sophisticated petitioning campaign conducted exclusively by disaffected members of the political nation. Since the prayer book riots of 23 July 1637 in Edinburgh, formal petitions on behalf of the elite had replaced mass demonstrations. Organised strictly according to rank and status, they were issued in the name of the three Estates as well as of the clergy, and co-ordinated by a central planning committee made up of nobles, gentry, burgesses and ministers. Collectively, this group of protestors bombarded the privy council with supplications demanding a reversal of Caroline religious policy: most notably, on 20 September, 18 October and 21 December of 1637. Although the tone and content of the petitions became increasingly critical over the eight-month period, all condemned the administration's new vision for the church on a number of grounds. Concern was expressed that the changes would have an immediate impact on the existing church service, wide implications for the future direction of the church, and a deleterious effect on the presbyterian court system of church government. For instance, the liturgy as outlined in the Caroline prayer book was attacked for the emphasis it placed on ritual and ceremony in worship, which included 'Mattins and evening songs, and canonicall services to be [per]formeis by the Minister and deacon' and for the prescription of the celebration of festivals and feast days.[2] While ordinary communicants may have given little thought to theological distinctions, few could have overlooked the impact of these changes on the style of worship with the introduction of a more ritualistic service. The establishment of a set liturgy had significantly redefined the image and function of the clergy, largely because presbyterian ministers were required to abandon their practice of extempore preaching and prayer. This proved controversial since it transformed the ministry into readers, thereby downgrading their importance as preachers.[3] The proposed communion service came under heavy criticism, too, for both its format and content. No longer were communicants to sit around a communion table, they were now expected to kneel before the minister to take the sacrament.[4] And, in receiving the bread and wine, there was an implicit recognition of Christ's Real Presence. This was a fundamental doctrinal change for presbyterians who conventionally viewed the elements as purely symbolic, preferring to adhere to memorialism.[5] If the Scottish clergy put the new prayer book into practice then both the laity and ministry would witness an immediate alteration in the character and substance of religious services.

As the petitions also made clear, the Caroline prayer book was only one part of a complex package of unpopular ecclesiastical reforms, which included a revised psalms book and a new book of canons. In providing the theoretical basis for recasting the Scottish Church, both had already eclipsed its conventional theology; hence, their real significance was that they legitimised the liturgical changes incorporated in the new prayer book. Of the two, the book of canons of 1635 was the most important in this respect. Critics denounced it for its advocacy of high church practices that were said to be 'fostering Abolisheid Su[per]sticons' – that is, to be moving the church closer to Roman Catholicism.[6] As an administrative guide, it was also instrumental in refashioning church government by centralising authority. Since it increased the jurisdiction of bishops, for instance, the autonomy of the remaining tiers of the church court system were said to be under threat. Moreover, the allocation of wider powers to the episcopate was unacceptable to presbyterian purists because it smacked of state interference. Even routine church business now came under the aegis of bishops as Crown appointees. It was the book of canons, for example, which gave bishops additional powers such as the right to license ministers. While the initial selection was still processed through each level of the church courts – from kirk session to presbytery to synod and, theoretically, to the General Assembly – ministerial candidates had to gain this new form of state sanction to take up their livings. The episcopate therefore gained a greater measure of control over the appointment of parish ministers.[7] This concentration of power into the hands of the higher clergy was therefore thought to diminish the importance of the lower church courts. Furthermore, the jurisdictional authority of the court of high commission, the highest ecclesiastical court, presided over by laymen and bishops but not presbyters and elders, was widened to accommodate the transition.[8] Since its primary function was to discipline church dissidents, radical presbyterians saw it as the Crown's enforcement agency for conformity, causing Samuel Rutherford to observe that 'We are in great fears of a great and fearfull trial to come upon the kirk of God; for these who would build their houses and nests upon the ashes of mourning Jerusalem, have drawn our King upon hard and dangerous conclusions against such as are termed Puritans, for the rooting them out. Our prelates . . . assure us that, for such as will not conform, there is nothing but imprisonment and deprivation . . . . All sorts of crying sins without controlement abound in our land'.[9] Therefore, as the petitioners made clear, Charles I's religious policy was contentious since it called for a complete restructuring of church policy and polity.

While the details of the new ecclesiastical order were important, their broader implications for the future direction of the church were of equal significance to the protestors. In effect, they signalled a clear departure from the traditional, Calvinist base in doctrine and administration with their promotion of Arminianism. It is perhaps worth recalling that after the Reformation, the established church adopted the Genevan model of policy and polity. It was doctrinally Calvinistic in its beliefs and practices and it relied on the presbyterian court system for its administration. This theological basis remained intact until the Caroline reforms of the 1630s. Modifications, however, had been made to the form of church government under James VI when bishops were reintroduced into the hierarchy and gradually acquired increased authority from 1606 to 1610, thereby assuming the supreme jurisdiction of the General Assembly.[10] Supporters of a pure presbyterian church polity acquiesced in the episcopalian ascendency by remaining within the established church; however, their presence created a certain tension, for they constituted a small but overtly critical faction. By the 1620s, these administrative divisions affecting the ministry, higher clergy and laity were widened over theological disputes occasioned by the introduction of Arminian beliefs and practices in the established church. It was through the writings of the Dutch theologian, Jacobus Arminius, that this new system gained converts among influential clergy and laity alike – including Charles I – so that eventually it became part of a key government strategy to establish religious uniformity in the multiple kingdom. Since religion was regarded as the 'base and foundation' of the early modern state,[11] conformity was sought by the king as an instrument of political stability. This policy gained momentum in 1633 when Charles appointed William Laud to the archbishopric of Canterbury and allowed him to oversee ecclesiastical affairs not only in England but, effectively, in Scotland and Ireland as well.

For its detractors, Arminianism threatened the integrity and character of the church in two distinct ways; thus, opposition derived from both the theological nature of the changes as well as from their effect on church–state relations.[12] First of all, Arminian beliefs and practices as incorporated in the new religious policies challenged the theological underpinnings of the established church. Certainly, doctrines emphasising ritual and ceremony in religious services as well as hierarchical discipline and order in church government were novelties for the average church-goer. But it spawned controversy in Scotland, where radical presbyterians saw it as a dismantling of the Reformation with the trend towards Arminianism leading inexorably to Catholicism. It was a common assumption that Arminianism (in the British sense) and Catholicism were essentially compatible; hence, they were readily equated. This was not too far-fetched, for they shared a number of beliefs and practices including the doctrines of universal atonement, free will and the Real Presence in the Eucharist; sacraments such as private baptism and private communion; concepts such as the Apostolic Succession of bishops; and worship practices emphasising church rites and ceremonies. Indeed, the similarity of Arminian and Catholic tenets was promoted by prominent Arminians themselves such as Richard Montague, later bishop of Chichester and Norwich. In the celebrated English test case against censorship which attracted attention in Scotland, Montague's work, *New Gag*, reduced the fundamental doctrinal differences between the Church of England and the Roman Catholic Church from forty-seven to eight.[13] For the average church-goer in Scotland, such beliefs contradicted everything their ministers had ever instilled in them through their sermons about the reformed faith. They were at odds, too, with the traditional Calvinism that formed the basis of church policy and polity. That is why, with the proposal for the introduction of the new prayer book, there was a general reluctance to have the English service book applied to Scotland. When comparisons were made between the books, critics always stressed that the English Reformation had been too indeterminate in its incorporation of reformed doctrine, leaving the Anglican Church in a sort of theological limbo between Protestantism and Catholicism. Typically, it was argued that while the Scottish prayer book was the 'same but more subtillye polisheid wth some alteracons and addicons' than its English counterpart, its acceptance was regressive in moving the church doctrinally closer to Catholicism.[14] Thus, the Caroline church's adoption of Arminianism was unpopular because it not only altered the whole character of the church but seemed to subvert the Reformation.

Secondly, Caroline ecclesiastical policy proved controversial because it was overtly Erastian. With the introduction of the book of canons and the prayer book, royal control over the church was tightened. So much was clear in the methods used to impose the reforms. Charles introduced his new religious policy in a piecemeal fashion through royal decrees. Although he consulted extensively with the Scottish bishops, he did not seek any of the standard endorsements of parliament or the General Assembly. While royal interference in ecclesiastical matters was common, state control over the worship practices, administration and regulation of the church had never been so blatant. What is more, this made a nonsense of presbyterian assertions that the church should be an independent and self-regulating institution. From the late sixteenth century, when the Genevan model of church government gained a foothold in Scotland, the ideal of full autonomy for the church had become more sacrosanct for presbyterian purists. Indeed, this had been one of the main principles underlying Andrew Melville's theory of the 'Two Kingdoms'. Granted, political realities such as the universal acknowledgement of the Crown's supreme authority and the reintroduction of episcopacy in 1606 had amply demonstrated the falsity of that ideal. Nonetheless, it was a theoretical tenet of critical importance for two reasons. First, for radical presbyterians, Erastianism was denounced on the grounds that the state had no right to dictate conscience.[15] Sir George Maxwell of Pollok, a prominent covenanting laird, spoke for many when he observed that the interests of the church were incompatible with those of the state: 'Sarah & Hagar would sooner dwell contendedlie in ane house then conscience & policie can duell under ane roofe; conscience is an ingenious piece & will still be speakeing policie is a deep plodding thing & will still be acteing its oun game'.[16] Secondly, it was linked to the presbyterian belief that the Scottish Church represented the quintessential reformed church which stood as a model of Protestant ideology. This, at least, was the substance of the arguments used in the petitioning campaign by the politically active, who as radical presbyterians deplored the government's extension of state control over the church.

It was only when the sociopolitical elite's campaign against Caroline religious policy ended in stalemate that the protest took on a truly populist dimension culminating in the National Covenant. By mid-February of 1638, it had become evident that the government was more interested in breaking the unity of the protestors than in redressing their grievances.[17] With negotiations at an apparent impasse, some of the leading protestors, including Archibald Johnston of Wariston and Lord Rothes, called for a major re-evaluation of the opposition's campaign. And after extensive consultation among the hundreds of members of the three Estates and the clergy gathered in Edinburgh, it was agreed that the only effective way to break the political deadlock and obtain the redress of grievances was to revitalise the anti-prayer book protest by adopting a more ambitious approach.[18] At a meeting of the nobles, gentry, burgesses and ministers, the decision was thus made to broaden support for the cause by 'reneuing that same Covenant subscribed be our ancestours, with such additions as the corruptiones of this tyme necessarilie requyred to be joyned, and such Acts of Parliament as was against Poperie and in favour of the true religione'.[19] This involved, rather than a continuation of formal petitioning on behalf of the political nation, an unprecedented departure from the accepted norms of public protest: a direct, formal canvass of the Scottish people for a loyalty oath known as the National Covenant. Thus, the actual decision to mount a public appeal owed little to popular protest since it arose directly from the inadequacies of the elitist campaign.

The National Covenant itself is a somewhat unlikely document to be heralded as a populist manifesto. In its style, content and language it is distinguished more by a cerebral legalism than by any visceral appeals to popular sentiment. Theoretically, it was to be subscribed by all church-going communicants on behalf of themselves as well as their followers and families; yet its complex syntax and sheer length – running to almost forty-three hundred words – probably prevented the majority of Scots from having a good grasp of its finer points. What would have been perfectly comprehensible to all, however, was the dual purpose of the exercise. Subscription meant that one had signed, first, a loyalty oath affirming commitment to Calvinist doctrine and presbyterian polity and, second, a national petition calling for a halt to the government's promotion of Arminianism. As the dual objectives of the petitioning campaign, these demands were common knowledge. Not only were they repeatedly expressed in sermons given in parishes located throughout the country but they were widely circulated through the numerous pamphlets and news-sheets that had been distributed in Scotland for more than half a year. Nowhere was the National Covenant's basic intent made more explicit, though, than in its five main sections: that is, the Negative Confession of 1581, the compendium of anti-Catholic legislation, the list of laws formally constituting the established church, the civil loyalty oath and the general band. Each had to be reworked by Archibald Johnston of Wariston, an Edinburgh lawyer, and Alexander Henderson, a Fifeshire minister, after extensive consultation with representatives of the three Estates and the ministry. And all were designed to emphasise objections to the dismantling of the Calvinist doctrines and presbyterian polity which commanded the support of church activists and, perhaps, the majority of communicants in Scotland. However, if the National Covenant represented the aspirations of the disaffected elite, what did the average layman think he was signing?

If we examine the text of the National Covenant, it is apparent that people were made aware that a threat to established worship practices necessitated a band.[20] So much is evident with the inclusion of the Negative Confession, a 'confessione of the true Christian faith', which was simply a pledge affirming the subscriber's commitment to Protestantism. Originally, when James VI and his chief political advisers signed it in 1581, it had been issued to allay fears about the Jacobean administration's alleged affinity for Catholicism which, it was feared, would result in a counter-Reformation.[21] Reference to an oath taken almost three generations earlier by the king's father was not as obscure as it might seem since it could be exploited to political advantage. It lent a certain legitimacy to the National Covenant by establishing its signators as emulators of a royal tradition, thereby providing the historical, legal and moral justification for the national petition. And its historic importance as a band of faith flattered them as the church's vanguard, occupying the high moral ground. What is more, by citing the Negative Confession, opponents of Caroline religious policy drew attention to parallel circumstances in an earlier age that had resulted in similar action. Both external and internal threats to the established church prompted a backlash in 1581 as they did in 1638, requiring a formal reaffirmation of Protestantism. Where the circumstances differed, however, was in the source of the external threat, with English Arminianism replacing the hegemony of continental Catholicism.

For this reason, the singularity of the church's policy and polity is emphasised in the Negative Confession, in which support for the Scottish brand of Protestantism, i.e. that faith 'receaved, beleved and defended by manie and sindrie notable kyrkis and relames, but chiefly by the kyrk of Scotland,' is pledged. In a sense, then, the Negative Confession provided a convenient shorthand for contemporaries, allowing the opposition to express their dissatisfaction about recent church reforms without specific reference to existing, government policies. This was a purely political expedient enabling protestors to maintain a veneer of legality while skirting the treason laws.[22] Moreover, with a blanket condemnation of 'all contrarie religion and doctrine, but cheifly all kynd of papistrie in generall', the renewed confession hit a responsive, populist chord by playing on the deeply ingrained anti-Catholic sentiment of the time. This had a broader significance, too, given the association in the public mind of Charles's church reforms with the unmaking of the Reformation. When Catholic ritual, ceremony and doctrine were enumerated and condemned in the Negative Confession, the Arminian church reforms promoted under the stewardship of Archbishop Laud were tarred with the same brush. Thus, by inference, the Negative Confession encapsulates all of the radical presbyterian criticisms of the Caroline church.

The second section of the National Covenant is a selective compendium of laws passed by parliament since the Reformation against Catholicism. Here, acts condemning Catholic worship, practices and beliefs and denying papal authority and jurisdiction are referred to by title. It also encompasses some of the penal laws enforcing civil penalties against practising Catholics as 'common enemies to all Christian government'; as 'rebellers and gainstanders of our sovereign Lords Authority'; and, as 'Idolators'. This view of Catholics as constituting a political and religious threat reflected early modern Protestant assumptions. In an era when religion was a badge of civil loyalty and a bench-mark of political dependability, political orthodoxy associated Protestant interests with the viability of the nation-state; thus, Catholicism was equated with subversion. Although an undercurrent had existed since the Reformation, popular hostility towards Catholicism in the seventeenth century was triggered by the outbreak of the Thirty Years War in 1618 and intensified after 1625 because of King Charles's marriage to Henrietta Maria, a French Catholic.[23] Concern about increased Catholic influence at court had resulted in parliamentary demands for more rigorous implementation of the penal statutes in the early years of Charles's rule; most notably at the convention of 1625.[24] This reflected the general expectation that a government crackdown on recusancy was necessary to confirm the administration's political orthodoxy.[25] Both the political nation and the Scottish people then sought tangible proof of the Caroline administration's willingness to suppress Catholicism. The anti-Catholic laws in the National Covenant therefore served as a timely reminder of popular apprehensions about Charles and his immediate circle, the court.

Juxtaposed with these negative expressions of populist sentiment is a litany of positive belief outlining the 'perfect Religion'; thus, the third section of the National Covenant contains a list of the pro-Protestant statutes 'conceaved for maintenance of Gods true and Christian Religion'. For the laity, these laws embodied the clearest expression of all that they were fighting for as signators to the national petition. When the sixteenth-century laws were read out to them, prefaced by the statement that 'there is none other Face of Kirk, nor other Face of Religion, then was presently at that time, by the Favour of God established within this Realme', they understood that it was the church of Andrew Melville that was referred to when presbyterianism had been in the ascendancy. If any missed this reference to the pre-episcopal church as the ideal, they had further opportunities to grasp the point in subsequent passages of the Covenant. There is, for instance, a direct call for official confirmation of the legal basis of presbyterian polity. And demands for the protection of the 'liberty & freedom' of the 'true Church of God' are unequivocal in specifying the presbyterian court system as the quintessential church polity. The ideal form of church government is thus defined as consisting of the 'National Synodal Assemblies, Presbyteries, Sessions . . . as that purity of Religion and liberty of the Church was used, professed, exercised, preached and confessed according to the reformation of Religion in this Realm'. Conspicuously, there is no mention of bishops in this definition of the church's hierarchy, for only the presbyterian model is regarded as legitimate for the 'true church'. Thus, with the compendium of legislation outlining the development of the established church, the laity pledged themselves to a dual commitment. In general, they were to oppose any measure that might threaten Protestantism. And, more specifically, they were to work towards the reconstruction of the sixteenth-century model of Scottish presbyterianism; a church based on a Calvinist vision of church government, shorn of the subsequent seventeenth-century addition of bishops.

What are too often overlooked as innocuous lists of Jacobean statutes were actually a political minefield of condemnation of the spirit and direction of Caroline religious policy. Certainly, the two separate lists of acts serve a number of purposes in terms of legitimising the protest against recent church reforms. Simply the emphasis on legality – a marked feature of the petitioning campaign – is sustained by their inclusion. Moreover, by listing parliamentary statutes instead of church ordinances, the political rather than the religious justification of the protest is given prominence. This provided a convenient framework for the claim that recent changes in the church infringed the spirit if not the letter of the law, thereby implying that the Caroline administration and not the protestors had acted illegally. However, in the National Covenant, criticism of the government is based as much on perception as on reality. When mention is made of the circulation of 'erronious doctrine' and 'erronious bookes and writtes' with the demand that the 'home-bringers of them' should be punished, the reference is not exclusively directed to Catholic literature. There is also the inference that Arminian literature has been allowed to spread through the authorities' indifference. That is why civil officials are reminded of their duty to suppress any contraventions of established kirk practices. Therefore, the lists of parliamentary acts gave signators of the National Covenant the distinct impression that not only was the existing system of church policy and polity under threat, but the ideal vision of the Scottish Church as the model of Genevan Calvinism faced extinction if Caroline church reforms were allowed to proceed.

The fourth part of the National Covenant ostensibly contains a conventional statement of civic loyalty to the Crown. But it is accompanied by three clauses drawing attention to existing political conditions affecting the relationship between ruler and ruled that make it distinctly unorthodox. First, it is prefaced by a statement asserting the supremacy of parliamentary statute.[26] This would have struck contemporaries as a radical constitutional assertion. Traditionally, parliament had functioned as an instrument for royal policy; thus the king, rather than parliament, was regarded as the chief law-maker. This clause may well have been taken, however, as an oblique reference to Charles's tendency to govern without parliamentary consensus and his reliance on royal decrees for the implementation of ecclesiastical policy. Secondly, the civic loyalty oath is made concomitant with an assertion of Scottish nationalism when reference is made to the findings of a Jacobean commission which had examined the possibilities of a formal, political union between Scotland and

England in 1604. Here, the commission's conclusions are reiterated to underline the dangers of conformity with England for national autonomy; thus, if the common laws of Scotland 'be innovated or prejudged, the commission . . . declares such confusion would ensue, as this Realme could be no more a free Monarchy'.[27] By citing the warning of this bilateral committee, supporters of the Covenant expressed concern for what they saw as the creeping anglicisation inherent in the administration. And this was exemplified in the popular mind by its recasting of the Scottish Church to conform with the Church of England. Thirdly, the statement of allegiance is coupled with a specific clause reminding Charles that his coronation oath included a pledge to defend the 'true religion'. That the king's commitment to Protestantism should have been questioned with this seemingly mild rebuke reflected popular assumptions that Caroline church reforms were reactionary. Nonetheless, there would have been no mistaking of its broader implications by supporters of the Covenant. The accusation embodied their chief complaint that Charles had been derelict in his duty as a 'godly magistrate': the key Calvinistic concept that justified their resistance. Thus, taken together, the clauses summed up the broader issues involved in the protest against the religious reforms. Not only their substance but their method of introduction and their intent were viewed as symptomatic of Charles's autocratic style of governing, which subjugated Scottish needs to English imperatives. The civic loyalty oath as expressed in the National Covenant thus encapsulated all of the protestors' misgivings about Charles's ability to provide good government for Scotland.

This willingness to question Charles's style of kingship is evident, too, in the fifth section of the National Covenant containing the general band. Recent changes in worship practice are condemned as constituting 'dangers in the nation to religion, the king's honour and the public peace'. Although the demand that they be suspended had sparked the initial public protests of July 1637, this was accompanied by a new condition in the National Covenant that the 'corruptions of the publicke Government of the Kirk, or civil places and power of kirk-men' be withheld 'till they be tryed & allowed in free assemblies and in Parliaments'. Such bold statements came perilously close to an outright denial of the royal prerogative in civil matters. Should the demands be met, they would infringe on the king's traditional right to formulate government policy, to select his advisers, to call parliament and to hold a General Assembly. When accompanied by a call for the restoration of the 'purity and liberty of the Gospel, as it was stablished and professed before the foresaid Novations', the general band had as its twin objectives the overturning of the church reforms and the modification of the Caroline style of government.[28] With the wide scope of this declaration of intent, signatories of the National Covenant were required to make three separate pledges: to defend presbyterian policy and polity (the 'true religion'); to uphold monarchical authority 'in the defence and preservation of the foresaid true Religion, Liberties and Lawes of the Kingdom'; and to support 'every one of us of another in the same cause'. Indeed, it is this intention of defending both the Church and the Crown when the self-styled champions of the two institutions seemed to be pursuing rival visions that is often dismissed as contradictory and disingenuous.[29] Yet, it is important to realise that this 'medley of loyalties' involving simultaneously an expression of opposition to royal policy and a declaration of loyalty to the king is a common feature of early modern popular revolts, especially against absolute regimes.[30] What is more, in the National Covenant defence of the Church and the Crown are regarded as inseparable: the 'true worship of God and the Kings authority, being so straitly joined, as that they had the same Friends, and common enemies, and did stand and fall together'. This reflected two contemporary characterisations of the sovereignty of the king. In the first, the king was seen as the embodiment of the natural order; in the second, as a Christian magistrate fulfilling his destiny as God's vice-regent on earth by performing his functions as the defender of the faith.[31] Proper fulfilment of the Christian magistrate's duty clearly mitigated against any conflict of interest. Moreover, in what features essentially as an escape clause, allegiance to the monarchy is stated to be conditional, predicated on the king's unequivocal support of the established church because 'we perceave that the quietnes and stabilitie of our religion and kirk doth depend upon the savetie and good behaviour of the kyngis majestie'. Few signators of the National Covenant would have believed that Charles was incapable of this stipulation as it was considered integral to good kingship. Thus, the dual pledge to defend the king and the church was the expression of an ideal and Charles, as a Christian magistrate, had an obligation to fulfil it by his subsequent actions.

The National Covenant's attack on the royal prerogative in itself made adherence to the band for mutual support all the more vital for the success of the opposition's campaign. However, this begs the question of why the protestors decided to resort to a pledge joining themselves together to defend the king and the church when, previously, petitions without any reference to collective action had been regarded as sufficient. Although it was part of the tradition of public banding, it is possible, too, that the new emphasis on communal responsibility was a direct consequence of the petitioners' recent experience of the government's handling of the prayer book controversy; thus, the oath of mutual assistance was the result of repeated attempts to divide and weaken the protestors. In comparison with earlier supplications, it constituted a fundamental shift in attitude, signalling the protestors' more aggressive strategy. Swearing to defend one another in pursuit of their objectives offered the persuasiveness and high morale of collective action.[32] But, it also had the effect of acting as a warning to the authorities that what had been a peaceful protest so far could escalate into civil disobedience. In making the bold declaration that 'whatsoever shall be done to the least of us for that cause, shall be taken as done to us all in general, and to every one of us in particular', the dissidents offered an open challenge to the government's authority with the threat of mass protest. When allied to the sense of mission underlying the oaths and the recurring linkage between religious freedom and 'civill liberties' throughout the National Covenant, the general band can be said to have been a dangerous recipe for rebellion. Yet, to its subscribers, it was not their own actions but those of the king which had brought them to articulate such revolutionary principles.[33]

The National Covenant, then, was the culmination of eight months of unsuccessful, political lobbying by the sociopolitical elite. Although this campaign had been launched in the aftermath of the prayer book riots, mass demonstrations were not an important feature of the protest against Caroline religious reform until the unveiling of the National Covenant itself. Why this should be so relates largely to the contemporary view of the social order. In a highly stratified, paternalistic society, the use of the mob as an instrument of political protest was regarded as dangerous because it contravened notions of the natural order, having the potential to destabilise society. Within the context of the petitioning campaign, then, the National Covenant constituted a major departure for the protestors for five reasons. First, it was more forthright in its definition of the opposition's worries than earlier petitions had dared to be; secondly, it was more radical in its content and tone; and, thirdly, it was more ambitious in its scope and aims. Fourthly, it had far-reaching consequences for Scottish politics. Canvassing popular support amongst a broad base of the population with the active solicitation of church-going communicants, in effect, redefined the political landscape. Although members of the nobility, gentry, burgh oligarchies and clergy were required to take civil oaths prior to 1638, never had so many ordinary Scots been personally involved in a political act of this type. This unprecedented solicitation of popular support in a formal oath involving matters of state thus significantly altered conventional precepts about who should testify personally as to their political loyalty – as the subsequent subscription campaign for the rival King's Covenant testifies. By embodying a spirit of public participation that was antithetical to constitutional practice, formal recognition was given in effect to a wider political franchise, establishing the validity of an extra-parliamentary pressure group. Fifthly, the success of the National Covenant was also responsible for altering contemporary perceptions of obedience and deference. Loyalty to the Crown had always been regarded as a natural attribute of kingship; thus, to affirm that tie with a public pledge was unnecessary for either the bulk of the political nation or the general populace. With the National Covenant, however, there was a recognition that the body of the people had to join in an act of public affirmation of their loyalty. But, if the National Covenant revolutionalised political life through its alteration of the perception of public trust, where did such ideas come from and how were they popularised so that ordinary men and women were willing to openly question the actions of their divinely-appointed king?

Certainly, the use of a formal contract binding its signatories to a specified obligation in pursuit of common objectives had a long history in Scotland, falling well within the bounds of accepted political and religious orthodoxy. When faced with a political stalemate, the protestors thus turned to the familiar remedy of issuing a band of mutual support to both clarify and publicly acknowledge their intentions. This impulse was part of the early modern convention of political banding. Although few of the surviving bands are comparable to the National Covenant, they do show commonality of purpose in their shared sense of political obligation in the face of a threat to the *status quo* and in their signatories' commitment to a specified political end.[34] It was also part of the tradition of religious banding in Scotland. Spurred on by the Calvinistic belief that a covenant is a mark of true faith, Scots showed a predilection for religious bands beginning in the late sixteenth century. Renewal of such covenants was a well-established ritual with no less than thirty-one extant documents of this type dating from the Reformation, the earliest known being the Duns Covenant of 1556 which was drafted on John Knox's return from exile on the Continent.[35] In terms of subscription, these ranged from covenants signed by a handful of nobles, such as the First Band of the Lords of the Congregation issued in 1557 in response to the pro-French policy of the Queen Regent, Mary of Guise, and subscribed by the earls of Argyll, Glencairn, and Morton along with Lord Lorne and John Erskine of Dun,[36] to those involving mass subscriptions, such as that solicited in March of 1596 at the General Assembly in response to the 'defections' of the ministry. This latter covenant was publicly witnessed by a show of hands of about four hundred clergymen attending the Assembly and was then sanctioned by the members of the kirk synods as a 'new Covenant'.[37] Yet, even though the National Covenant does bear some resemblance to these previous religious bands, it is nonetheless strikingly different. Not only is it more ambitious in the scope of its intentions but, in the unprecedented numbers of its public subscribers, it draws on a broader social base. These are critical distinctions that made the National Covenant not a personal but an emphatically public alliance forged in the name of the common good.[38] Thus, while its underlying dynamic may have been shaped by the tradition of political and religious banding, the National Covenant was politically precocious, going well beyond established conventions.

What made the National Covenant truly unique was its embodiment of the concept of a covenanted nation involving the people of Scotland. This was an all-embracing, perpetual commitment that had never been put into practice before; a realisation of the Old Testament ideal of the covenant between man and God referred to by the church fathers, including Irenaeus and Augustine. The concept gained new currency in the late sixteenth century because of the development of Federal Theology, a system of Calvinist belief characterised by its evangelical millenarianism. Continental reformers such as David Pareus, Zacharias Ursinus and Caspar Olevanius, and English reformed thinkers including William Tyndale and John Hooper were all prominent exponents of this theological system. Their preoccupation with the idea of a covenant – a word which appears no less than three hundred times in the Bible – made it a basic feature of mainstream Calvinist teachings.[39] Although grounded primarily in the German and Dutch scholastic tradition, Scottish theologians made significant ideological contributions to Federal Theology. John Forbes of Carse, a Divinity professor at Aberdeen from 1620, studied under David Pareus in Heidelberg. In 1616 he published an important study of the doctrine of the covenants, *Justification*, a comparative analysis of the Covenant of Works and the Covenant of Grace.[40] Forbes's work was grounded in the intellectual heritage of continental reformed thought, for his former instructor, Pareus, was himself a follower of Zacharias Ursinus, co-author of the Heidelberg Catechism, the authoritative text used in catechetical preaching for Calvinist congregations throughout the Low Countries and Germany.[41] Indeed, it was Ursinus' detailed examination of the Covenant of Works which was seminal to the evolution of what later became known as Federal Theology.[42] Equally influential were the writings of Caspar Olevanius, a legalist and theologian, who studied for a short time under Jean Calvin at Geneva and co-authored the Heidelberg Catechism with Ursinus. It was Olevanius' *De Substantia Foederus Gratuiti inter Deum et Electos* that used the concept of a covenant as the matrix of his theological system. Furthermore, this provided the philosophical basis for the works of two eminent Scottish theologians: Robert Howie, principal of Marischal College in Aberdeen and, later, principal of New College in St Andrews, and Robert Rollock, the rector of the University of Edinburgh. As Robert Howie was a former student of Olevanius at Herborn, his book, published in 1591, *Theses at Basil De Reconciliatione Hominus cum Deo*, owes much to his mentor.[43] Olevanius' influence is perhaps most notable, however, in Rollock's tract, *Treatise on Effectual Calling* which first appeared in 1597 in both Latin and English. As 'one of the earliest, systematic discussions of the Covenants', the monograph was central to the development of Federal Theology.[44] It was Rollock, for instance, who coined the phrase *foedus operum* or 'covenant of works': a theme examined in turn by some of his most eminent students, including Robert Boyd, who later assumed the principalship of the universities of Edinburgh and Glasgow.[45] What is of critical importance for our purposes, however, is that Rollock may be credited with establishing the more overt political overtones associated with Federal Theology.[46] By placing greater emphasis on divine intervention in relation to the Covenant of Grace, he altered the Calvinist belief in unilateral decrees, thereby providing the basis for the concept of a covenanted nation which underpinned the National Covenant.[47] Through his work, then, Rollock played a pivotal role in the formulation of Calvinist political ideology.[48]

The close personal ties among western European intellectuals were crucial to the transference of Federal Theology to Scotland. The scholarly links between native theologians and their continental mentors helped to introduce it. Its broader dissemination, however, was guaranteed by the influential academic positions held by its proponents, with the result that successive generations of ministerial candidates and other university students were tutored in the centrality of the covenant ideal. Indeed, by the 1620s, Federal Theology had become one of the most dominant theological systems adhered to in the Scottish Church. One measure of its acceptance was that David Pareus's notes on the Heidelberg Catechism were made part of the university curriculum by order of the General Assembly, serving as mandatory reading for all divinity students in the seventeenth century.[49] Its incorporation into mainstream thought is evidenced, too, by the subsequent practice of publishing and binding *The Sum of Saving Knowledge* – a seminal work of Federal Theology written by David Dickson and James Durham – along with the Westminster Confession.[50] The ideology gained wider exposure, however, through the mechanism of evangelising with the result that it became common currency among the laity of the church. Given their academic background, the presbyterian clergy promoted the covenant ideal in their sermons to the extent that it became a predominate theme of seventeenth-century pastoral theology. A case in point is a sermon by John Hamilton dating from 1638. Hamilton urged his parishioners to subscribe the National Covenant because it was part of Scotland's destiny; 'the children of Izrael schal come . . . . They schal ask the way to Zion with thair faces thitherward, saying, Come, and let us joyne ourselves to the Lord in a perpetual covenant that schal not be forgotten. My people haith been lost scheip'.[51] By drawing on the ideological base of Federal Theology, the perpetual nature of the National Covenant itself was therefore emphasised for, as another radical presbyterian minister put it, 'it was not a temporal Covenant of temporary things but a covenant forever'.[52]

In Federal Theology, the significance of the covenant between man and God was that it acted as the only verification of true faith. Since God was expected to call on the elect to covenant with him at some unspecified time, then it was incumbent on each individual to formally enter a covenant with God as proof of their election.[53] The enduring centrality of this concept thus led many laymen to make a formal, personal commitment to the covenant ideal on a regular basis. Jean Campbell made annual renewals of a 'Covenant with God', mainly at Ferniehurst, for a decade starting when she was twenty years of age in 1691.[54] And Sir George Maxwell of Nether Pollok signed such a covenant on his death-bed in 1656.[55] That Federal Theology had a strong populist appeal is perhaps no more evident than in the introspective commonplace books kept by members of the laity. With the Calvinist stress on self-examination of conscience as proof of faith, many were motivated to record their inner thoughts out of obligation to their doctrinal beliefs.[56] Extant diaries such as that of the Spreul family thus help to shed some light on the inner religious life of presbyterian radicals.[57] Many seem to have found solace in keeping commonplace books filled with highly idiosyncratic yet personally meaningful lists of appropriate religious or moral phrases – often biblical passages – copied out as many as a dozen times like a school child writing out lines.[58] But it is the writers' preoccupations with universal themes such as faith, love and liberty, along with their tortuous inner struggle with conscience, that make the diaries particularly relevant. The diary of Sir George Maxwell of Pollock, or the notes of Sir William Scott of Harden, entitled 'Anent personall covenanting,' illustrate how deeply the ideals of Federal Theology were imbedded in the presbyterian psyche.[59] When Sir Archibald Johnston of Wariston, as a leading covenanting polemicist, needed to justify resistance to the Crown in 1638 after a provisional covenanting government had seized power, he turned to the writings of prominent Federal Theologians for inspiration. According to his diary entries for the better part of the year, he made notes on the question of civil disobedience after resolving 'to wryte al thoughts as they cam in thy heed doune in paiper, and to studie som laues upon sik sort of subjects, as rebellion, sedition, tumult, convocation'.[60] He examined a treatise, *Politica Methodice Digesta*, by the Dutch Calvinist, Johannes Althusius,[61] which stresses the 'co-operation of all citizens under two contracts, social and governmental . . . in which both the "ephors", or lower magistrates, and the chief rulers function as delegates of the people'.[62] Wariston refers as well to the work of Robert Parker, William Ames and Thomas Cartwright which 'for ane yeir or tuo was thereby praepairing me (by my knowledge and expectation) for this present imployment'.[63] For instance, on the question of the King's prerogative, he consulted Robert Parker's *De Politeia Ecclesiastica Christi et hierarcha opposita, libri tres* while racking his memory for 'sik things, books, reasons as might conduce to the cause'.[64] He also studied David Pareus's *In divinam St. Pauli Apostoli and Romanos Epistolam Commentaries*, a monograph analysing Romans 13 on the question of obedience to rulers.[65] Wariston's attitudes on the issue of civil disobedience – and, by extension, those of the covenanting movement in general – were thus heavily imbued with the covenant ideal. It is not too much to say then that Federal Theology was so widely diffused in Scotland by the 1620s that it had permeated the consciences of laymen to become an integral part of the belief system.

Evidence suggests too that, in the early part of the seventeenth century, educated laymen took a more active interest in theological questions that had traditionally been the preserve of the ministry. The variety and proliferation of books and tracts dealing with religious subjects and specific topics of theological exposition provides one tangible indicator of their pronounced religious enthusiasm. Between 1600 and 1640 the number of monographs printed in Scotland rose overall by four hundred per cent. Each succeeding decade saw a steady if uneven growth; forty works were printed from 1610 to 1619, whereas the previous decade's total was thirty. But, starting in the 1620s, the numbers escalated by fifty per cent with sixty monographs appearing. This figure almost doubled in the 1630s, when one hundred and fourteen religious works were published.[66] The growth in publishing activity was partly an outcome of the reprinting of basic scriptural works and partly the result of the writing of new didactic monographs on religious and moral subjects. The Psalms of David were published in twenty-five editions between 1625 and 1638, with more than half of these appearing in 1633 alone. Similarly, the new King James version of the Bible was printed six times between 1633 and 1638 while the New Testament was reissued thirteen times between 1625 and 1637, with a royal version produced in 1628 and a new translation from the Greek printed in 1631. John Calvin's Catechism was published in 1628 and, at the same time, as a Catechism in Gaelic, in 1631. While this greater demand for scriptural works may suggest popular interest in religion, more active involvement in theological debates by the laity is discernible too in the increasing number of prose works appearing on a variety of religious and moral themes. A range of theological positions was represented in the writings. Arminian treatises by John Forbes and Thomas Valesius as well as moral essays such as *The triumph of a christian*, written in 1632 by William Couper, bishop of Galloway, rolled off the presses only to compete with the offerings of radical presbyterians, such as *Garden of spirituall flowers*, produced in 1634 by Zachary Boyd. In response to public demand, tracts on specific biblical passages, including *The loves of the Lord with his troth-plight spouse, contained in the Song of Songs paraphrased* written by the anonymous D. W. and the Psalms of David by A. Johnston were printed. Published sermons, especially those delivered by radical, presbyterian ministers such as Robert

Rollock, found a wide lay readership as well. Taken together, the writing and consumption of religious works, their unprecedented rate of reprinting and the growing diversity of devotional literature made available through the printing presses reflect the religious revivalism affecting Caroline Scotland.[67]

The impulse to analyse the inner spiritual life, although rooted in Augustinian tradition, enjoyed a revival in the early seventeenth century because it was often fuelled by the evangelistic millenarian component of Federal Theology. Belief in the prophetic authenticity of the Revelation of St John and the visions of Daniel was part of the mainstream cosmology attracting the attention of leading contemporary thinkers, including men of science prominent amongst whom were men like John Napier of Merchiston in Scotland; however, it took on important political implications when allied to the Federal Theologians' concept of a covenanted nation. Elaborate schemes for the calculation of the precise date of the Second Coming, which would either precede or follow one thousand years of 'godly rule' and hence 'heaven on earth' became a major intellectual preoccupation.[68] The exact interpretation of biblical allusions to the 'Beast', the 'ten horns', the 'little horn' and the 'whore of Babylon' varied widely. Yet millenarians shared the view that the Reformation signalled the onset of the apocalyptic struggle marking the defeat of the AntiChrist and thus the hegemony of the Catholic Church. Moreover, this was an event that they felt sure would be resolved in their own lifetime.[69] That is why there was the broadly held perception among contemporaries that theirs was an age of moral decay badly in need of spiritual regeneration. Tracts such as *An Abstract of some late characters. Or, How the principall means appointed for our Reformation is become the main fuell of our Wickedness* lament the moral and spiritual laxity of the time.[70] Allied to this prevailing sense of foreboding, however, was the surety of the dawning of a new age, for which men had to prepare since 'life on earth was only valuable as a metaphor for life in heaven'.[71] The promise of salvation was said to exist if God's will was adhered to, the anticipated reward being that 'thyn eys shall see Jerusalem'.[72] Comfort was found, then, in prophetic writings such as *Christs kingdom on earth, opened according to the Scriptures*, which offered detailed studies of the book of Revelation as proof that the Second Coming of Christ was imminent.[73]

Central to this typology was the concept of the 'godly prince' modelled on Constantine, the first Christian king, who would take the lead in what was essentially a pan-Protestant crusade against the AntiChrist, interpreted by contemporaries as the pope. Although in

England the tradition of the dynamic Christian emperor was popularised largely by works such as John Foxe's *Actes and Monuments of the Church* or, as it is more commonly known, 'Foxe's Book of Martyrs',[74] there is evidence to suggest that even in the absence of a powerful native tradition a comparable ideology prevailed in Scotland.[75] James VI, for instance, saw himself as a Christian king whose duty to God, the law and then to nature were among his first responsibilities, as his book on kingship, *Basilikon Doron*, outlines.[76] This view was also articulated in the coronation oath taken by each Stewart king after the Reformation, which stressed the central importance of the 'Christian Monarch' to maintain and champion the established church and to act as a 'godly magistrate' by punishing any who sought to alter it.[77] As well, millenarian influence surfaced in the appeals made to Charles I as the new Constantine to become actively involved in the Thirty Years War against international Catholicism.[78] Indeed, as a belief system, millenarianism (and chiliasm) ran so deep that occasionally it produced self-proclaimed demagogues like Ryce Crane who in 1646 publicly announced that he was Jesus Christ and that 'he did ryse to justifie nane but his elect and further that he is ye judge of the world and of all men'.[79] That there existed a broad interest and awareness of this ideology in Scotland is perhaps no more apparent than in the fact that extracts were taken from Foxe's Book of Martyrs, reprinted, and sold as tracts.[80]

Given that millenarian thinking was widely accepted as part of the early modern belief system, fulfilment of these prophecies must have seemed very near at hand with the public unveiling of the National Covenant in March of 1638. For more than a generation, both the ministry and laity of the presbyterian wing of the church had been schooled in the chiliastic rhetoric of Federal Theology; thus, for radical presbyterians, the National Covenant offered tangible confirmation of the dawning of a new age. Furthermore, evidence suggests that the National Covenant became such a vital force in seventeenth-century politics largely because the imagery and rhetoric of millenarianism was relied on to sustain popular interest. So much is clear in the public pronouncements of covenanting activists who were anxious to popularise their cause. Contemporary perceptions about the erosion of acceptable Christian values were linked by propagandists to the Caroline administration's attempts to alter church policy and polity. Samuel Rutherford, a leading dissident, regarded the new religious practices as a 'fiery trial upon the Church'.[81] According to George Gillespie, the political upheaval that resulted was taken as confirmation that 'God seemes of late to be in a veine of working miracles and miracles for us . . . as if God were about a new creation, and as if the new heavens and the new earth were neere at hand'.[82] To achieve the 'new heaven and new earth', emphasis was laid on the need to rejuvenate the reformation of religion, as the sermons of Alexander Henderson make clear. In one given to members of the House of Lords in England in May 1645, Henderson spoke of an evangelical revival as imperative: 'Doth not the present posture of religion, and the constitution of the church (which yet is not so independent, as it is by some desired to be) call as loud for a Reformation, and for settling of religion, as the former did, before a Reformation was begun?'[83] In emulating the work of the sixteenth-century reformers, he argued, the church would be restored to its rightful place as a focal point for national unity. He was adamant, then, that without religious peace there could be no civil peace for, as he put it, the 'reformation is suspended, because the people are distracted; reformation being the only means to reduce them to unity'.[84] Thus the main arguments used in persuading the general populace to support the National Covenant relied heavily on millenarian thinking.

Perhaps the most significant feature of the covenanting ministry's use of millenarianism was the sense of destiny that it imparted so that rank-and-file supporters believed that they were engaged in a divine plan.[85] That Scotland held a special place in the reformed movement was frequently alluded to by covenanting leaders to underscore the momentous nature of the National Covenant, its timeliness and the unique opportunity it presented to complete the process begun by the sixteenth-century reformers. There was the popular assumption among presbyterian radicals that Scots were one of the chosen people practising the purest form of Protestantism; thus, analogies between Scotland and Israel as nations of the elect were common in seventeenth-century sermons.[86] When Henry Rollock wanted to gain adherents to the National Covenant, he made specific reference to this concept: the 'covenant betwixt God and Izrael . . . and betwixt God and this land, now renewed upon most pressing reasons, as the renovation of our infeftments, putting our naime in our faythers hands and the schaiking hands a new after our former schedding, as the only means to kmet us eyther to God or amongst ourselves, as the most gracious, glorious work that ever our God of glory did to this land'.[87] For this reason, too, the nation had a unique part to play in the reformation of religion as a world leader for pan-Protestantism.[88] Scotland then was thought to be in the vanguard of a European crusade modelled on the 'Precedents and Example . . . of the people of God of old, of the reformed Churches of Germany, and the low countrie'.[89] Overtly conscious that they shared a commonality of purpose and an identity of interests with militant Protestants elsewhere, propagandists thus maintained that the outcome of their cause was predicated on the success of their continental counterparts:

> The changes and revolutions which we heare of in other Kingdomes, are documents, that the divine Providence is about some great worke, in which we are now called to act our part, in the sicht of men and angels. The opportunity of Reformation is rare and singular and cannot be parrallel'd in any History, and therefore to be used in all reverence, with heavenly prudence, and abstractnesse of spirit, from earthly considerations. We are zealous of our oune 'liberties', let us be more zealous of the liberties of the Kingdome of Christ that both we ourselves, and the Posterity may have a well grounded and blessed Peace.[90]

It was this acute awareness of their present image and their future legacy then that gave sympathisers their collective sense of destiny. And, by drawing on this readily understood and commonplace imagery in the near hysterical atmosphere of evangelical revival meetings, the popular appeal of the National Covenant was assured.

However, what Federal Theology offered those ordinary communicants drawn from all social ranks was, most of all, a political morality that legitimised resistance to monarchical authority. With its millenarian view of the Reformation and the central role given to the head of state as a 'Christian prince', the new Constantine, traditional assumptions about natural obedience and sovereignty were overturned. Granted, the conventional hierarchical typology of the natural order – consisting of the diety followed by Christ and then the king as God's 'vice-regent' or 'supreme magistrate' on earth ruling over a subservient people – was taken as the inviolable protector of social and political stability. However, in interpreting the relationship between the constituent levels of authority, the emphasis in Federal Theology on contractual obligation as the agent holding this arrangement together made resistance to authority possible.[91] Under this paradigm, there was nothing natural about obedience and deference; instead, in a sense, it had to be earned by proven legitimacy and the authority's demonstrable commitment to legality. So much is evident in a sermon preached at the Glasgow Assembly of 1638 when Alexander Henderson stated that loyalty to a superior was contingent on three conditions. First, on whether he had his 'calling from God' and was thus a legitimate ruler; secondly, whether his 'commandments be lawful'.[92] If the authority of superiors derives from an unlawful office 'we owe them no obedience' and if they were legitimate superiors who 'command what is unlawful we are not bound to obey them'.[93] Thirdly, if civil or ecclesiastical authorities did not fulfil their responsibility by acting according to the wishes of their immediate superiors then the expected obedience of those under them was no longer guaranteed. As Henderson phrased it, 'whenever men begin to go out of line, forget their own subordination, then these that are under them become no way subject to them, because they go out of the right order'.[94] Essentially, these principles account for the Covenanters' aggressive opposition, embodied in the National Covenant, to Caroline religious reforms. As early as December of 1637, at a meeting between government officials and representatives of the protesters held at Holyroodhouse to discuss the implications of the king's latest proclamation, it was the legality of Charles's ecclesiastical policy that was questioned. And despite assurances that there were no plans for further reform and that the service book's use had been suspended, the dissidents were still unwilling to abandon their campaign until the legal issue was addressed. The new book of canons and the revival of the court of high commission were singled out on this score because 'they everted all church discipline, and the lawfull judicatories of the kingdome . . . and yitt wer introduced without, yea contrair to all order of law appoynted in this kirk and countrey, for establishing ecclesiastick constitutiones or lawfull judicatories'.[95] Thus, the Chain of Being which had served so long as a metaphor for the hierarchical paternalism of early modern society was in effect reassembled by covenanting propagandists to accommodate their promotion of a new political and social order. Their watchword on the question of deference seemed to be obedience when necessary but not necessarily obedience. And this view was informed by godly approval, thereby making it legitimate and indeed compulsory for rank-and-file supporters.

It is important to note, however, that the attitudes to kingship fostered by Federal Theology did not encourage popular republicanism. Royalists might regularly identify evangelical presbyterianism as a destructive force threatening religious and political stability[96] and 'anticovenanters' might naturally equate its aspirations with sedition,[97] but it was a point of honour among supporters of the National Covenant that they were committed to the preservation of monarchical government and, in that sense, considered themselves loyal Scotsmen.[98] Throughout the course of the elite's petitioning campaign, every opportunity was taken to dispel royalist allegations about attempts to encroach on the king's authority. A case in point was the Instrument of Protest which was unveiled at the market-cross of Edinburgh on 22 February 1638 by Archibald Johnston of Wariston and John, earl of Cassillis, on behalf of the nobles, barons, burgesses and ministers. In response to charges of sedition made in a recent royal proclamation, it emphasises that all previous petitions against the imposition of the prayer book grew out of a 'preposterous zeall and not out of any disloyaltie or dissafectioun'.[99] Such sentiments were not solely a mechanism for self-preservation; rather, they were reflective of the social and political reality that Scotland was a royalist nation. And it was as monarchists that the people of Scotland questioned the king's sovereignty with the National Covenant. Why this should be so relates to what later became the matrix of covenanting ideology: the concept of a 'covenanted king'. The phrase itself does not appear in the National Covenant and is rarely used before the 1640s. But, during the seventeenth century, it came to be associated with the attainment of civil rights and liberties; or, as was frequently mentioned by radical presbyterians, the 'Magna Charta of our religion'.[100] In essence, the notion of a 'covenanted king' embodied an alternative vision of kingship. What was meant by this ideal as it evolved was a limited monarchy co-existing in a theocratic state. In terms of sovereignty then, the Crown was thus accountable to a human rather than divine authority for, within the theocratic system of government, it was assumed that the national church court, the General Assembly, would function as the ultimate source of power. There was the clear implication that the royal prerogative was restricted. Yet there was no hint of republican government. Under the terms of the National Covenant, the 'people of God' owed allegiance to a civil power; however, it was conditional and contingent on the king fulfilling his prescribed role as the 'godly magistrate' by defending the church. Since the necessity of ensuring the 'preservation and defence of the trew religion'[101] was considered a fundamental duty, any attack on Calvinist doctrine and presbyterian polity regardless of its source was to be challenged. Loyalty to the Crown was therefore warranted only 'if kings, and princes and superior powers, would all strive to have their laws and actions, especially and principally in the worship of God, conform to the will of Jesus Christ'.[102] 'Blind obedience' to a king was undesirable when it directly conflicted with a higher allegiance to religious beliefs or when there was the perception that the 'King comand contrary to God'.[103]

This was not a licence for private individuals to defy authority; on the contrary, resistance was acceptable only if it was a collective action on the part of the community to effect a 'popular reformation'.[104] With the moral imperative to protect the radical presbyterian ideal of the church, it was believed, too, that rebellion under these particular conditions constituted a 'defensive war': a fundamental principle of Calvinist resistance theory in general.[105] How unorthodox this attitude to the social order was may be gauged from the reaction of royalists. They were quick to dismiss notions of a 'popular reformation' and a 'defensive war' as 'a most reall Rebellion and Treason' in which religion was used merely as a pretext for civil disobedience.[106] In *The Remonstrance of the Assemblie of Scotland arraigned of 1650*, the Engagers argued that the war party's continuance of a 'defensive war' was incompatible with monarchical government, for it neither served the public interest nor had any legal or constitutional basis.[107] But, it is the effect of a 'defensive war' on the social order which is identified as particularly alarming for it makes 'popular license the Supreame law, which is the destroyer of all lawes, and the most dangerous evill to all humane societies'.[108] It was within the context of these charges, then, that radical presbyterians sought to justify what amounted to their advocation of popular rebellion. Both scriptural and historical precedent were commonly mustered to legitimise this form of civil disobedience throughout the seventeenth century, for it was regarded as the 'chife mean quherby formerly we wresteled ourselves from under the yocke of tiranie'.[109] For his opponents, Charles I's promotion of Arminianism was taken as an indication that he had contravened divine will. That is why ministers reminded their parishioners of the failings of the Crown due to the inadequacies of the man occupying the sacred office. Preaching at St Giles in 1638, James Rowe urged support for the National Covenant on the grounds that 'theres but a man that stands betweene yea & god, yet by that man & gang tew god'.[110] Such radical thinking was heavily promoted by the covenanting ministry. David Dickson, in a sermon given in August of 1638, declared that obedience to rulers was neither mandatory nor necessary since it was 'Better to obey God than man; quher he prooved that disobedience to God could not be obedience to authoritie, it might weal be disobedience to man'.[111] Therefore, as an expression of communal will, rebellion was justified as a last resort when the individual holding the office of authority failed to retain the public trust.

With Covenant ideology, there was an explicit rejection of the collectivist, sociopolitical obligation to obey out of natural deference to authority in favour of an individualistic responsibility to conscience based on religious conviction. As the criterion for loyalty, the designation of conscience was recognised as a radical choice with potentially serious political repercussions.[112] Those opposed to Caroline religious reforms were well aware that their activities bordered on sedition; nonetheless, they believed that their faith provided the moral imperative. William Rait, a laird who was responsible in his locality for collecting signatures to the National Covenant, shared this attitude. In a letter to the parish minister dated April 1638 informing him of a shire meeting about the National Covenant, Rait gives this same rationale for civil disobedience: 'ye know, Sr, better nor I, that all things ought to be done to edification & not to destruction & many gud men will somtyme absteine from Lawll things & go very far on in indifferent things, for the weaknes of ther christian brethren This is not Sr to urge you or anyman to due any thing against yor mynd and conscience But only most earnestly to intreat you not to suffer any carnall worldly or human respect to any [per]sone ecclesiastick or civill'.[113] Why this mode of thought was particularly remarkable was that it redefined the traditional relationship between ruler and ruled. It was completely at odds with the prevailing view of authority because it introduced an element of choice into the paternalistic system of deference. If personal conviction replaced obligation, then the standard concept of natural, collective loyalty and obedience owed to the established order no longer held. With all of society bound by a covenant in subordination to God, conventional social and political allegiance thus took a back seat to faith and the 'Politick Christian'[114] was created.

Therefore, when ordinary communicants were asked to sign the National Covenant, they did so with a sense of anticipation cultivated by over a generation of proselytising. Religious enthusiasm imbued with millenarianism had uniquely prepared them for this momentous occasion; thus, they were eager to fulfil their collective destiny by making the commitment urged by the radical presbyterian clergy. The covenanting ministry were themselves among the strongest advocates of this evangelical, revivalist sentiment because of their acceptance of Federal Theology. But, at the same time, they were able to tap into this powerful belief system to benefit the cause of the National Covenant. The readily understandable imagery and rhetoric

# The 'Politick Christian' 

of the apocalypse which could be invoked made the covenanting activists' demands and aspirations easily accessible to the Scottish peasantry. By identifying what subsequently became the covenanting movement as the champion of such popular assumptions, the polemicists were able to more clearly define their essential objectives in the public mind; question the political credibility of their royalist opponents; obtain social and political legitimacy for their views; and rally popular support for their campaigns in the country at large. Central to the ideological debate, which resulted in civil disobedience ranging from armed resistance to civil war to rebellion, punctuating each decade from the 1630s to the 1680s, was the seminal issue of sovereignty; that is, the extent of the Crown's right to exercise power. In the process, traditional ideas about the social order and conventional views of deference and obedience came under public scrutiny. What proved so valuable for the continuing popularity of covenanting principles, then, was not only that the Covenanters were seen to be on the right side of the religio-political debate in the popular mind but that the political implications of the Protestant, evangelical and millenarian impulse were of central importance to that public discourse.

## NOTES

1. *Diary of Archibald Johnston of Wariston, 1632-1639*, 2 vols, ed. G. M. Paul (Edinburgh, 1911), I, 327-8. Similar evangelical meetings were held in Cramond and Prestonpans.
2. Edinburgh, Scottish Record Office [S.R.O.], Clerk of Penicuick, MS GD 18/3957[a].
3. S.R.O., Clerk of Penicuick, MS GD 18/3957[a], fo. 2. The 'reading Minister' was seen as a dangerous regression in church practice for 'therewith all ignorance, & blyndnes upon the people for if an ignorant asse, canne but raed this book and gett orders; he may solemnize mariage, minister the supper of the Lorde; and sufficientlye discharge the function of Ministration, on the other side, the ablest preacher that is, may use noe other worde in the time of the Comon prayer and Ministracon of the Sacram[ent]s, then are proscribed in the booke. Soe wee shall make an asse minister, and ablest minister an Asse'.
4. S.R.O., Dalhousie Muniments, MS GD 45/1/45; *Historical Manuscripts Commission, 9th Report* (1885), II, 254.
5. S.R.O., Clerk of Penicuick, MS GD 18/3957[a]. In the communion service, it was said that the 'Minister must pray that God would so blesse and sanctifye the elements of bread

and wyne, that they maye be unto us the waye, bodye and blood of Christ'.
6. S.R.O., Clerk of Penicuick, MS GD 18/3957[b]. For contemporary arguments of the same point see: S.R.O., Airlie Muniments, MS GD 16/46/40; *Reasons Why the Service-Booke was Refused of the Church of Scotland in Certain Grievances, or, The Popish Errors and Ungodlinesse of so much of the Service Book as Antichristian. Plainly laid open, by way of Conference between a Countrey Gentleman and a Minister of Gods Word*, ed. L. Hughes (London, 1642), pp.51-7.
7. S.R.O., Dalhousie Muniments, MS GD 45/1/46.
8. M. Lee, *The Road to Revolution: Scotland under Charles I, 1625-37* (Urbana, 1985), p.199. Although there was continuity in its operation between the Jacobean and Caroline eras, the court of high commission was given wider discretionary powers under a new commission issued in 1634 extending, for instance, to the authority to prosecute pamphleteers.
9. *Letters of Samuel Rutherford*, ed. A. A. Bonar (Edinburgh, n.d.), p.52.
10. No General Assembly met between 1618 and 1638.
11. A. Henderson, *Arguments given in by the Commissioners of Scotland unto the Lords of the Treaty persuading Conformity of Church government, as one principall meanes of a continued peace between the two Nations* (1641), [n.p.], p.2.
12. *Historical Manuscripts Commission*, II, pp.253-4; S.R.O., Dalhousie Muniments, MS GD 45/1/46. W. Ferguson, *Scotland's Relations with England: A Survey to 1707* (Edinburgh, 1977), p.112.
13. C. Russell, *The Crisis of Parliaments: English History 1509-1660* (Oxford, 1985), p.213.
14. S.R.O., Clerk of Penicuik, MS GD 18/3957[a], fo. 2.
15. S.R.O., Dalhousie Muniments, MS GD 45/1/41, fo. 2.
16. Glasgow, Strathclyde Regional Archives [S.R.A.], Records of the Maxwell family of Nether Pollok, subsequently the Stirling Maxwells, MS T-PM 114/7.
17. J. Leslie, *A Relation of Proceedings Concerning the Affairs of the Kirk of Scotland from August 1637 to July 1638* (Edinburgh, 1830), p.69.
18. *Ibid.*, pp.69-70.
19. *Ibid.*, p.70.
20. For the discussion which follows, all quotations from the Negative Confession and the National Covenant are taken from the versions provided in G. Donaldson, *Scottish Historical Documents* (Edinburgh, 1974), vol. III, pp.150-3, 194-201.
21. The Negative Confession of 1581 was subscribed by James VI, his Household and the privy council and then ratified by the General Assembly with a 'general band for the maintenance of religion and the king's person'. The band was also signed by

noblemen, barons, gentlemen, burgesses, ministers and commoners. Its chief purpose had been to 'maintain the said true religion, and the King's Majesty according to the confession aforesaid and acts of parliament'. Rumours about growing Catholic influence gained credibility by the political ascendancy of Esme Stewart, the duke of Lennox.
22. D. Stevenson, *The Scottish Revolution: 1637-1644: The Triumph of the Covenanters* (Newton Abbot, 1973), p.86.
23. C. Hibbard, *Charles I and the Popish Plot* (Chapel Hill, 1983), pp.92-4.
24. *The Acts of Parliament of Scotland* [A.P.S.], 12 vols (Edinburgh, 1814-74), V, pp.184, 179-180.
25. Rae to Campbell, 17 Nov. 1634, in S.R.O., Breadalbane Muniments, MS GD 112/39/556.
26. It reads: 'all lieges are bound to maintaine the King's Majesty's Royal Person and Authority, the Authority of Parliaments, without the which neither any lawes or lawful judicatories can be established . . . and the subjects Liberties, who ought onely to live and be governed by the Kings lawes, the common lawes of this Realme allernerly'.
27. The statement reads in full: 'This Realme could be no more a free Monarchy because by the fundementall lawes, ancient privileges, offices and liberties of this Kingdome not onely the Princely Authority of his Majesty's Royal discent hath been these many ages maintained, but also the peoples security of their Lands, livings, rights, offices, liberties, and dignities preserved'.
28. The call for parliamentary sanction of government policies was a reaction to the almost total absence of parliament since 1625. Prior to the parliament held in 1633, Charles called only one parliament in September of 1628 which lasted one day and produced no legislation. One convention was also held in October and November of 1625 during which twenty-six acts were passed. The last parliament of James VI was in June-August of 1621.
29. I. B. Cowan, *The Scottish Covenanters* (London, 1976), pp.24-5; G. Donaldson, *Scotland: James V-James VII* (Edinburgh, 1971), p.315.
30. G. Rudé, *Ideology and Popular Protest* (London, 1980), p.32.
31. [J. Craig], *An Act published by the General Assembly of Scotland. Being a forme of examination at the speciall desire of the kirke; by them thought to be so needfull, that every Pastor exhort his flocke, to buy the said Booke, and reade the same in the Families; whereby they may be better instructed. And that the same may be read, and learned in Lector Schooles* (London, 1641), p.5. This was a reprint of John Craig's *Ane forme of examination before the Communion* (Edinburgh, 1592).
32. S.R.O., Dalhousie Muniments, MS GD 45/1/50. In recruiting

public support, the protestors commonly argued that 'If we Joyne or selffis wt ye rest & sa ye bodie of the kingdome befound of one mynd it is not unliklie bot so Just a king will give a gracious ans[wer]'.

33. *The Letters and Journals of Robert Baillie*, 3 vols (Edinburgh, 1841), I, pp.67-8. Even moderate Covenanters like Robert Baillie spoke of the necessity of taking an effectual course to 'crosse the undermyners of our whole religion and civil liberties'.

34. J. M. Brown, 'Bonds of Manrent in Scotland before 1603' (Ph.D. dissertation, University of Glasgow, 1974), esp. pp. 334-43, 552-8. This analysis of the significance of political and religious bands in general has been expanded on in Dr Brown's subsequent book. See: J. Wormald, *Lords and Men in Scotland 1442-1603* (Edinburgh, 1985).

35. J. Lumsden, *The Covenants of Scotland* (Paisley, 1914), p.1; F. N. McCoy, *Robert Baillie and the Second Scots Reformation* (Berkeley, 1974), pp.49-50. The Duns Covenant was an anti-Catholic bond subscribed by five lords in 1556 to coincide with Knox's visit to Scotland.

36. Like the National Covenant, fear of foreign domination in the face of a threat to the established church prompted the public declaration. It contained a denunciation of Catholicism and a pledge to uphold the reformed religion 'aganis Sathan and all wicked power that dois intend tyrannye or troubill aganis the forsaid Congregationne'. Two years later, the Lords of Congregation signed another bond declaring that they acted for 'God's cause'. And in April of 1560, the 'contract and band' made at Leith resulting in the removal of French troops from Scotland with English military aid cited the 'reformation of religion according to God's Word' as the chief motivation for the band. See G. D. Henderson, ed., *The Burning Bush: Studies in Scottish Church History* (Edinburgh, 1957), p.61; Donaldson, *Scottish Documents*, III, pp.116-17.

37. *Ibid*.

38. As Dr Brown (Wormald) suggests, the pre-1600 bands were 'quite consciously short-term agreements' involving a number of individuals that emphasized the value of the formal personal alliance'. Brown, 'Bonds of Manrent', pp.552-8.

39. P. R. Beard, 'Martin Bucer and the Covenanted Nation' (unpublished M.A. dissertation, University of Guelph, 1976), p.24; G. Marshall, *Presbyteries and Profits: Calvinism and the development of capitalism in Scotland, 1560-1707* (Oxford, 1980), p.110. The word 'covenant' appears most notably in Joshua, Ezra, Nehemiah and Hebrews. The concept itself figures prominently in the work of Bohatec and Budaeus, the latter, in an examination of God's relationship to man, spoke of the covenant as *'foedus et pactum admirabile'*. It was also explored by the German writer, Musculus, in *Lois Communes*, a book

published in England in 1563. See: Henderson, *Burning Bush*, pp.62, 63, 65-9; R. Greaves, 'The Knoxian Paradox: Ecumenism and Nationalism in the Scottish Reformation', *Records of the Scottish Church History Society*, XVIII (1972), pp.95-6.
40. Henderson, *Burning Bush*, p.67.
41. J. T. McNeil, *The History and Character of Calvinism* (London, 1954), p.269. Ursinus spent seven years in Wittenburg studying under Melanchthon before going to Heidelberg in 1561.
42. Translated into English in 1587, it was accessible in Scotland soon thereafter, for three years later David Rait of Aberdeen University had acquired it. *Ibid.*, pp.270-2.
43. Henderson, *Burning Bush*, pp.65-9.
44. McNeil, *History and Character of Calvinism*, p.307.
45. Henderson, *Burning Bush*, pp.65-9.
46. This ideology as expressed in the National Covenant found an echo in the writings of John Knox. In *Apellation to the nobility, and the estates of Scotland*, he states that collective responsibility to God and to one another joins the people of a community in a common purpose in obedience to the idea of a covenant. He depicts the idea of mutual obligation as an agreement binding man and God in resistance against idolatry. Elsewhere, he refers to the covenant between man and God as a 'conditional promise calling for man's reciprocal obedience', thereby giving emphasis to the notion of the covenant as contract. But, unlike Rollock, Knox does not talk about Scotland as a covenanted nation or of the people of Scotland bound together in a national covenant. See: John Knox, *Apellation to the nobility, and the estates of Scotland*, in *John Knox: A Biography*, ed. P. Hume Brown (London, 1895), pp.353-4; Greaves, 'Knoxian Paradox', pp.95-7.
47. This ideology was also promoted by William Ames or Amesius, the English reformer, who worked mostly in Holland. His work, *Medulla*, first published in 1623, was translated into English in 1642 and quickly became a standard text in Scotland. McNeil, *History and Character of Calvinism*, p.266.
48. S. A. Burrell, 'The Apocalyptic Vision of the early Covenanters', *The Scottish Historical Review*, XLIII (1964), p.13.
49. McNeil, *History and Character of Calvinism*, pp.270-2. Inventories of Scottish university libraries as well as the personal libraries of Covenanters such as Robert Baillie reveal that the work of the Federal Theologist, Cloppenburgius, was also popular. See: Henderson, *Burning Bush*, pp.71-2.
50. Henderson, *Burning Bush*, pp.69-70. The culmination of this tradition was the appearance in 1655 of Samuel Rutherford's *The Covenant of Life Opened*.
51. *Diary of Sir Archibald Johnston*, I, p.326.
52. Glasgow, University of Glasgow - Special Collections (G.U.S.C.), Sermons by Covenanters, MS Gen 32, fos 3-76.
53. Marshall, *Presbyteries and Profits*, p.111.

54. *Historical Manuscript Commission, 6th Report Appendix* (1877), No. 253, p.634.
55. S.R.A., Maxwell of Pollok, MS T-PM 102/21.
56. Marshall, *Presbyteries and Profits*, p.80.
57. Glasgow, G.U.S.C., Commonplace book – Religious thoughts of the Spreul Family, MS Gen 70.
58. Glasgow, G.U.S.C., Commonplace book 17th cent., MS Gen 378; Glasgow, G.U.S.C., Commonplace book on theology 17th cent., MS Gen 1243.
59. S.R.A., Maxwell of Pollok, Diary of Sir George Maxwell, MS T-PM 114/7; Edinburgh, S.R.O., Scott of Harden Lord Polwarth, MS GD 157/1885.
60. *Diary of Sir Archibald Johnston*, I, p.308.
61. *Ibid.*, p.408.
62. McNeill, *History and the character of Calvinism*, p.416. Althusius was a German lawyer who worked as a local official in Emden in the Low Countries.
63. *Diary of Sir Archibald Johnston of Wariston*, p.379.
64. *Ibid.*, pp.292-3.
65. *Ibid.*, p.310.
66. Moreover, the marked growth in publishing activity was actually of greater magnitude than the figures suggest since they purposely do not include the large number of pamphlets and books produced in response to the Caroline religious reforms. All figures are based on an analysis of the data provided in H. C. Aldis, *A List of Books Printed in Scotland before 1700: Including those printed furth of the realm for Scottish Booksellers: With Brief Notes on the Printers and Stationers* (Edinburgh, 1970).
67. *Ibid.* All of these examples are taken from Aldis's list.
68. P. G. Rogers, *The Fifth Monarchy Men* (London, 1966), pp. 138-9. An interesting study of popular millenarianism is B. S. Capp, 'The Fifth Monarchists and Popular Millenarianism', *Radical Religion in the English Revolution*, ed. J. F. McGregor and B. Reay, (Oxford, 1984), pp.165-89.
69. S. A. Burrell, 'Apocalyptic Vision', p.5.
70. *An Abstract of some late Characters. Or, How the principall means appointed for our Reformation is become the main fuell of our Wickedness* (London, 1643).
71. R. D. S. Jack, 'Sir William Mure and the Covenant', *Records of the Scottish Church History Society*, XVII (1969), p.8.
72. J. Nimmo, *Narrative of Mr. James Nimmo: Written for his own satisfaction to keep in some Remembrance the Lord's Way in Dealing and Kindness towards Him, 1654-1709*, ed. W. G. Scott-Moncrieff (Edinburgh, 1889), p.42.
73. T. Hayre, *Christs kingdom on earth, opened according to the Scriptures. Herein is examined what Mr. Tho. Brightman, D. J. Alstede, Mr. J. Mede, Mr. H. Archer, The Glimpse of Sions Glory, and such as concurre in opinion with them, hold*

*concerning the thousand years of the Saints Reigne with Christ, And of Satans binding: Herein also their Arguments are answered* (London, 1645).
74. P. Collinson, 'A Chosen People? The English Church and the Reformation', *History Today*, XXXVI (1986), pp.14–20.
75. For a different view see A. Williamson, *Scottish National Consciousness in the age of James VI* (Edinburgh, 1979). Here, Dr Williamson argues that the millenarian tradition and the concept of a 'godly prince' did not exist to any great extent in Scotland.
76. *Basilikon Doron of King James VI*, ed. J. Craigie (Edinburgh, 1944).
77. *The Booke of the Universal Kirk, Acts and Proceedings of the General Assemblies of the Kirk of Scotland* (Edinburgh, 1839–45), I, pp.108–9.
78. A. Henderson, *Reformation of Church-Government in Scotland, Cleared from some mistakes and prejudices: By the Commissioners of the General Assembly of the Church of Scotland, now at London* (Edinburgh, 1644), p.5a.
79. S.R.O., Dalhousie Muniments, MS GD 45/1/79.
80. Aldis, *List of Books*, No. 747.
81. *Letters of Samuel Rutherford*, p.79. Rutherford often alludes to the degeneration of moral and spiritual values which he believes are reflected in Caroline church reforms; thus, the Church is 'decaying – she is like Ephraim's cake . . . and the grey hairs are here and there upon her'. See: *Ibid.*, p.48.
82. G. Gillespie, *Certaine Reasons tending to prove the unlawfulnesse and inexpediencie of all Diocesan Episcopacy (even the most moderate). Together with some needfull points suddenly suggested considering the season. Untill by the good providence of God a more full and mature discourse may bee prepared and published (if neede so require) by some better hand* ([Edinburgh], 1641), p.15.
83. A. Henderson, *A Sermon, Preached before the Right Honourable House of Lords, in the Abbey Church of Westminster, upon Wednesday the 28th of May 1645* (Edinburgh, [1846]), p.105.
84. A. Henderson, *A Sermon, Preached before the Lords and Commons, at Margaret's Church in Westminster, upon Thursday the 18th of July, 1644* ([Edinburgh], [1846]), p.78.
85. Burrell, 'Apocalyptic Vision', p.6.
86. For example, John Sterling's sermon notes dating from 1 June 1673 on the text Hos: 8:2 'Let the trumpet to thy mouth' offer a classic example of this apocalyptic vision. See: S.R.A., Maxwell of Pollok, MS T-PM 114.
87. *Diary of Archibald Johnston*, I, p.326.
88. Burrell, 'Apocalyptic Vision', p.10.
89. A. Henderson, *A Speech delivered by Mr. Alexander Henderson, immediately before the taking of the Covenant by the House of*

*Commons and the Assembly of Divines* (Edinburgh, 1643), pp.26-7.
90. A. Henderson, *The Unlawfullness and Danger of Limited Prelacie or Perpetuall Precidencie, in the Church, Briefly discovered* (London, 1641), p.19.
91. Burrell, 'Apocalyptic Vision', p.13.
92. A. Henderson, *The Bishops Doom. A Sermon Preached before the General Assembly which sat at Glasgow anno. 1638. On occasion of pronouncing the sentence of the greater excommunication against eight of the bishops, and deposing or suspending the other six. By Alexander Henderson, moderator of that and several subsequent assemblies. With a Postscript on the present decay of church discipline* (Edinburgh, 1792), p.18.
93. *Ibid.*
94. *Ibid.*, p.17.
95. Leslie, *Relation of Proceedings*, p.35.
96. Edinburgh, National Library of Scotland [N.L.S.], Lauriston Castle Collection – 'Sermons 1644', MSS 153, fos 99-106, 181-213, 214.
97. An especially good though highly exaggerated example of this rhetoric is found in the paper 'Wittie queries anent the settling of government', in which the anonymous writer dismisses presbyterian polity as the 'platonicke imaginarie perfection of the newe fangled presbiterian anarchie, which cannot be reached by Sence nor evidenced by experience unlesse it be in utopia or in the world of the Moone'. See: Edinburgh, S.R.O., Guthrie of Guthrie Manuscript, MS GD 188/20/13/12.
98. S.R.O., Airlie Muniments, MS GD 16/46/40.
99. S.R.O., Leven and Melville Muniments, MS GD 26/14/15.
100. N.L.S., Wodrow Papers, MSS Oct V., fos 356v-357r.
101. N.L.S., 'Papers of the Earls of Lauderdale' – in Watson Collection, MSS 597 fos 140-141v.
102. Henderson, *Bishops Doom*, p.16.
103. *A Scriptural Chronicle of Satans Incendiaries, Viz. Hard-hearted Persecutors and Malicious Informers, With their Work, Wages, and Ends, who were Instruments of Cruelty against true Worshippers*, ed. Charles Hariss (London, 1670), p.16.
104. Propagandists were always careful to emphasise that civil disobedience was undertaken as part of a public cause and not as a private initiative. Indeed, this was one of the chief points of contention between the moderate Covenanters and the Cameronians in the 1680s. See: N.L.S., Wodrow MSS Oct. V., fos 356v-357r; fo. 360; fos 367-8.
105. In a seminal article on the origins of resistance theory, Quentin Skinner questions the view of Calvinism as an unique ideology that inspired revolutionary impulses in the sixteenth-century wars of religion throughout western Europe, as articulated most succinctly by Michael Walzer. Although Professor Skinner

agrees with the basic premise of Walzer's thesis that the most prominent defenders of a populist and secular theory of civil disobedience in the early modern period were Calvinists themselves, he points out that the Calvinist theory of revolution was not original, for it draws heavily on Catholic theories of good government and Lutheran arguments on the justification for revolution. See: Q. R. D. Skinner, 'The Origins of the Calvinist Theory of Revolution' in *After the Reformation*, ed. B. C. Malament (Manchester, 1980), pp.309-30; M. Walzer, *The Revolution of the Saints: A Study in the Origins of Radical Politics* (Cambridge, Mass., 1965).

106. S.R.O., Dalhousie Muniments, MS GD 45/24/2, 3. See also: S.R.O., Scott of Harden, MS GD 157/1828/2.
107. *Remonstrance of the Assemblie of Scotland arraigned* (1650), [n.p.], pp.8, 10.
108. *Ibid.*, pp.18-19.
109. *Register of the Privy Council of Scotland*, 38 vols, Edinburgh (1905), XII, p.489.
110. N.L.S., 'A Sermon preached att St Giles ye great church in Edinburgh uppon a fast day ye last Sunday in July by Mr James Rowe', MSS 498 fo. 27. Although the inside cover of the manuscript bears the date 1646, it is obvious from the content of the sermon that it dates from 1638. See also: *Letters of Samuel Rutherford*, p.485.
111. *Diary of Sir Archibald Johnston*, I, p.377.
112. S.R.O., Shairp of Houston Muniments, MS GD 30/1723. As the exemplar of Divine Right theory, Charles I naturally deplored the idea of a 'popular reformation' because the 'inferior Magistrate or People (take it which way you will)' had no authority to instigate change in any manner; least of all by an uprising. Thus, he was unequivocal in his attitude to the subject: 'I shall think all popular Reformation, little better than Rebellion'. Furthermore, as he made clear, it had no foundation in law: 'as I doe acknowledge it a great sinne for any King to oppress the Church, so I hold it absolutely unlawfull for subjects (upon any pretense whatsoever) to make Warre (though defensive) against their lawfull Sovreigne'. See: *The Papers which passed at New-castle betwixt His Sacred Majestie and Mr Al: Henderson: Concerning the change of Church-Government Anno Dom. 1646* (London, 1649), pp.37, 38, 44.
113. S.R.O., Rait of Hallgreen General Papers 1509-1723, MS RH 15/37/200.
114. S.R.A., Maxwell of Pollok, Diary of Sir George Maxwell, MS T-PM 114/7.

# Three

## THE MAKING OF
## THE NATIONAL COVENANT

Edward J. Cowan

On 1 April 1638, the 'gloriousest day that ever Edinburgh enjoyed', the National Covenant was reaffirmed yet again. As the people lifted their hands to swear, according to Archibald Johnston, 'thair rayse sik a yelloch . . . as the lyk was never seien nor heard of'.[1] Three hundred and fifty years later it is worth asking what caused the 'yelloch' and whether, in the longer historical perspective, it was truly justified. This paper will argue that the formulation, and subsequently the subscription, of the Covenant constituted one of the most profound experiences in Scottish history. The author, however, must confess a similar unworthiness for the task of investigation as that articulated by the great architect of the Covenant himself: 'Thou knowest the stammerings, or rather the unskraiped overhaistings of my tongue, the schilpitnes of my wit, the unclean, unsolid undistinctnes of my judgement, the sliperie sliderines of my memory . . . how ungifted, unfit, unready, unable for so weighty a piece of service of sic importance.'[2]

To the making of papers about the making of the National Covenant there is potentially no end. Charles I's alienation of his Scottish subjects has been recounted in numerous publications.[3] There are abundant details as to how the Covenant actually took shape from 1637 onwards in the pages of contemporary sources such as Wariston's *Diary*, the *Large Declaration*, Rothes' *Relation*, Baillie's *Letters and Journals*, the works of historians of the Troubles such as Spalding and the various Gordons, and in the pamphlet literature, to name no others.[4] But such an account would prove excessively tedious, a lang sang set to a dismal tune, about a subject that has claimed during these past three and a half centuries more than its fair share of stunningly boring historical commentary. This paper will, rather, attempt a fresh look at a phenomenon which was essentially a Scottish response to a contemporary European preoccupation with the nature of power and authority. There were peculiar reasons as to why the Covenant should have developed in Scotland and there were equally peculiar Scots standing in the wings to orchestrate such developments. If many individuals responded haphazardly to the bewildering historical forces which engulfed Scotland in the first half of the seventeenth century,[5] a reconsideration of the evidence suggests that almost every stage in the process was carefully and consciously planned by some of the brightest minds ever to grace a Scottish leadership. Consideration will also be given to some of the inspirational forces on which these men drew and to their extensive labours that would be rewarded on Wednesday, 28 February 1638, 'that glorious marriage day of the Kingdome with God'[6] when the Covenant was first subscribed in Greyfriars Kirk.

The discussion that follows is no doubt influenced by a myriad of assumptions but two of these might be specifically mentioned. First, there is good evidence for arguing that Scotland before 1638 manifested many of the symptoms of what has long been distinguished as the 'General Crisis of the Seventeenth Century'.[7] Secondly, a related though probably less contentious point, Scotland was placed in a revolutionary situation as a result of the subscription of the Covenant. Modern theory on the subject tends to distinguish between rebellion and revolution by considering their respective consequences: a revolution is described as such if it succeeds; a rebellion if it does not.[8] This convention of defining the means in terms of the end seems curiously ahistorical. If such tenets are adopted we might ask when did the Wars of Independence end, when did Scotland become a nation, or when was the Scottish Reformation accomplished?

It is perhaps permissible to seek some guidance on this problem in the tangled roots of the legendary past, when Finn asked the *fianna* what was the best music they had ever heard. Conan thought it was the music of sport, Diarmid conversation with a woman, another the cry of his hounds. Oisin loved the music of the woods, 'the sound of the wind and of the cuckoo and the blackbird, and the sweet silence of the crane' while Osgar relished the striking of swords in battle. But Finn believed it was the music of the thing as it happened.[9] It is one of the tasks of the historian to record and analyse this music. We need not fear the label 'Scottish Revolution' and we can perhaps even agree that the Revolution had been accomplished by June 1641. If it was subsequently lost that is another matter.

It has been convincingly demonstrated that a preoccupation with the idea of the *covenant* predated the Reformation of 1560.[10] A covenant was essentially a compact, contract or promise for eternity to which God and his people were parties, as in the Old Testament. There is now a voluminous literature on the notion of the covenant, much of it distinctly unhelpful as far as the student of seventeenth-century Scotland is concerned.[11] People of the period undeniably studied the Bible but they were not necessarily biblical scholars. They regarded the Bible as divinely inspired and monolithic; though they could split theological atoms with the best of them they were, basically, credulous fundamentalists.

It is important to note that the Scots derived their notion of the covenant as much from Zwingli and Bullinger as they did from Calvin and that they particularly stressed the idea of the double covenant – that one entered into a covenant for purposes of civil as well as religious reform. It is one of the tragedies of Scottish historiography that the Covenant was for so long regarded by deluded presbyterian ministers and their opponents as being exclusively concerned with matters of religion. It emphatically was not. Religion was a convenient pretext for the exploitation of a device which would enable the constitutional remoulding of the small world that was Scotland; it is the civil component which makes the Scottish movement truly revolutionary. Yet, despite the earlier, and best, efforts of such luminaries as Robert Rollock, the first and distinguished principal of Edinburgh University, who is credited with being 'the first Scot to expound the notion of the double covenant systematically',[12] it would appear that by the late 1630s Scots sympathetic to the covenanting cause shared a less-than-perfect understanding of covenant theology. The evidence suggests that in the heady days of subscription the ministers, less concerned with matters of grace and redemption than they were with some kind of manifest destiny, would happily preach on any biblical reference to the covenant.[13] Many of their references would be considered by modern authorities to be of doubtful value and perhaps even irrelevant to the concept as it is now rigorously defined.

To James Carmichael, minister of Haddington, belongs the credit for first distinguishing the Negative Confession of 1581 – the total abjuration of popery sworn by the household of James VI in the aftermath of the Esme Stewart scandal – as a covenant.[14] Linguist, poet and collector of proverbs, Carmichael was described by his friend, mentor and associate, Andrew Melville, as 'the profound dreamer' and 'our Corydon of Haddington'. The two were forced into English exile in 1584, Carmichael subsequently devoting himself, for some three years, to collecting materials for a presbyterian apologia.[15] His inspirational example accounts for the presence of the Negative Confession as the first part of the National Covenant. Nonetheless, it might be suggested that talk about a covenant during what was to all intents and purposes an evangelical revival in 1596[16] has been misinterpreted. It has been hailed by some authorities[17] as the morning star of the National Covenant whereas it may be more convincingly viewed as the evening star of the Melvillian dusk. The 1596 episode was a temporary aberration. By that date the presbyterian lights were going out over Scotland and with them the phantom glimmerings of the Covenant; the Jacobean episcopal moon was in the ascendant.

Even before he departed Scotland for the glories of the English throne, James had placed himself at the centre of a debate that would consume all of Europe.[18] As the American scholar, Francis Oakley,[19] shows, the debate focused upon the apparent demise of the Great Chain of Being; medieval constrictions upon monarchy were giving way to royal absolutism. That absolutism was to be challenged, throughout Europe, by ideas about popular sovereignty. James's own ideas about Divine Right, enshrined in his *Basilikon Doron* and *The Trew Law of Free Monarchies*, were in themselves a specific response to the Scottish situation – the twin threats of presbyterian parity and the political propaganda of the king's old tutor, George Buchanan.[20] However opportunistic or anachronistic James's arguments were, they pointed the way to the future, towards Stewart despotism and to the era of the Sun King himself.[21]

As James indicated in his speech to the House of Lords in 1609, the rival theories on ultimate authority were enshrined in two rival covenants.[22] This same view was admirably summarised in the tract *Vindiciae Contra Tyrannos* anonymously published, allegedly at Edinburgh in 1579 and, needless to state, full of ideas for which James himself would later have nothing save contempt. The *Vindiciae* is thought to have been compiled by Philippe Duplessis Mornay and it was given an Edinburgh location in the hope that it might be passed off as the work of none other than George Buchanan, who survived until 1582.[23] Mornay argued that a two-fold covenant was sworn at the coronations of Old Testament kings: 'the first between God, the king, and the people, that the people might be the people of God; the second between the king and the people, that the people shall obey faithfully, and the king command justly.' The essential thrust of his argument is best described by himself. 'In the first covenant or contract there is only an obligation to piety; in the second to justice. In one the king promises to serve God religiously: in the other, to rule the people justly. By the one he is obliged with the utmost of his endeavours to procure the glory of God; by the other the profit of his people'.[24] Since Mornay believed in popular sovereignty he was in no doubt whatsoever that if the ruler broke the contract, or compact, the people's representatives not only had the right, but the duty, to resist him.

Even those who could not agree with the radical ideas of Mornay were aware that the rival positions were encapsulated, on the one hand, in the Mosaic covenants (in Deuteronomy) which Moses mediated between God and his people and, on the other, in the covenant in 2 Samuel 7 in which God promises that as a reward for his loyalty David's descendants will rule forever,[25] a covenant which could be interpreted in terms of Divine Right, thus tracing the origins of the seventeenth-century sovereignty debate back to the covenants in the Old Testament. Margaret Judson long ago pointed to the 'poverty of political thinking of men participating in the great controversy between king and parliament' in England,[26] a view that might now be modified, for the same accusation could hardly be made of the Scots who had been discussing the covenant for well over half a century and who had been quite familiar with the arguments of George Buchanan concerning the deposition of a monarch who had clearly infringed the covenant, namely, Mary Queen of Scots. Indeed one might venture further, beyond the Scottish 'conjectural historians' of the sixteenth century, such as John Major and Hector Boece, to the discussions on the nature of kingship preserved in such medieval compilations as Walter Bower's *Scotichronicon* and the *Liber Pluscardensis*, to suggest that Jacobean concerns had long been entrenched in Scottish political thought.

But the situation after 1603 lent further point to the debate; the problem of the kingless kingdom after the departure of James VI for England created a profound crisis which manifested itself in numerous ways. In brief, the Scots, or many of them, feared absorption by the larger kingdom with consequent loss of identity and the suppression of their institutions. There were acute concerns – well justified, as it turned out – about the status of Scots law, about religion, and about matters cultural and economic.[27] Such anxieties were fine-tuned through a combination of chauvinism and anglophobia but, above all, by the sheer sense of bewilderment engendered by the removal of the monarch.

Indeed, that single fact of the absentee king is one of the major counters to those who would dispute the existence of a 'crisis' in

## The Making of the National Covenant

seventeenth-century Scotland.[28] Symptoms of crisis are not hard to detect. In the space of barely one generation the *ecclesia Scoticana* had experienced the Knoxian reformation and the substitution of bishops by superintendents who were, in turn, suppressed, as well as Andrew Melville's introduction of presbyterianism outlawed by the Black Acts and then apparently established in 1592 only to be rapidly subject to the reimposition of bishops. What *was* the true polity of the reformed Scottish church? Crisis-fixated historians have so far failed adequately to explain the state of the Scottish economy in the early seventeenth century[29] but James's parting gesture in 1603 of setting the value of the Scottish pound at one-twelfth that of the English one, is surely diagnostic as was the perception, even if it was no more than that, that henceforth Scottish wealth would be drawn to London.[30] The Scottish aristocracy clearly believed itself to be under threat (admittedly a perennial problem) trapped as, emphatically, it was between feudalism and feuars. Its anxieties were greatly reinforced by the king's creation of a *noblesse de robe*. Nor can the nobility have received much comfort from the attack on kinship orchestrated by Kirk and Crown.[31] The savagery of the assault upon clanship was unprecedented[32] and as obsessional as the contemporary preoccupation with the witch-hunt[33] and the suppression of Scottish popular culture.[34] Elite culture also perceptibly suffered in the absence of royal patronage.

It has been observed that 'there was nothing inevitable about the Scottish revolution; the king provoked it by his own ineptitude';[35] this, despite the obvious rejoinder that no one has so far argued the inevitability of revolution. Another unavoidable question is that if monarchical ineptitude was a cause of developments in the 1630s why had revolution not taken place long before? The seventeenth century had no monopoly on ineffectual kings, which had been a Stewart legacy ever since the accession of the dynasty in 1371. To deny that there was a crisis seems to fly in the face of contemporary opinion. Robert Baillie was to refer to the Solemn League as marking 'a new period and crise which these hundred years has exercised thir dominions',[36] while Alexander Henderson argued that the National Covenant was 'qualified by expresse limitations and restrictions to this kirk and kingdome, to the Religion, Lawes and Liberties of Scotland' and as such could not be extended to England;[37] in other words, the Covenant had a structural relationship to Scottish society and institutions. In 1633 William Lithgow preserved, in a poem as tedious as it was tendentious, arguments which had been in circulation at the time of the Union. Towns and trade were in a state of decay while the nobility squandered their wealth in England – two million pounds worth of gold having been transported to London since 1603. Scottish noblemen cultivate English accents, Lithgow observes, and have

> growne effeminat, weare womens loks
> Freize hanging, combd o're shoulders, necks and cloks,
> That many doubt, if they bee mayds or men
> Till that their beards sprout forth and then then ken.[38]

There is doubtless much exaggeration in Lithgow's effusion, which, remarkably, was designed to be personally addressed to Charles on the occasion of his Scottish coronation, but he admirably demonstrates the petty attribution of Scotland's ills to the absentee monarch as well as the sense of *ennui* such absence had generated.

As opposition to the absolutism of Charles I increased, the major dissidents sought to appeal to precedent or example. The major thrust of contemporary dialectic was, of course, geared precisely in the direction of discerning some justification for present action in the Bible, classical literature, various theoretical writers and historical experience. George Buchanan, among others, had satisfactorily (to partisan contemporaries) demonstrated how this could be done. The trouble was that the situation in early seventeenth-century Scotland was absolutely without Scottish precedent. Scotland claimed to be one of the oldest monarchies in Europe but until 1603 the rulers had always existed amidst their own people. Novel mechanisms now had to be distinguished in order to cope with the alien, or foreign, ruler. As early as 1620, Sir John Gordon of Gordonstoun put his finger on the matter when he observed that James as 'absolute King of all Great Britain may when he listeth daunt the proudest and mightiest of you all'. Things were not as they had been a generation before.[39] And while James was regarded as a native son, the problem intensified under Charles who, despite being born at Dunfermline, was viewed as a foreigner by virtue of his upbringing and instinct. It is apparent from the voluminous writings of covenanting apologists that their major source of inspiration in refining resistance to Stewart despotism was the Dutch Revolt.

Modern Dutch scholars – or at least those whose writings it has been possible to consult – stress the haphazard nature of developments in the Netherlands from the 1560s onwards. Fairly typical of such opinion is the observation that 'the Dutch Republic came into existence less as a result of a pre-conceived plan, than as a consequence of an unexpected combination of political events'.[40]

E. H. Kossman has tirelessly argued in several places that the

## The Making of the National Covenant

historical literature on the Revolt is as 'chaotic and inconclusive' as the historical events themselves; that 'the Revolt was not made by theorists', nor was it 'based upon a solid set of political doctrines'.[41] The parallels between the sixteenth-century Netherlands and seventeenth-century Scotland are potentially as suggestive and intriguing to modern commentators as they were to anxious activists in the 1630s. It could be argued that while historical developments are almost always chaotic the Dutch experience ensured that the Scottish response was less so – indeed, that it was quite the opposite.

It should be stressed that the chronicle of covenanting achievement between 1637 (perhaps even 1633) and 1643 was one of virtually unmitigated success. Painful though the admission may be, it must be confessed that the triumph of the covenanting leadership was not typically Scottish; it is even more remarkable that these men were presbyterians, individuals who might have been expected to create endless possibilities for dissent, disagreement and disaster. There is much truth in the old adage that only one idea is required to create twenty new Scottish kirks. The single-minded orchestration of protestation and petition, culminating in the Covenant itself, is truly astonishing. It is, above all, the clarity of expression, the sophisticated level of articulation, the lucidity of argument in these documents which impress. The accomplishment is the greater when it is considered that many of the perorations were conceived to answer various purposes: they had to answer legal objections from opponents in both England and Scotland; they served as political propaganda for the interested population at large; and they were designed to settle the doubts of a generation trained in theological disputation of the most obtuse and hair-splitting variety. In many cases they had to get by committees and commissions before they could be published, and even among supporters they had to satisfy the often disparate and competing carpings of the nobility, the ministers and the lawyers, not to mention the entrenched views of individuals among the leadership.

Before we enquire further into the impact of the Dutch Revolt it is worthwhile to review briefly the covenanting leaders if only for the reason that these men have, by and large, not received the credit they deserve. They succeeded in a few months, to paraphrase the famous response of Spottiswoode, in throwing down at once 'all that we have been doing these thirty years past'.[42] There has been an unfortunate conspiracy over the years – probably less real than it is apparent – to detract from this achievement.

It is, for example, something of a disservice to Archibald Johnston of Wariston that his diaries have survived. These are truly remarkable productions but they almost defy scholarly investigation, at least by historians; they are better suited to the interests of psychologists or psychiatrists. Couched in braid Scots the nuggets of historical value are frequently overwhelmed by the dross of Johnston's endless ravings with his God. His prose can be delightful but his alternating moods of self-doubt and buoyancy, reported as actual conversations with God, ultimately repel. The reader is frequently drawn up short, as when Johnston solemnly reports, 'the Lord remembered me to remember him back again', a neat allusion to a temporary lapse in omniscience. The diaries provide an invaluable portrait of Johnston holding forth to his family on the finer points of the Negative Confession, discoursing with his brother-in-law on 'the power of the king and the three estates', imbibing literature on the French Wars of Religion or the Dutch Revolt, reviewing the legislation of the Scottish Parliament or reflecting on 'the insupportable burden of drawing up the Band . . . laid upon my weak shoulders'. But the overall effect is of a religious maniac – thanking God for placing him in his mother's womb, complaining about the destination of his estates, sobbing, weeping, shrieking, fainting like some deluded member of an American televangelical show in which God is virtually reduced to some divine personal property.[43] It has been well observed that it is one of the 'peculiarities of Calvinism that it should have credited God with the values of a small-town notary public and to explain to Him what He could not do'.[44] There were doubtless many around like Johnston who had a highly subjective and familiar approach to their God and who, indeed, created Him in their own image. The revivalism which swept presbyterian Scotland in the 1630s was, potentially, extremely difficult to contain but the leadership took pains to harness it for political ends; many shared Argyll's conviction that 'popular furies would never have end if not awed by their superiors'.[45] Yet in the midst of his most demented confessional ramblings Johnston can casually inform his readers that he framed a protestation while riding from Wariston to Edinburgh. There is an important point to be noted here – namely, that there is a huge gulf between Johnston's private and public personae, but the bizarre documentation about the former is so voluminous as to almost overwhelm the latter. Yet Johnston's public prose is as lucid as his diary is convoluted and obtuse; the clarity and economy of his legalistic style stand out in an age which worshipped verbiage and which often refused to accept one word where twenty would suffice.[46]

Similarly dismissive evaluations are made of Johnston's colleagues, with the exception of the highly gifted Alexander Henderson, who is almost alone in the enjoyment of near-universal approbation. Balmerino's masterly supplication of 1634 is devalued because he was supposedly a minor individual with personal grievances to settle. The earl of Rothes, on the basis of an eighteenth-century statement grounded in the most profound ignorance,[47] is dismissed as a frivolous character given to 'light living' despite the impressive counter-testimony preserved in his own *Relation*,[48] commissioned in two parts and intended to preserve an accurate record of events leading to the Covenanting Revolution, almost a testament in the biblical sense of the word. The worst (and the best) that could be said of him was that he enjoyed a joke. He was always jesting, a man who could reduce the pomposity and tediousness of endless disputation with humour. There is much mournful joy in covenanting chronicles but not a lot of laughter. Is it possible that Rothes understood, with François Rabelais and Sir Thomas Urquhart of Cromarty, that all the world's great historical dramas unfold before the chorus of the laughing people?[49] If so, he is to be cherished rather than condemned. Lord Loudoun is yet another scorned. He has been characterised as one of the most acquisitive and grasping of all of the great Clan Campbell (which is to say a lot),[50] despite the gravity of his speeches, his invaluable participation in the debates and the certainty that his prominent role was potentially placing his neck in a noose. All of these men were very well aware that they were engaged upon one of the headiest experiments in Scottish history. What should not be in doubt is that they possessed in full measure the mental equipment and the requisite moral rigour to achieve their ends.

Nonetheless, the covenanting leaders and their supporters faced the problem of finding the necessary arguments to achieve their goals. The appeal to Scottish history could take them only part of the way. George Buchanan had shown how and why a monarch could be deposed, but what procedure should be adopted if the king happened to be absentee? At this point they returned to the inspirational example of the Dutch Revolt. Charles I became Philip II; Archbishop Laud was Cardinal Granvelle. As episcopacy had been thrust upon the Netherlands, so it had been imposed upon Scotland. There was even a parallel and inconclusive debate, in which both Scots and Dutch participated, as to whether each represented God's chosen people, their countries a second Israel.[51] Far from suffering an 'embarrassment of riches',[52] the Scots experienced what might be called a 'want of plenty', but this lack of economic wealth was in part compensated for by an abundance of theoretical ideas.

It might be tentatively suggested – though this would require further investigation – that the idea of the covenant was somewhat eclipsed during the post-Union reigns of James VI and his son. For one thing, the Godly Ruler or Covenanted King was neither present, godly nor covenanted. The covenanting idea and ideal survived among the fanatical few, among the conventiclers and the presbyterian preachers who took themselves off to Ireland, but as a mainstream notion it almost evaporated along with precise knowledge (later to be resurrected by Johnston) about the presbyterian establishment. Here again, in the matter of the Covenant, the Dutch Revolt was to prove inspirational. In 1638 Archibald Johnston was studying the *Politica Methodice Digesta* of Johannes Althusius, or Johann Althaus, the great apologist for the Revolt.[53] First published in 1603, the *Politica* can be seen as providing a blueprint for the Scottish Revolution. In what follows only some of the possible influences of Althaus will be indicated. The *Method* of his title was Ramist; that is, Althaus followed the logic of Peter Ramus, whose ideas were by no means unknown in Scotland.[54] Ramism was concerned with the proper organisation of materials in order to discover and clarify knowledge. Ramus himself wrote that 'those who think wisely and methodically descend from the most general idea to the various divisions thereof, and thence to the particular cases it comprehends'.[55] As this methodology informs the work of Althaus, his, in turn, influences that employed in pamphlet after covenanting pamphlet.[56]

Althaus regards politics as 'symbiotics', the art of living together, *symbioses* translating as 'associations' or 'federations'. Each of those ascending associations, from the basic Aristotelian unit of the family to federations of states, is governed by a compact (*pactum*).[57] A few examples, with minimum comment, should illustrate the significance of his ideas upon Scottish thinking. The other point to note is that Althaus himself was heavily influenced by the so-called 'monarchomachs',[58] by Duplessis Mornay and, above all, by George Buchanan. In a sense he was returning the Scottish tradition in political thinking to the Scots via the medium of the Dutch Revolt.

The basic or most primitive association is that which embraces relatives, kinsmen and friends. Althaus discusses kinship at some length, considering how the head of a kin may be a *princeps*, investigating the obligations of blood right, marriage and so on; he might almost have had kin-thirled Scotland in mind as he wrote. What governs such relationships is a *pactum* or covenant.[59] Johnston of

Wariston refers to his own marriage as a 'paction', he, for his part, 'promising never to gloume nor glunche on hir befor folks, and shoe vowing never to disobey me in any companie'.[60]

Outside of the family there exist *collegia*, associations of farmers, merchants, craftsmen, workers, scholars, clergymen, and so on. They associate for specific purposes, usually occupational or professional, and this relationship is similarly governed by a modicum of regulation and right: a *pactum*. These collegia are, in turn, incorporated into the city, cities into the province. Consideration of the province leads Althaus into a discussion of the ruler and the bottom line here is that rulers are still emphatically governed by the *pactum*: 'the less the power of those who rule, the more lasting and stable the imperium is and remains'.[61] The responsibility for constituting the supreme magistrate (which description could, of course, embrace the king) is entrusted to a body that Althaus calls the 'Ephors' – a generic term for the elders, the estates or the nobility who by one name or another are 'protectors of the covenant entered into between the supreme magistrate and the people'.[62] These ephors are 'superior to the supreme magistrate to the extent that, representing the people, they do something in its name'.[63] An example of such superiority in action was the resistance of the Dutch ephors against Philip of Spain. Althaus takes time out to refute William Barclay's *The Kingdom and Regal Power*, which argued *contra* Buchanan that the people through the *pactum* alienated their power to the king.[64] James VI had, of course, advanced a similar argument and Charles was to carry those identical prejudices to the block. To anyone who has even superficially investigated Scottish political ideas from the Declaration of Arbroath onwards, Althaus's theories on popular sovereignty require no elaboration; they reinforced existing elements in the Scottish political psyche.

Equally familiar from 1597, when the term is first used in Scotland, are Althaus's remarks on fundamental law. He cautions that in constituting the supreme magistrate 'the highest concern must be had for the fundamental law of the realm. For under this law the universal association has been constituted in the realm. This law serves as the foundation, so to speak, of the realm and is sustained by the common consent and approval of the members of the realm'.[65] It is no mere coincidence that the Scots felt compelled to stress fundamental law in the aftermath of the personal Union and the concept was to become an obsession of the Covenanters.[66]

His section on Ecclesiastical Administration was pure Calvin and here again there was little that was unfamiliar. Interestingly, in view of the contentious way in which the phrase was later used by the Covenanters,[67] this passage contains several instances of the ominous expression 'according to the word of God'. Ecclesiastical administration comprises two tasks for which the magistrate is responsible – the introduction of orthodox religious doctrine and practice and, secondly, the conservation, defence and transmission to posterity of this doctrine and practice. The fulfilment of these duties is promised in a religious covenant (*pactum religiosum*).[68] The implications are elaborated in almost text-book fashion as they were later to be by covenanting propagandists.

A section on civil administration contains advice on a variety of topics, from representation to the conduct of warfare, but it was the virtually inevitable conclusion of the *Politica* that would most appeal to the Covenanters. The opposite of 'just and upright administration' is tyranny.[69] Not all rulers who fail are to be described as tyrants; there is always the possibility of reform. But the unrepentant tyrant must be removed by the ephors, and not, be it noted, by the private citizen – a point fudged by Buchanan.[70] Tyranny exists and consists in the overthrow and destruction of the fundamental laws of the realm. A second type occurs when the magistrate 'like an enemy plunders, perverts and upsets church and commonwealth'.[71]

Charles I was clearly guilty on both counts; yet, just as Althaus counselled that 'remedies other than deposition for curbing and coercing tyranny should be first attempted time and again until they prove to be without effect',[72] so the National Covenant was initially designed to bring the king to his senses. Against the possibility of failure, Althaus provided a programme leading to the next phase of action, a model which the Solemn Leaguers would adopt in 1643. The tyrant should be resisted by word and deed, 'by words when he by words only violates the worship of God and assaults the rights and foundations of the commonwealth and by force and arms when no alternative has succeeded'.[73] Althaus's greatest achievement was to bring together the moment and the tyrant, and his message was by no means lost on the Covenanters.

What is remarkable throughout the *Politica* is Althaus's confidence. Hardly any of his statements are qualified; there are no 'ifs' or 'buts' and opponents such as William Barclay are blown away. E. H. Kossman has argued that Althaus's theories ultimately had 'a paralysing rather than a stimulating effect on the Dutch Calvinists of the seventeenth century' – and the same point could be made about their Scottish counterparts in the same period and during the following century. However, he goes on to make a further interesting

## The Making of the National Covenant

point which provides yet another Scottish parallel. Althaus's work, says Kossman, was 'monarchical not so much because it preferred the monarchy to all other forms of government . . . but simply out of inner logical necessity. It was monarchical because it was constitutional'.[74] Scottish belief in the constitutional monarchy was to drive a very large nail into the coffin of the Covenant at Charles's execution in 1649. Not even the later Covenanters, the proud upholders of Christ's republic during the Killing Times, could escape the language of constitutional dialectic. Remarkably, that language still haunted constitutional debate in Scotland on the three hundred and fiftieth anniversary of the National Covenant.

So what evidence is there that the Covenanters were reading Althaus? Johnston of Wariston tells us that *he* was, and internal references suggest that he had been familiar with the *Politica* for some time.[75] Carl Friedrich observed that of all the writings of the seventeenth century, Samuel Rutherford's *Lex Rex* 'comes closest to the Althusian position'.[76] That is because Rutherford had clearly devoured the whole of Althaus. There are echoes of Althaus in Rothes' *Relation* and in the correspondence of Archibald Campbell, marquis of Argyll who would become the great leader of the covenanting cause.[77] One of the most inspiring passages that Alexander Henderson ever penned appeared in his *Instructions for Defensive Arms* (1639) – 'The people make the magistrate [king], but the magistrate maketh not the people. The people may be without the magistrate but the magistrate cannot be without the people. The body of the magistrate is mortal, but the people as a society is immortal'.[78] A powerful sentiment! Great words that make one proud to belong to the same nation as the man who wrote them! But they were lifted straight out of chapter nineteen of Johann Althaus's *Politica Methodice Digesta*.[79]

There were other suggestions in Althaus which almost certainly influenced Johnston and his cohorts. To select just one among many, the following recommendation could be seen as something of a double-edged weapon:

> One of the estates, or one part of the realm can abandon the remaining body to which it belonged and choose for itself a separate ruler or a new form of commonwealth when the public and manifest welfare of this entire part altogether requires it, or when fundamental laws of the country are not observed by the magistrate but are obstinately and outrageously violated, or when the true worship and disclosed command of God clearly require and demand that this be done.[80]

This is fine if a person is part of the dissenting or separating minority but a fatal notion to the cause if different estates decide to pursue different courses; and this the Covenanters realised full well. Johnston was as worried about the ministers as he was about the 'grandee lawyers'. There was tremendous apprehension, even in 1638, about the 'small men' of the south and southwest. There were equally grave suspicions about the motives and inclinations of the nobility, while so outraged were the burgesses of Glasgow by the excesses of Charles I that they cancelled Guy Fawkes Day.[81] To make matters worse, many within these different factions would not have given an oatcake for religion.

What was truly remarkable in the covenanting experience of 1638 was that there should have been a physical document that one could actually sign in the knowledge that it was a covenant. In the writings of the sixteenth century, in Althaus and the others, the covenant was an abstraction. It was, for example, understood that the king at his coronation undertook to uphold the true religion. Why then demand an actual document or copies thereof in 1638? Why an actual subscription? Why not a verbal oath, a swearing on the Bible, as would have been more typical of the period?

It is the remarkable, coincidental collision between religion and absolutism that provides the explanation. Religious alienation provided the opportunity, one might even suggest the excuse, for constitutional reform. The civil issue was just as important (and, of course, it was included) but no single secular issue could have generated such universal reaction. Religious innovation was symptomatic of what appeared to be an attack upon Scottish identity.[82] The Covenanters were serving notice to their monarch that a new age had dawned. But it was not just a new era of contract and legal justification so far as the monarch was concerned. The insistence upon signatures also heralded a new age of social and civil responsibility, of a written constitution, a truly inspirational example which signposted the long road through the American and French revolutions. It was an assertion of individual human dignity and a reinforcement of civic responsibility which still has relevance three hundred and fifty years later as we contemplate the forces of repression throughout the world. This is not to deny that the Covenant itself ultimately became an instrument of rigid totalitarian repression – but, for one fleeting moment in 1638, Scotland provided an example to a world in which the unrestrained hounds of tyranny were a universal problem.

At that same moment in Greyfriars in February of 1638 Johnston, Henderson, Loudoun, Rothes and the rest provided the Covenanters with a potent myth to compensate for the history that had been lost in 1603. Successful myths must encompass the past, the present and the future; what was, what is and evermore shall be. The invention of the Covenanters' myth, predicated upon none other than God Himself, was inspired, ingenious, brilliant, above all perverse and ultimately it failed catastrophically. But it happened and we should listen to its music.

NOTES

1. *Johnston of Wariston's Memento Quamdiu Vivas and Diary from 1632 to 1639*, ed. G. M. Paul (Edinburgh, 1911), p.331.
2. Johnston, *Diary*, I, 276.
3. The most useful accounts are those contained in Gordon Donaldson, *Scotland James V to James VII* (Edinburgh, 1965); David Stevenson, *The Scottish Revolution 1637-1644: The Triumph of the Covenanters* (Newton Abbot, 1973); Walter Makey, *The Church of the Covenant 1637-1651* (Edinburgh, 1979); Maurice Lee, *The Road to Revolution* (Urbana, 1985). For a recent review article see David Stevenson 'Scottish Church History 1600-1660: A Select Critical Bibliography', *Records of the Scottish Church History Society* XXI (1982), 209-20.
4. W. Balcanquhal, *A Large Declaration Concerning the Late Tumults in Scotland* (London, 1639); John, Earl of Rothes, *A Relation of Proceedings Concerning the Affairs of the Kirk of Scotland* (Edinburgh, 1835); Robert Baillie, *The Letters and Journals*, ed. D. Laing, 3 vols (Edinburgh, 1841-2); John Spalding, *Memorialls of the Trubles in Scotland and in England 1624-1645*, 2 vols (Aberdeen, 1850); J. Gordon of Rothemay, *History of Scots Affairs from MDCXXXVII to MDCXLI*, ed. J. Robertson and G. Grub, 3 vols (Aberdeen, 1841); Patrick Gordon of Ruthven, *A Short Abridgement of Britane's Distemper MDCXXXIX to MDCXLIX* (Aberdeen, 1844); Robert Mentet (Menteith) of Salmonet, *The History of the Troubles of Great Britain*, trans. James Ogilvie (London, 1735).
5. Edward J. Cowan, *Montrose For Covenant and King* (London, 1977), ch. 2 and p.101.
6. Johnston, *Diary*, I, 322.
7. Trevor Aston, ed., *Crisis in Europe 1560-1660* (London, 1965); Geoffrey Parker and Lesley M. Smith, eds, *The General Crisis of the Seventeenth Century* (London, 1978); Peter Clark, ed., *The European Crisis of the 1590s: Essays in Comparative History*

(London, 1985). The arguments of H. R. Trevor-Roper in 'Scotland and the Puritan Revolution', *Religion, the Reformation and Social Change* (London, 1967), pp.392-444 have been thoroughly discredited by, among others, William Ferguson, *Scotland's Relations with England: A Survey to 1707* (Edinburgh, 1977), pp.118-19. My own assessment of the problem, 'The Union of the Crowns and the Crisis of the Constitution in 17th Century Scotland', in *The Satellite State in the 17th and 18th centuries*, ed. S. Dyrvik, K. Mykland, J. Oldervoll (Bergen, 1979), pp.121-140 is totally at odds with Maurice Lee, Jr., 'Scotland and the "General Crisis" of the Seventeenth Century', *S.H.R.* LXIII No. 176 (1984), 136-154.

8. See Lawrence Stone, *The Causes of the English Revolution 1529-1642* (London, 1972); G. E. Aylmer, *Rebellion or Revolution: England 1640-1660* (Oxford, 1987), pp.204-5; Stevenson, *Scottish Revolution*, pp.315-26. One historian who is not troubled by the concept of 'defeated revolutions' is Perez Zagorin, *Rebels and Rulers 1500-1660*, 2 vols (Cambridge, 1982). On this problem there are some instructive comments in Christopher Hill, '"Reason" and "Reasonableness"', in *Change and Continuity in Seventeenth Century England* (London, 1974), 103-23. Two useful parallels to the Scottish situation can be found in Parker and Smith, *General Crisis* - John Elliott, 'Revolution and Continuity in Early Modern Europe', pp.110-33 and A. Lloyd Moore, 'The Preconditions of Revolution in Early Modern Europe: did they really exist?', pp.134-64. See also Martha Francois, 'Revolts in Late Medieval and Early Modern Europe - A Spiral Model', *Journal of Interdisciplinary History* V (1974-5), 19-43.

9. Lady Gregory, *Gods and Fighting Men: The Story of the Tuatha de Danaan and of the Fianna of Ireland* (repr. Gerrards Cross, 1976), pp.246-7.

10. Arthur Williamson, *Scottish National Consciousness in the Age of James VI* (Edinburgh, 1979), *passim*; Roger Mason, 'Covenant and Commonweal; the language of politics in Reformation Scotland', in Norman Macdougall, ed., *Church, Politics and Society: Scotland 1408-1929* (Edinburgh, 1983).

11. See, e.g., Delbert R. Hilliers, *Covenant: The History of a Biblical Idea* (Baltimore, 1969); Klaus Baltzer, *The Covenant Formulary in Old Testament Jewish and Christian Writings*, trans. David E. Green (Oxford, 1971); J. Wayne Baker, *Heinrich Bullinger and the Covenant: The Other Reformed Tradition* (Athens, Ohio, 1980). The covenant is a perfect illustration of how theologians and historians can look at exactly the same evidence and arrive at totally different conclusions; see J. B. Torrance, 'Covenant or Contract? A Study of the Theological Background of Worship in Seventeenth Century Scotland', *Scottish Journal of Theology* XXIII (1971). For two important articles (which, however,

require modification) by an historian see S. A. Burrell, 'The Covenant Idea as a Revolutionary Symbol: Scotland 1596-1637', *Church History* xxvii (1958), 338-50 and 'The Apocalyptic Vision of the Early Covenanters', *S.H.R.* xliii (1964), 1-24.
12. Williamson, *National Consciousness*, p.76.
13. Johnston, *Diary*, I, 320-1, 322, 327-9.
14. *The Miscellany of the Wodrow Society*, vol. 1, ed. David Laing (Edinburgh, 1844), pp.440-4; Cowan *Montrose*, pp.29-30.
15. On Carmichael see *The James Carmichael Collection of Proverbs in Scots*, ed. M. L. Anderson (Edinburgh, 1957), pp.31-42; *East Lothian Biographies*, ed. W. Forbes Gray and James H. Jamieson (Haddington, 1941), pp.31-2; Gordon Donaldson, 'Scottish Presbyterian Exiles in England 1584-8', in *Scottish Church History* (Edinburgh, 1985), pp.178-90 (reprinted from *Records of the Scottish Church History Society* xiv (1963), 67-80.)
16. David Calderwood, *The History of the Kirk of Scotland*, ed. T. Thomson, 7 vols (Edinburgh, 1842-9), V, 408, 433-7; Alexander Peterkin, ed., *The Book of the Universall Kirk of Scotland* (Edinburgh, 1839), 423-39.
17. The 1596 episode has held an entrenched place in presbyterian and covenanting historiography ever since the time of Calderwood. See, for example, D. Hay Fleming, *The Story of the Scottish Covenants in Outline* (Edinburgh, 1904), pp.26-7; R. Moffat Gillon, *John Davidson of Prestonpans* (London, 1936), pp.147-66. Although it is anachronistic to use the term 'revival', the contemporary language and metaphor are identical to those employed in later movements.
18. Margaret A. Judson, *The Crisis of the Constitution: An Essay in Constitutional and Political Thought in England 1603-1645* (New Brunswick, 1949); W. H. Greenleaf, *Order, Empiricism and Politics: Two Traditions of English Political Thought* (London, 1964); Gerald R. Cragg, *Freedom and Authority: A Study of English Thought in the Early Seventeenth Century* (Philadelphia, 1975); C. C. Weston and Ian J. R. Greenberg, *Subjects and Sovereigns: The Grand Controversy Over Legal Sovereignty in Stuart England* (Cambridge, 1981).
19. Francis Oakley, *Omnipotence, Covenant and Order: An Excursion in the History of Ideas From Abelard to Leibnitz* (Ithaca, 1984), p.93.
20. Cragg, *Freedom*; like all too many writers on this topic, Cragg fails to note James's Scottish antecedents, though they had long been well recognised. C. H. McIlwain, ed., *The Political Works of James I* (Cambridge, Mass., 1918), xxxvii.
21. Oakley, *Omnipotence*, pp.94-5; Greenleaf, *Order*, p.67.
22. Oakley, *Omnipotence*, p.103ff.
23. Harold J. Laski, *A Defence of Liberty Against Tyrants: A Translation of Vindiciae Contra Tyrannos* (London, 1924; rep. 1963), pp.57-9. On Mornay see Quentin Skinner, *The*

*Foundation of Modern Political Thought*, Vol. 2, *The Age of Reformation* (Cambridge, 1978), pp.315-18, 325-35.
24. Laski, *Defence*, pp.71, 175-6. There is a discussion of Mornay's possible debt to Bullinger in Baker, *Heinrich Bullinger*, pp.174-7.
25. Richard Elliott Friedman, *Who Wrote the Bible?* (New York, 1987), p.105.
26. Judson, *Crisis*, pp.8-9.
27. Cowan, 'Union of the Crowns' *passim*. Despite the fact that this article appears to have impacted upon the world of scholarship with all the force of a feather landing on the surface of Loch Ness many of its arguments are confirmed by Bruce Galloway in *The Union of England and Scotland 1603-1608* (Edinburgh, 1986) and Brian Levack in *The Formation of the British State* (Oxford, 1987). As these words are being written the parallels between the 1630s and the 1980s appear striking. An autocrat sitting in distant London still treats the Scots like errant schoolchildren while a handful of placemen dominate their native country, intent upon the imposition of an alien liturgy. Creeping anglicisation in Scottish institutions is still a lively issue, as is, unbelievably, the issue of increased taxation without representation. It would be the supreme irony if, on the anniversary of the subscription of the National Covenant car stickers were to appear bearing the legend: 'Come Back Charles I, all is forgiven!'
28. Lee, 'General Crisis', *passim*.
29. An honourable exception is Rosalind Mitchison, *Lordship to Patronage Scotland 1603-1745* (London, 1983), pp.48-51. See too the pioneering S. G. E. Lythe, *The Economy of Scotland in its European Setting 1550-1625* (Edinburgh, 1960). Further study of this topic is urgently required.
30. Sir Thomas Craig, *De Unione Regnorum Britanniae Tractatus*, ed. C. S. Terry (Edinburgh, 1909), pp.446-55.
31. Williamson, *National Consciousness*, pp.69-71, 33-8.
32. Edward J. Cowan, 'Clanship, Kinship and the Campbell Acquisition of Islay', *S.H.R.* LVIII (1978), 132-57, 'Fishers in Drumlie Waters: Clanship and Campbell Expansion in the Time of Gilleasbuig Gruamach', *Transactions of the Gaelic Society of Inverness* LIV (1986), 269-312.
33. Christina Larner, *Enemies of God: The Witch-hunt in Scotland* (London, 1981); Edward J. Cowan, 'The Darker Vision of the Scottish Renaissance: the Devil and Francis Stewart', in *The Renaissance and Reformation in Scotland: Essays in Honour of Gordon Donaldson*, ed. Ian B. Cowan and Duncan Shaw (Edinburgh, 1983), pp.125-40.
34. Edward J. Cowan, 'Calvinism and the Survival of Folk' in Edward J. Cowan, ed., *The People's Past* (Edinburgh, 1980), pp.32-57.
35. Lee, 'General Crisis', p.151.
36. Baillie, *Letters and Journals*, pp.11, 90.

37. *A Declaration Against a Cross Petition* (Edinburgh, 1643), pp.11-12.
38. Cowan, *Montrose*, p.38.
39. Sir William Fraser, *The Sutherland Book*, 3 vols. (Edinburgh, 1892), II, 357.
40. Eco Haitsma Mulier, 'The Language of seventeenth century republicanism in the United Provinces: Dutch or European?', in *The Languages of Political Theory in Early Modern Europe*, ed. Anthony Pagden (Cambridge, 1987), p.179.
41. E. H. Kossman and A. F. Millink, eds, *Texts Concerning the Revolt of the Netherlands* (Cambridge, 1974), pp.1-2.
42. J. Spottiswoode, *History of the Church of Scotland*, 3 vols (Edinburgh, 1851), I, cx.
43. Johnston, *Diary* I, 269, 312, 315, 319, 321, 356.
44. Mitchison, *Lordship to Patronage*, p.27.
45. Archibald Campbell, Marquis of Argyll, *Instructions to a Son* (Glasgow, 1743), p.6.
46. David Reid, 'Prose After Knox', in *The History of Scottish Literature*, Vol. 1, *Origins to 1660*, ed. R. D. S. Jack (Aberdeen, 1988), pp.183-97 recycles all the hoary clichés about Scottish prose in the 17th century. The voluminous writings of the Covenanters are virtually ignored, along with notably and lamentably, the extensive pamphlet literature. (Incredibly, the same omissions occur in *The Party-Coloured Mind*, ed. David Reid (Edinburgh, 1982), a volume of extracts ironically subtitled *Prose relating to the Conflict of Church and State in Seventeenth Century Scotland*, Reid, having dismissed the 'workmanlike style' and the 'plainness' of covenanting apologist prose (p.186), barely lingers over Johnston, presumably on account of his 'gross emotionalism' (p.190). It is truly remarkable that the lit. crit. fraternity (and sorority) appear to have totally overlooked the centrality of Johnston to the entire debate about Scottish letters in the 17th century and indeed beyond. The man retained Scots for the private language of his diaries and reserved English for his public prose. His verbal rendition of the latter was, no doubt, in Scots. This point has been reinforced in conversation with Billy Kay. See his stimulating discussion in *Scots: The Mither Tongue* (Edinburgh, 1986).
47. He was allegedly 'of a disposition prone to levity and addicted to pleasure', quoted Rothes, *Relation*, ii.
48. Rothes' *Relation* was to be revised by Balmerino according to Johnston's *Diary*.
49. Mikhail Bakhtin, *Rabelais and His World* (Bloomington, 1984), p.474. On Rothes' humour, see J. Gordon of Rothiemay, *History*, I, 33.
50. By this author among others, 'Drumlie waters', 292-3.
51. G. Groenhuis, 'Calvinism and National Consciousness: the Dutch

Republic as the New Israel', in *Britain and the Netherlands*, VII, *Church and State Since the Reformation*, ed. A. C. Duke and C. A. Tamse (The Hague, 1981), pp.118-33; Arthur Williamson, 'The Jewish Dimension of the Scottish Apocalypse: Climate, Covenant and World Renewal', in *Menasseh Ben Israel and His World*, ed. Yosef Kaplan, Henry Mechoulan and Richard H. Popkin (Leiden, 1989), pp.7-30.

52. Simon Schama, *The Embarrassment of Riches: An Interpretation of Dutch Culture in the Golden Age* (New York, 1987).
53. Johnston, *Diary*, I, 348. Johannes Althusius, *Politica Methodice Digesta*, ed. Carl J. Friedrich (Cambridge, Mass., 1932). In view of what follows it is an interesting coincidence that while this edition was the second volume in the *Harvard Political Classics* series, the first was McIlwain's *Political Works of James I*. For a translation see Frederick S. Carney, *The Politics of Johannes Althusius* (London, 1964). For commentary: Otto von Gierke, *The Development of Political Theory* (New York, 1966), original German text published 1880.
54. Williamson, *National Consciousness*, p.138.
55. As quoted by Carney, *Politica*, p.xviii.
56. Cf. Mitchison, *Lordship to Patronage*, p.24: Ramism 'merely reinforced the other influences which limited profound thinking'.
57. It seems to me that Skinner is too rigid when he states 'contract (*pactum*) is wholly separate from the idea of the religious covenant (*foedus*)', *Political Thought*, II, 331. Althaus in several places appears to use *pactum* in the latter sense, e.g. *pactum et contractum*, *Politica*, p.162. He also uses the term *pactum religiosum* (Carney, *Politics*, p.157).
58. As Friedrich observes, they could more accurately be termed tyrannicides, *Politica*, lvi.
59. Carney, *Politics*, p.22.
60. Johnston, *Diary*, I, 10.
61. Carney, *Politics*, p.92.
62. Carney, *Politics*, p.94.
63. Carney, *Politics*, p.100.
64. Carney, *Politics*, pp.103-4. William Barclay (c.1546-1608) studied at Aberdeen and spent most of his life in France. His best-known publication, a detailed refutation of Buchanan, was *De Regno et Regali Potestate* (Paris, 1600) [*The Kingdom and the Regal Power*]. He coined the term 'monarchomachs' - 'king killers'. See Skinner, *Political Thought*, II, 301.
65. Carney, *Politics*, p.123.
66. Williamson, *National Consciousness*, pp.79-82.
67. Edward J. Cowan, 'The Solemn League and Covenant', in *Scotland and England 1286-1815*, ed. Roger A. Mason (Edinburgh, 1987), pp.190-1.
68. Carney, *Politics*, p.156-7.
69. Carney, *Politics*, p.185.

70. Duncan H. MacNeill, *The Art and Science of Government Among the Scots, Being Buchanan's De Jure Regni Apud Scottos* (Glasgow, 1964), p.95ff; I.D. Macfarlane, *Buchanan* (London, 1981), p.399.
71. Carney, *Politics*, p.186.
72. Carney, *Politics*, p.189.
73. *Ibid*.
74. E. H. Kossman, 'The Development of Dutch Political Theory in the Seventeenth Century', in *Britain and the Netherlands. Papers Delivered to the Oxford-Netherlands Historical Conference 1959*, eds. J. S. Bromley and E. H. Kossman (London, 1960), p.95.
75. Johnston, *Diary*, I, 310, 348.
76. Carney, *Politics*, p.xii, intro. by C. J. Friedrich.
77. A superficial reading of both texts will demonstrate the indebtedness of the *Relation* to the *Politica*. Possible influence upon Argyll is more problematical since he explicitly communicated few of his ideas. His *Instructions to a Son* indicates that he shared many of Althaus's views on the family, and particularly the clan led by a *princeps*. It seems to me that Argyll's sentiments in the remarkable series of letters he addressed to Strafford in 1638-9 may owe something to Althaus's notions on the delegation of authority to the ephors. (In Knowler, ed., *The Earl of Strafford's Letters and Despatches*, 2 vols (Dublin, 1740), II, 220; Carney, *Politics*, p.191.) Argyll's actions would also suggest that he was quite persuaded by Althaus's argument on choosing a separate ruler, in this case, Campbell himself (cited below – note 80). This whole matter requires, and will receive, fuller investigation.
78. Printed in Andrew Stevenson, *The History of the Church and State in Scotland from the Accession of King Charles I to the Restoration of King Charles II*, 2 vols (Edinburgh, 1754), II, 686-95. The earliest edition of this pamphlet that I have been able to consult is one of 1642.
79. Carney, *Politics*, p.117.
80. Carney, *Politics*, p.191.
81. Johnston, *Diary*, I, 321; Lee, *Road to Revolution*, p.216.
82. Cowan, 'Union of the Crowns', 127-9.

# *Four*

## THE SCOTTISH NATIONAL COVENANT AND BRITISH POLITICS, 1638–1640

### Peter Donald

'Was there ever any realme since Christ's incarnation professed Christian religion so universally . . . in such puritie, discipline, and publike worship, with such liberties and for so many yeares together, as our realme hath done?'[1] Thus beginning his pamphlet, reissued in 1638, on the Scottish Church, David Calderwood captures the self-confidence and pride in the Reformation which undergirded the making of the Scottish National Covenant. History and faith together informed that vision. The heart of the Covenant was the Negative Confession of 1581 against popery. A second section extensively cited Acts of the Scottish Parliament going back to the Reformation. A third bound its present signatories in adherence to and in defence of the 'aforesaid true religion'.[2] As if to answer David Calderwood, much of Scotland joined in the cause.

As was made explicit in the text, the Covenant was a band against innovations. It was composed in 1638 against a background of protest at a string of innovating policies in the Church of Scotland, latterly and most infamously the Scottish Book of Common Prayer. The history of ecclesiastical troubles reached back further, to the Five Articles of Perth and, for some die-hards (Calderwood included), the revived episcopacy of James VI and I. Nonconformists made their defence through selective use of precedent and legislation. Some set their targets high, but the unity of the Covenant movement was more a constant goal than a fact. Ambiguity in the Covenant on the question of bishops elicited some dispute even at the outset, most prominently from Robert Baillie, who wished to be quite clear that he was not swearing commitment to the abolition of episcopacy.[3] Similar problems surrounded the matter of the Perth Articles. The strongest opponents condemned innovation contrary to the early achievements of the Scottish reformers: they felt that kneeling at Communion, feast days, episcopal confirmation and the private administration of the sacraments were highly suspect – practices that tended towards popery if they did not actually constitute it.[4]

The ambiguity as to what constituted innovation proper to be resisted can be explained simply. Episcopacy and the Five Articles both had substantial legislation in their support. Although the Covenant made much of the 1592 Act which, in its day, had upheld presbyterianism, it could not deny, but only overlook, what stood in contradiction to that high point for the anti-episcopal cause. In the period of the National Covenant, however, the momentum of the Troubles deriving from the introduction of the service book was fully exploited. During 1638, arguments already harnessed concerning both the alleged illegitimacy of the 1621 Act regarding the Five Articles and the abuses of episcopacy were taken far. By the end of the year, at the Glasgow Assembly, these were abjured and the Covenant, accordingly, officially reinterpreted. In copies of the Covenant subsequent to that assembly, a short addition was written at the foot to make explicit what was meant.[5]

The Covenant was signed by the noblemen, barons, gentlemen, burgesses, ministers and commons – an all-inclusive list purposely designed to convey a sense of unanimity in the country behind a common cause. A mark of the opposition to royal policy in Scotland was its social spread, which was acknowledged in the operation of the Tables in Edinburgh, but however wide the potential support in the localities, the importance of the leadership of the Covenant should not be underestimated. An emphasis on law and precedent, however selective it was, had much to offer, and the diligence of Archibald Johnston of Wariston alongside some prominent noblemen deserves to be singled out. Wariston did not work alone as a lawyer and draughtsman in the service of the Covenant, but he was – at least on the basis of the sources we have – the principal labourer. He was intensely committed to opposing what had come to Scotland by anglicising and ungodly means. He went as far as any, again at least in writing, in voicing antipathy to the ways of Charles himself.[6]

The regime behind the innovation was as much the focus of opposition as the recent changes themselves. The mutual band which comprised the third section of the Covenant was utterly political, implying that support of the king was conditional on his upholding the 'aforesaid religion, liberties and laws'. Despite the careful wording, designed to keep this from making an explicit challenge, Charles appreciated correctly its tenor.[7] For him, the band above all was offensive. It struck directly at what was dearest to him, his royal authority. Borrowing an image from King James's writings, he affirmed bitterly that as long as this Covenant was in force, he had no more authority than a Venetian Doge.[8]

The king's position is the first part of the British dimension of the National Covenant story. If we turn first to origins, we have to take into account the history of the Reformation in Scotland, effected against the will of the Crown, and the struggle thereafter for authority in the Church. James VI, more than his cousin Elizabeth, had to fight to assert his supremacy. The Scottish Church had further to contend for its special identity following the Union of the Crowns in 1603. Technically English churchmen kept well out; but their proximity to the king, together with the recommendations in a king's eyes of episcopal church government and a single order of worship, gave English divinity in practice a distinct advantage. Episcopacy was the order of church government most consonant with monarchy (as the bishops themselves were quick to maintain); a universally observed liturgy protected the people from the vagaries of individual ministries and bred them in a good faith.[9] James was not shy of telling the Scots that some things English were good and to be appropriated.[10] Both in disciplining Scottish presbyterians in 1605-6 and in the separate, contentious policies that led to the Five Articles of Perth, the king enjoyed the support of English churchmen.[11] It was nevertheless problematic that Englishness was joined with high claims for the royal prerogative.

James, more than Charles, acknowledged the reality of differences in the Scottish situation. Charles was ready for the most part to pay lip-service, but was remarkably insensitive to regional feeling. His general incapacity to suffer opposition was critical. He was unwilling to acknowledge sustained objections to policy that he approved: quick, rather, to suspect contradictory or modificatory advice and even to brand it as seditious. The politics of ruling over three kingdoms would always have been problematic in the early seventeenth-century situation; Charles exacerbated matters considerably. To take our present subject, he consistently overruled protest on ecclesiastical matters. In 1626 it had been ordered that only ministers being newly admitted would be forced to observe the Five Articles of Perth, a grudging compromise that solved little. In the Convention of Estates in 1630, and even more in the parliament of 1633 which Charles himself attended, written protest was fobbed off and ignored; those who dissented on the church legislation earned his particular displeasure.[12] Charles was standing firm on his absolutist notions of royal authority in a kingdom in which he was not even resident and in which, it appears, there was continuous discontent concerning matters of the Church. It was impolitic rule and in Scotland particularly it was to his cost. Opposition to the new liturgy and canons was expected, but the decision to avoid any form of national consultation was a major grievance around which the opposition could organise.[13]

The parties who embraced the idea of a Covenant stood therefore to a national cause against an absentee king. English history was no adequate recommendation for changes; Scots were quick to point to the long-standing divisions even there concerning proper practice. The Scottish Reformation was seen as more perfect than the English; as long as nothing had been or could be vouched against it, there was no reason to uproot it by changes smacking of popery. The tradition of general assemblies for the Scottish Church was blatantly being bypassed. Since the means of introducing the innovations as much as the changes themselves was the focus of opposition, the Scottish bishops – figures already highly vulnerable by virtue of animosities raised on other fronts – took the brunt of the attack. The liturgical policy dictated stood little chance. The opposition plausibly raised a charge of bad counsel and appealed to Charles for remedy.[14]

Initially, in 1637, the king preferred not to listen. Scotland was one of three kingdoms and therefore had to conform in obedience to his fiat. Nonconformity in the church was not a problem unique to Scotland. British as well as Scottish government was at stake. Archbishop Laud, whose part in the making of the service book Charles had been pleased to command, feared a likely conjuncture between the Scots and the puritan factions in England and Ireland.[15]

Scots clambered to influence the king but Charles kept a British perspective. Naturally and without hesitation, when it was felt that force might be needed to subdue the recalcitrants, the king turned to all three kingdoms for his support. As the marquis of Hamilton made his way north in May 1638, secret preparations were beginning in England; Lord Deputy Wentworth, to his displeasure alongside the Catholic earl of Antrim, was warned to prepare for a possible need for force from Ireland.[16] At the same time, efforts were stepped up in England and Ireland for detection of the passage of Covenanter propaganda and to guard against likely expressions of support.[17] Although in Scotland the National Covenant was distinctly Scottish, it had immediate British consequences.

While we have already remarked on the relevance of English divines to Scottish church policy, Charles I, like his father, accepted at least the general need for Scotsmen in his government. The decision to send the marquis of Hamilton to Scotland in 1638 as the king's personal representative was in line with this; Hamilton's strong position with Charles ensured that much of the subsequent direction of policy depended on his counsel. The aim was very much to confine the problem to Scotland. Through his troubled and demanding mission, Hamilton kept a ready awareness of the risk of outside ramifications of his work. Indeed it was to the advantage of the line he took, namely to try to effect a peaceful compromise to the Troubles, that he could play for time on account of the king's slow military preparations in his other kingdoms. There was something of a chain reaction here. At the outset, Charles was urged to hold back his anger while Hamilton tried to isolate the leading troublemakers. This obliged both a delay of stiff proceedings against their likely friends and a continuing secrecy surrounding what armed preparations there were. Ways of conciliation were advanced but they foundered probably as significantly on Charles's lack of responsiveness as on an unwillingness to negotiate in Scotland. The 'royal way' of force did little better. In Ireland, Wentworth's efforts helped to keep the large numbers of Scots there under control, but the privy English war administration was far from able to answer the king's wild expectations of it.[18]

The Covenant provided a powerful symbol for those who continued in protest. It was least secure in the latter part of 1638, when Hamilton, with support from other councillors, most prominently the earl of Traquair, organised a rival covenant for subscription in the country. Known as the King's Covenant, it took the Negative Confession and added a band of combination which had no implications for limiting Charles's authority; the alleged innovations of recent years were not mentioned.[19] Many signatures were procured in the face of opposition. However, the better organisation of the original Covenanters won through in the end. The general assembly allowed by Charles to meet at Glasgow at the end of 1638 was packed to ensure determinations that repealed all alleged innovations, including episcopacy, and that upheld the suitably interpreted original Covenant.[20]

In 1639 the prospect of war became very much more real. New subscription of the Covenant was taken to be a mark of loyalty, and royalists were systematically made powerless.[21] Precisely the opposite course was taken by the king. The Scots who went with the marquis of Hamilton in a sea offensive up the east coast were required to sign an oath that included a pledge to sign no covenant without the king's approval. In Ireland, Wentworth forced all Scots to take a similar oath specially composed.[22] There were Scots loyal to the king but Scottish identity had become something suspect. Judging by the evidence which survives of correspondence intercepted for Secretary Windebank in England, Scottish mail was systematically interfered with in the hope of discovering seditious contacts. In June 1639, all Scots in and around London were obliged to take the oath already used in Ireland against the Covenant.[23] Subscription of the Covenant was not supposedly enforced in Scotland before late 1639; it had become a touchstone of loyalty long before.

Domestic politics obviously were thrown into disarray by the Scottish Troubles, first in Scotland and then elsewhere as the war effort gained momentum. Foreign politics too were affected, and the possibility of the king taking action in Europe became increasingly unlikely. Though many Protestants in the British kingdoms wished Charles to take a lead on the Continent, the king's tendency had been to keep at a distance; this was accentuated under the strains of the Scottish crisis. Furthermore, first Spanish, then French intervention was suspected for the Covenanters; efforts were made to block the Scots' import of arms, not to mention experienced soldiers, from the Continent.[24]

Charles clearly never would give way willingly to the Covenanters. In some limited measure he heeded the counsels of Hamilton and Traquair; thus far pragmatic, but always responding slowly to the course of events, he nevertheless remained devoted to his ultimate ideals – which could make him shifting and devious, ready to nurse sinister intentions for the future if present prospects were bad. He affirmed the value of the contentious service book at Berwick in 1639, long after it had ceased to be the matter of explicit contention.[25] Charles seemed to believe that the problem was how to overcome the subjection of his people to a factious minority; in fact the royal will faced widespread protest over an increasing variety of concerns. Hopes for what might be achieved were not just in the king's mind. His preparedness to lead armies not once but twice against the Covenanters bore witness to his determination. In 1640 he summoned an English parliament for the first time in eleven years in the hope that it might give him good backing for the war. The failure there of the royal imperative – to some extent in both houses – caused the parliament's dissolution with deleterious effects upon the king's standing in England. Scotland, however, remained the priority. Charles feared for his prerogative. Readily he undertook what was seen to be civil war.

Neither in 1639 nor in 1640 was there any sustained engagement between the royal and covenanting forces. Some blood was spilt in the north-east of Scotland and other royalist strongholds, but the battles were as much of nerves and propaganda. In 1639 Charles seems fully to have expected a capitulation before he came himself to battle. The Covenanters too desired no fighting, although no surrender either. The result was an interim settlement which both sides hoped might anticipate the end of the Troubles. Given the intransigency of those taking part and the issues raised, it was not surprising that this 'pacification', as it was called, failed to achieve its end.[26] The second campaign was altogether more serious. It called for greater efforts of militarisation; it also involved more underhand dealing, which aimed to effect some lasting solution.

We might now consider the British dimension of the National Covenant story on the other side of the coin, so to speak, by asking how far the fears of the king and his councillors of Anglo-Scottish collusion were justified. As in our discussion of the king's side of things, we might begin with origins. In the mid-sixteenth century reforming Englishmen and Scotsmen had mixed happily. The differing fortunes of presbyterianism in the two countries lay behind a negative critique of the English Reformation that was subsequently sustained in the north.[27] One of the tensions for the English Crown was that nonconformity flourished across national borders. If the problem was felt to be more remediable after the Union of 1603, a problem it nevertheless remained. Peter Smart apparently published his complaint against practice in the see of Durham in Scotland in 1628.[28] Before the Troubles, Scottish divines fearful of anglicisation in the Church noted their increasing concern when they saw popish and Arminian doctrine go apparently uncensured in England (not to mention its increase within Scotland). Equally, these divines, and others interested such as Archibald Johnston, read the works of English nonconformists.[29] The extent of personal as opposed to reading contacts remains somewhat unclear, but the sheer distance was prohibitive. Mutual encouragement through the written word was most important.

Of the very many items of Covenanter propaganda, most were written primarily for circulation within Scotland. But the organisation of the covenanting movement, so impressive in word and deed, by no means neglected the sending of information to friends in England and Ireland. Whether the channels were through Court or private contacts – or as time went on through the promotion of tracts written specifically for the English market – the gathering of support was important. The Covenant cause, however Scottish, claimed to be both the cause of Christ and of laws and liberties; it could have a general appeal.[30] The Scots were persecuted, and would draw on friends for encouragement, hopeful that many would see their opposition as reasonable.

Charles tried to confine the Troubles within Scotland. Circulation of news was not encouraged; not until 1639 did he offer a full account to his English subjects of a military initiative that was already well under way.[31] But it was in vain. Archbishop Laud's part in the Troubles was discussed almost more quickly south of the Border than in Scotland. Rumour that Laud was heavily struck by the Scottish defence was current in Court from late 1637.[32] Copies of the October 1637 Supplication to Charles circulated in English hands in a corrupted version which, rather than blaming the Scottish bishops, named the English. One of our sources here was also alert enough to Scottish as well as English church problems to have noted earlier in his diary the issues at contention in the 1633 parliament.[33]

A public appeal outside Scotland by the Covenanters was held back until necessity seemed to demand it. A Scottish national cause did not willingly open itself to the judgements and opinions of outsiders. Much more was done surreptitiously – requests were made for information on how the king was acting; contacts were cultivated in the Low Countries and Sweden to bring powder and weapons into Scotland should a need arise.[34] However, when Hamilton was in Edinburgh in June 1638, he warned and indeed threatened the Covenanters that the king was ready to mount an offensive. He was not bluffing, sadly, and the other side responded. It seems clear in chronological terms that the Covenanters consciously acted reactively – albeit with singular determination. At this time a defence by arms was planned in detail; and a tract for the benefit of the English was published – *A short relation . . . for information and advertisement to our brethren in the kirk of England. By an hearty well-wisher to both kingdomes.*[35]

Archibald Johnston of Wariston was chiefly responsible for the *Short relation*. The tract offered an account of how the Troubles had come to their present height. It was unashamedly critical of Scottish episcopacy; the English were to be concerned since threats had been made of an English army to oppose the Covenanters. Johnston invoked the fraternity of the two nations but, even more, the fear of the corruption of the Reformation. His readers should watch lest they be called to fight against God himself. Although he was largely silent on the subject of the church established in England, Johnston warned that disruption was to be expected there. The changes made to the prayer book in its Scottish version were said to be also a preparative for popish change in England which the English bishops along with the Catholics might champion. Vision as well as necessity, as yet only cautiously advanced, shaped this first pamphlet for the English.[36]

The use of the printing press from the middle of 1638 greatly increased the availability of Covenanter propaganda, wherever it was directed. Longstanding links with the Low Countries led to the publication of the *Short relation* and subsequent works in translation; in Leiden, William Haig, presumably of 1633 fame, was having editions turned out of the proceedings of that fateful parliament.[37] The next major item for England came in February 1639: *An Information to all good Christians within the kingdome of England*. Again, the immediate context was the threat of war, and the *Information* took yet further the idea of the popish plot as the basic danger to both kingdoms. The English hierarchy was now explicitly described as tyrannous. As provocatively, in the eyes of Archbishop Laud, the *Information* suggested that although Scotland was by no means bound to answer to any outside judicatory, the cause of the Covenant might well be declared within an English parliament. The appeal was to have the rule of Christ Jesus confirmed in the whole island.[38]

The power of the vision for reformation meant that, as Laud and the king suspected, the earliest contacts with the outside looked for from Scotland were on sympathetic religious ground. Although religious politics was not of exclusive importance in the Scottish Troubles, it was a singularly pervasive factor, as the contacts story bears out. The critique of Scottish bishops for their conduct as churchmen was the dominating theme of the handwritten propaganda of late 1637 sent into England. This continued, as we have seen, in the more widely read printed works. The ploughing up of common ground struck hard against Archbishop Laud; at the time of the decisive attack against him in the Long Parliament, Scots lent a helping, even a co-ordinating hand.[39]

A more difficult area for investigation is the nature of the English response to this. The most interesting of the contacts in 1638 was the case of the well-connected Sir John Clotworthy, for which some good evidence has now come to light. Clotworthy met Johnston of Wariston early in June 1638, and when he had gone on to England assisted his friend by sending the latest possible news of the king's armed preparations. This, if you like, was the necessity aspect of

Anglo-Scottish contacts – although, of course, sympathetic Scots at Court could provide as useful a function. But Clotworthy frequently affirmed his own sympathies. In the first of his letters that we have, he related how the 'protestants' and 'precisians' joined in wishing the Scots happy success. As his own word of encouragement, he urged the Covenanters beyond temptations to compromise: 'cleere ye roote & branch'.[40]

Given the speeches he would have heard in Edinburgh, we can make no mistake about the meaning of that latter phrase.[41] But did readiness to see episcopacy abolished correlate with Clotworthy's apparent distinction between Protestants and precisians? While the Covenanters' later thrust on that issue in England met with a complex response, it is worth noting that they did not all go blindly into such a troublesome area. Even before the Covenanters' invasion of England in 1640, Johnston of Wariston anticipated difficulties in talks with Englishmen who had 'doubts & scrouples anent the kirk governement'.[42] Perhaps, though, he had been encouraged that the possibilities of radical change were open, whatever the nature of the change was to be.

The success of the Covenant gave heart to some who were disaffected in the England of the 1630s. Some peers thought of drawing up a petition to the king for remedy of grievances. This was again reported in 1639 from another source. A connection might be made, possibly, with the peers' petition of August 1640.[43] In July 1638 two peers in particular were prominent – most likely Lord Brooke and Viscount Saye and Sele, who were reported to be intending a voluntary exile in Scotland, should the Covenanters win through: there they would find their 'America'.[44]

A novel part of the impact of the Scottish Troubles in England was the forced awakening of a truly British dimension in English politics. Certainly the causes of grievances differed in particulars; but the Scots were asked to send information about their national cause, to send Covenants to keep the English informed. Clotworthy acknowledged economic realities when describing the possible large-scale exodus of wealthy and influential figures to Scotland, by giving assurance that the exiles would spend well – to the locals' benefit; in return, they hoped for full freedom in passing to and fro. An additional grievance at home was the feared royal exploitation of ship money. Let us be clear that no one contemplated replacing Charles. Yet while triple sovereignty was central to the king's strategy of attack – for it promised him extra strength – those in defence on the other side contemplated far-reaching reforms. People learned by stages what might be done to go forward. In developing a British vision, some Scots were better informed than others. When Sir Alexander Gibson of Durie drafted the *Information* of 1639, he advocated a general assembly as well as a parliament in England; Wariston corrected the mistake to read parliament only.[45]

It should be emphasised that rebellion against royal authority could take no automatic or easy course. Many in Scotland needed to be persuaded that concerted, let alone armed, resistance to the king was legitimate; national prejudice added to similar opinions disposed many in England against the Covenanters. The covenanting cause always had first to stand up in Scottish terms, as a letter from the earl of Rothes in 1639 to a hesitant domestic supporter clearly bears out. Whatever the 'best affected' in England thought or wanted, Rothes maintained, the Scottish cause obliged defence even by arms: 'so will we ventur all befor we lose Chryst or part fra his cleir & undenyabl treuth'.[46] Not everyone dared to face the full implications of this. The significant contacts described here were confined always to a few, although leading, figures in the two countries.

While the king remained unyielding, ways and means of opposition evolved. Saye and Sele and Brooke stood out in England, first resisting the summons of 1639, then refusing an oath offered to the king's following at York. Scots put effort into keeping the English as well informed as possible; after the agreement was made at Berwick, they entertained various individuals in their camp. In turn they were encouraged by the attendance of one of Saye and Sele's sons, almost certainly Nathaniel, at the general assembly in July 1639 that re-enacted the constitutions of Glasgow; later in the year, it seems that Samuel Rutherford did some preaching around Lord Brooke's establishment.[47]

An English parliament called for April 1640, when the king's preparations were underway for a second major drive northwards, provided an important forum for the Covenanters. Charles hoped for a ready supply for his armies. In Scottish eyes, this was a test of English sympathies. With the English aroused for all kinds of reasons of their own, there was rather more to it than that, but the Covenanters did what they could by secret communications to achieve their end. By this stage they reckoned that they had already done all that they could in print and public dispute; it was for their English friends, as they would answer before God, to bring the cause before the parliament. The seriousness of the now very prolonged crisis had broadened out the issues. Robert Baillie's *Ladensium* Αυτοκατακρισις: *the Canterburians' Self-Conviction* was a tract more specifically than ever aimed at undermining the English hierarchy.[48] Covenanter contacts with foreign countries, long hesitated over, had been advanced for the purposes of strengthening their appeal to Charles. It was a worry that the king tried to exploit invalid evidence of an approach to the king of France. But the English friends were warned that should the truth of contacts not only with France but Holland and Denmark too be uncovered, they should be ready to come to the Covenanters' defence.[49]

Charles's early dissolution of the English parliament in May 1640 precluded what expression there might have been of pro-Covenant sentiment.[50] The wide spectrum of English opinion on the Scottish Troubles, if fully known, would probably have given the Covenanters limited comfort. The political impasse set up by the king forced further action. On the one hand, Charles tried but failed to muster an effective fighting force from the English with any speed. The Covenanters, faced with increasing hardship at home, and with encouragement enough from the south, prepared themselves for the novel approach of attack.

The vision that accompanied necessity became open in its hopes for reformation in England as well as in Scotland. Union of a kind rather different from that which Charles had intended was seen as the way forward. That this Covenanter perspective on a fuller union was as problematic as anything that had come from the Crown can be noted in passing. The hard business of British politics would be thrashed out in the next decades. At the outset, the Scots saw co-ordination of religious aims as requiring some action on, or possibly modification of, the National Covenant. Wariston with his support engaged in talks of pushing on towards a presbyterian settlement. There was some talk of a covenant that might be subscribed by both nations.[51]

The popish plot theme was voiced with increasing intensity, but advances of political daring were also significant. Charles had wanted to prorogue the meeting of the Scottish Estates scheduled for June 1640, but the Covenanters had held it against his will, and passed a far-ranging body of legislation. In private, the king's right to rule was disputed, but nothing came of it; instead, the Estates ended by sending something of an ultimatum to Charles, demanding that he give his consent to the legislation. Charles's refusal was all but ignored in determined preparation for the invasion of England. The purpose, simply stated, was to secure a final settlement of these costly and demanding Troubles.[52]

It is well known that the programme of the Covenanters by the time of the invasion went far beyond the infamous demand for unity of religion and uniformity of church government in the king's dominions. Charles's failure to manage the crisis unleashed demands for reform over a whole range of topics, from the constitution of parliaments to the finer points of commercial policy, and the tensions of the British union were frequently addressed.[53] The broad message had emerged that Charles had failed as king and would have to submit to be guided as his subjects, in their collective wisdom, thought best.

The most secret contacts between Scots and English around the time of the invasion confirm the far-reaching seriousness of the crisis. Friends in England did more than convey and distribute information. No close agreement was reached on aims or a covenant, but colonels and their regiments within the king's army were persuaded to be ready to comprise 'armys for the comounwealth'. Should Charles actually choose to meet the Covenanters in battle, he would be faced by rebellion within his own ranks which would force him to submit. Members of the English nobility took the lead, to act 'in regard of their great entresse [in religion, liberties and laws] for the saftie of both king and kingdomes and their awne nighbour natioun and church of Scotland'. The Covenanters were advertised of the petition timeously signed by twelve peers shortly after the invasion, which in its conclusion appealed for an end to the Scottish struggle.[54] The Covenanters for their part resolved to accept no settlement except within the respective parliaments. The king's powers of discretion were to be limited in both kingdoms – or rather, with Ireland included, in all three.

We leave the story there, in advance of the meeting of the English parliament where the treaty and further political battles were fought out. The extent of the king's authority had to be the key issue in the Scottish Troubles. The noise that the Covenanters made struck at something to which Charles in particular had so deeply committed himself, namely a prerogative not to be challenged. The Covenant movement came to stand for an alternative line. Royal government made too many incursions in this fragile period of union. On matters surrounding the church, land and office as well as theology and disliked practices, it created serious troubles. With relative ease, the Covenanters paralysed its operation and gradually replaced it with their own. They had an extraordinary organisation which shaped an impressive unity out of a heterogeneous whole. Ambiguities, divisions, and lack of commitment were problems never wholly overcome, but the leadership took on board a wide programme.

Charles in normal circumstances had wanted to stifle opposition. In the Scottish crisis, with the successes of the National Covenant movement, his regime collapsed. An outlet was made for the expression of English grievances; in time, Irish Catholics were frightened to rebel for their own preservation. Thus a king of three kingdoms, attempting to overcome or better annihilate one seriously discontented party, brought on a major crisis all round.

NOTES
1. D. Calderwood, *Quaeres concerning the state of the church of Scotland* (n.p., 1621, reprinted 1638), p.3.
2. S. R. Gardiner, *The constitutional documents of the puritan revolution* (3rd edn., Oxford, 1906), pp.124-34.
3. R. Baillie, *The letters and journals*, ed. D. Laing, Bannatyne Club (3 vols, Edinburgh, 1841-2), I, 52-4; see also National Library of Scotland [N.L.S.] Advocates' MS 29.2.8, fos. 263-4.
4. For careful phrasing in the third section of the Covenant, see the draft in N.L.S. Wodrow MSS, Folio series (Wod.Fo.) 64, fo. 210.
5. D. Stevenson, *The Scottish revolution* (Newton Abbot, 1974), pp.123-5.
6. See, for example, N.L.S. Wod.Fo.64, fos. 218-19; *Diary of Sir Archibald Johnston of Wariston, 1632-1639*, ed. G. M. Paul, Scottish History Society (Edinburgh, 1911), p.410.
7. Again see N.L.S. Wod.Fo.64, fo. 210.
8. G. Burnet, *The memoires of the lives and actions of James and William, dukes of Hamilton and Castleherald . . .* (1677), p.60; 'The true lawe of free monarchies', in J. Craigie and A. Law, eds, *Minor prose works of King James VI and I*, Scottish Text Society (Edinburgh, 1982), p.73.
9. *The register of the privy council of Scotland* (2nd Series, 8 vols, 1899-1908) [hereafter *R.P.C.S.*] I, 91-2; B. Botfield, ed., *Original letters relating to the ecclesiastical affairs of Scotland* (2 vols, Edinburgh, 1851), II, 445, 483.
10. E.g. in a speech in 1617 – Cambridge University Library MSS, Ee.5.23, fos. 442-5.
11. D. G. Mullan, *Episcopacy in Scotland: the history of an idea, 1560-1638* (Edinburgh, 1986), pp.98-103, 151.
12. M. Lee, Jr., *The road to revolution: Scotland under Charles I, 1625-37* (Urbana and Chicago, 1985), pp.31, 99-100, 128-37.
13. For the general problem, see C. Russell, 'The British problem and the English civil war', *History*, LXII (1986), 395-415.
14. See N.L.S. Wod.Fo.43, fos. 260-1; J. M. Henderson, 'An "advertisement" about the service book, 1637', *Scottish Historical Review (S.H.R.)*, xxiii (1925-6), 199-204; D. H. Fleming,

*Scotland's supplication and complaint against the book of common prayer . . . the book of canons and the prelates* (Edinburgh, 1927).
15. *The works of the most reverend father in God, William Laud, D.D.*, eds. W. Scott and J. Bliss (7 vols, Oxford, 1847-60 – hereafter *Laud*), VII, 387, 389-90, 401-2, 468, 502.
16. *Laud*, VII, 444; W. Knowler, ed., *The earl of Strafforde's letters and dispatches* (2 vols, 1739), II, 184, 187-8, 208-9.
17. Cf. *Calendar of state papers, domestic series [C.S.P.D.], 1637-8*, 393/38, 45, 397/58; Public Record Office [P.R.O.], SP 16/397/34; M. P. Maxwell, 'Strafford, the Ulster Scots and the Covenanters', *Irish Historical Studies*, xviii (1973), 524-51.
18. This is argued in greater detail in P. Donald, *An uncounselled king: Charles I and the Scottish troubles 1637-1641* (Cambridge, 1991), ch. 3.
19. *R.P.C.S.*, VII, 64-78.
20. Stevenson, *Scottish revolution*, pp.112-26; W. Makey, *The church of the Covenant 1637-1651* (Edinburgh, 1979), pp. 36-53.
21. Baillie, *Letters*, I, 181-3.
22. British Library (B.L.) Add.MS 5754, fo. 41; Maxwell, 'Strafford, the Ulster Scots and the Covenanters', 536-48.
23. Most of the evidence for letters intercepted survives in State Papers, Domestic; for the oath see *Privy council registers in facsimile* (12 vols, 1967-8), VI, 412ff.
24. P.R.O. SP 84/154, fo. 146v; A. Collins, ed., *Letters and memorials of state*, vol. II (1746), p.572; A. H. Williamson, *Scottish national consciousness in the age of James VI* (Edinburgh, 1979), pp.143-5; C. Hibbard, *Charles I and the popish plot* (Chapel Hill, N.C., 1983), pp.20-37.
25. B.L. Add.MS 38847, fo. 11; *Diary of Sir Archibald Johnston, Lord Wariston, 1639*, ed. G. M. Paul, Scottish History Society (Edinburgh, 1896), p.79.
26. For a full account, see Donald, *An uncounselled king*, ch. 4.
27. G. Donaldson, *The making of the Scottish prayer book of 1637* (Edinburgh, 1954), pp.4-23; Williamson, *Scottish national consciousness*, pp.97-107.
28. P. Smart, *The vanitie and downfall of superstitious popish ceremonies* (1628); *R.P.C.S.*, II, 449-50.
29. E.g. Baillie, *Letters*, I, 1-2, 10; N.L.S. Wod.Fo.43, fo. 254; Johnston, *Diary . . . 1632-1639*, pp.94ff.
30. Cf. S. Burrell, 'The apocalyptic vision of the early Covenanters', *S.H.R.*, XLIII (1964), 1-24.
31. Charles I, *A large declaration* (1639); for an emergency anticipation of this, see J. F. Larkin, ed., *Stuart royal proclamations*, vol. II (Oxford, 1983), pp.662-7.
32. B.L. Add.MS 27962H, fos. 75-6; *Calendar of state papers, Venetian series, 1636-39*, pp.259-60, 273; *C.S.P.D. 1637*, 369/41.

33. B.L. Add.MS 35331, fos 67-8, 52v; Bedfordshire Record Office J.1347.
34. Baillie, *Letters*, I, 72, 89-90, 111-12, 117; S.R.O. GD 112/40/2/1/5; N.L.S. MS 2263, fos 71-2; Wod.Fo. 61, fo. 264v.
35. N.L.S. Adv.MS 29.2.8, fos. 243-5; *A short relation* . . . (n.p., 1638).
36. *A short relation*; an incomplete draft is in N.L.S. Wod.Fo. 64, fos. 215-16.
37. P.R.O. SP 16/387/79.
38. *An information to all good Christians* . . . (Edinburgh, 1639).
39. Baillie, *Letters*, I, 273-5, 280. Laud first came to the fore in Scottish propaganda in the draft of the February 1639 *Information* - N.L.S. Wod.Fo. 63, fos. 24-6; P.R.O. SP 84/155, fo. 6.
40. Johnston, *Diary . . . 1632-1639*, p.351; P.R.O. SP 16/393/31, 33 (anonymous, but Clotworthy holograph).
41. Cf. S.R.O. GD 406/1/10775, 556; Baillie, *Letters*, I, 85-6.
42. N.L.S. Wod.Fo. 64, fo. 203.
43. D. Dalrymple, *Memorials and letters relating to the history of Britain in the reign of Charles the first* (Glasgow, 1766), p.41; S.R.O. GD 406/1/985; *C.S.P.D.* 1640, 465/16.
44. Dalrymple, *Memorials*, p.41.
45. Dalrymple, *Memorials*, pp.39-45 (original is N.L.S. Wod.Fo. 66, fos 109-10, Clotworthy holograph); N.L.S. Wod.Fo. 63, fos 24-6; Johnston, *Diary . . . 1632-1639*, p.408; Baillie, *Letters*, I, 188.
46. Crawford MS 14/7/45 (now deposited in N.L.S. I am grateful to the Rt. Hon. the earl of Crawford and Balcarres for permission to cite from his family papers.)
47. B.L. Add.MS 11045, fo. 52; Traqr.MSS bundle 28 [iii], letter of 10 August 1639; B.L. Add.MS 23146, fos 87, 88v. I am grateful to the late Mr Peter Maxwell Stuart for permission to consult the manuscripts in his possession at Traquair House.
48. *Ladensium* Αυτοκατακρισις. Printed in April 1640.
49. N.L.S. Wod.Fo. 64, fos 163, 165-6.
50. Cf. S. R. Gardiner, *History of England . . . 1603-1642* (10 vols, 1884), IX, 117.
51. See *Intentions of the army of Scotland* (n.p., 1640); *Information from the Scottish nation to all English* [1640]; N.L.S. Wod.Fo. 66, fo. 223v.
52. Stevenson, *Scottish revolution*, pp.190-6, 206.
53. C. L. Hamilton, 'The Anglo-Scottish negotiations of 1640-1', *S.H.R.*, XLI (1962), 84-6; D. Stevenson, 'The early Covenanters and the federal union of Britain', in R. Mason, ed., *Scotland and England, 1286-1815* (Edinburgh, 1987), pp.163-81.
54. P. H. Donald, 'New light on the Anglo-Scottish contacts of 1640', *Historical Research*, LXII (1989), 221-9.

# Five

## THE SCOTTISH CONSTITUTION, 1638-51: THE RISE AND FALL OF OLIGARCHIC CENTRALISM

Allan I. Macinnes

Although religious issues had acted as precipitants, the emergence of the covenanting movement accords with the classical definition of a revolution as the outcome of a long process of dissatisfaction, disaffection and organisation culminating in a successful, but violent, change of government.[1] Within three years of the publication of the National Covenant prescribing the fundamental reordering of the relationship between God, Crown and people, the Tables – as the revolutionary embodiment of the covenanting movement – had accomplished, by persuasion and coercion, a thorough transformation of government within Scotland. In turn, the covenanting revolution served as a British model for terminating the Personal Rule of Charles I.[2] While no attempt was made to replace the Stewart monarchy in Scotland, Charles I was obliged to accept permanent checks on the royal prerogative in Kirk and State. He was also obliged to recognise that adherence to the National Covenant replaced acquiescence in the dictates of absentee monarchy as the vital prerequisite for the exercise of political power north of the Border. Constitutional and ideological attainments notwithstanding, the covenanting movement was concerned primarily with the collective interests of the political nation, not with the protection of individual liberties or with social engineering. Despite the nobles being in the vanguard of the movement, respect for aristocratic privilege tempered but did not prevent the wholescale restructuring of central and local government. Indeed, the radical cutting edge of the covenanting revolution, honed by constitutional defiance and by recourse to war, found expression through institutional development, notably the reorientation of Scottish government toward a form which can be depicted as oligarchic centralism.

This essay will suggest that the oligarchic involvement of the nobles, gentry and burgesses in running Scotland imparts three distinctive characteristics to constitutional history between 1638 and 1651. In the first instance, primacy must be accorded to the political process, not to ecclesiastical issues, a primacy upheld by the leading ideologues among the ministers of the Kirk and especially evident in Alexander Henderson's contribution to the Defensive Arms Controversy of 1639, in Samuel Rutherford's *Lex Rex* of 1644 and in Robert Douglas's sermon for the coronation of Charles II in 1651.[3] Secondly, the labelling of political parties must be reappraised. The distinction between moderates and extremists within the covenanting movement is essentially a product, if not a fabrication, of the Restoration era. In like manner, the appellation of 'the Kirk Party', applied to the opponents of the Engagement of 1648,[4] obscures the basic continuity of the radical mainstream dominating the covenanting movement between 1638 and 1651. Thirdly, the radical mainstream's fundamentalist approach to politics was not only enshrined in, but wholly consistent with, the National Covenant of 1638, which was in essence a written Scottish constitution by social compact.

The National Covenant must be placed within its immediate political context, the 'crisis by monthly instalments' which had followed on from the riots against the Service Book in Edinburgh on 23 July 1637.[5] Particular attention should be paid to the series of supplications which culminated in the National Covenant, notably the National Petition of 20 September against the Service Book; the National Supplication of 17 October against the Service Book and the Book of Canons, which first served notice against breaches of the covenant between God, Crown and people: and the Composite Supplication of 21 December which added the Court of High Commission to those things petitioned against and which was supplemented by a declinator against the bishops. Nationwide petitioning was co-ordinated by the disaffected element opposed to the authoritarian absenteeism that had stamped the Personal Rule of Charles I. Initial co-ordination was based informally on the political Estates, the gentry, burgesses and ministers taking their lead from the nobility. From 15 November, co-ordination was effectively directed by the Tables, each Estate composing a Table with representatives from the other three joining the nobles to form a revolutionary executive which was constituted formally as the Fifth Table on 6 December. The operation of a provisional government under the direction of the Fifth Table was not institutionalised publicly until 23 February 1638, five days before the promulgation of the National Covenant.[6]

In essence, the National Covenant was a revolutionary enterprise binding the Scottish people together to justify and consolidate the revolt against absentee monarchy.[7] Its moderate tenor, coupled with its conservative format and appeal to precedents, has led to the National Covenant being described as 'a constitutional, and not a revolutionary document'[8] – a description which undoubtedly belies its radical nature.[9] The finalised version having been approved by all four Tables before subscriptions commenced on 28 February, its appearance of unanimity was not deceptive. The National Covenant deliberately maintained 'a shrewd vagueness' not just to attract support from all classes and from every locality,[10] but primarily to avoid specific imputations of treason. Indeed, the Fifth Table had the contents cleared by legal counsel to ensure that the National Covenant did not come within the scope of the enactment of 1585 against private banding without royal consent.[11] For the National Covenant was not a private league of rebellious subjects, nor even an aristocratic reaction against the Personal Rule of Charles I,[12] but a nationalist manifesto asserting the independence of a sovereign people under God. It was the explicit intent of the Fifth Table that the National Covenant should be propagated as a tripartite public band embracing God, Crown and people, 'for the maintenance of religione and the King's Majesteis authority, and for the preservatione of the lawes and liberties of the kingdome against all troubles and seditione'.[13] Accordingly, the National Covenant can be split into three components, which demonstrated the immediate cause, the dual imperatives and the fundamental priorities of this public banding.[14]

The first component rehearsed the Negative Confession of 1581 in association with a detailed, if selective, series of parliamentary enactments perpetrated to maintain the 'true religion, and the King's Majesty'. The radical implication of this component was that loyalty to the Crown was conditional on expunging idolatrous, superstitious and popish practices from the Kirk, on protecting the purity of the reformed tradition and on upholding the right of the Scottish people to be governed according to the common laws of the realm as grounded in statute.[15] The selection of parliamentary statutes reveals the radical astuteness of the Fifth Table. Precedents for the removal of erroneous doctrines and prejudicial practices culminated in the collation and codification of the penal laws in 1609, which served to increase the urgency of an uncompromising Protestant crusade to ward off the unabated threat from the Counter-Reformation.[16] Precedents for sustaining the established Kirk's purity of doctrine, discipline and worship did not extend beyond the era of the first presbyterian experiment during the 1590s; there was a calculated omission of all subsequent legislation in favour of episcopacy – but not a categorical declaration 'to extirpate the bishops'. Indeed, recourse to such Erastian precedents demonstrates no convincing support for Melvillianism nor any resolve to establish a theocracy.[17] At the same time, the intention of the Fifth Table to restore a 'moderate episcopal regime', as typified by the Jacobean episcopate, cannot be substantiated. Nor was the appeal to statute a deliberate oversight of the General Assemblies, which were commended specifically for having promoted the Negative Confession and its reissue in 1590.[18]

The attack on episcopacy, though muted, was not a secondary aspect of the National Covenant[19] but was subsumed within the resolve of the Fifth Table to sweep away all innovations, religious or secular, which had threatened national independence and the subjects' liberties since the Union of the Crowns. Hence, precedents emphasising the vital importance of respecting the 'fundamental lawes' of the kingdom drew chiefly on the legislation of the 1604 parliament[20] (which had been called to discuss union with England) to warn against innovations prejudicial to parliamentary authority, 'as this Realme could be no more a free Monarchy'. In effect, the apparent appeal to constitutional tradition masked a revolutionary determination to vest sovereignty in the king-in-parliament at the expense of the royal prerogative.

The limitations imposed on monarchy by statute – as Charles I was held to have recognised in 1633 – were accepted formally in the solemn oath taken by 'all Kings and Princes at their Coronation and reception of their Princely Authority' to preserve the 'true Religion, Lawes and Liberties of this Kingdome'. The true religion 'now receaved and preached' was Protestantism in accord with the Negative Confession of 1581 – that is, prior to the readmission of bishops in the Kirk (1606–10) and the Five Articles of Perth (1618) as well as the recent liturgical innovations (1636–37). Moreover, true religion and royal authority were so linked that it was impossible to be truly loyal to the Crown without being loyal to the true religion. Although the first priority of the Crown was to rule the people according to the will of God as revealed by scripture, royal authority had to respect, at the same time, 'the laudable Lawes and Constitutions received in this Realme, no ways repugnant to the said will of God'.[21]

The second component of the National Covenant went on to elaborate the concept of a two-fold contract on which the whole life of the Scottish kingdom was based. This two-fold contract encapsulated the dual imperatives of covenanting by drawing on historical, biblical and political precepts which, in their opposition to the Divine Right of kings and absolute monarchy, were inspired as much by the ideology of French Huguenots and, to a lesser extent, of Dutch Calvinists as by the Knoxian legacy of resistance to an ungodly monarch.[22] Although recourse to covenanting was justified historically in terms of past examples of banding by the Scottish people in defence of civil and religious liberties and of national sovereignty, the contents of past bands – including that of 1596, the last to receive nationwide circulation and subscribed by 'many yet living amongst us' – bore little relation to the religious and political imperatives currently acclaimed in the National Covenant.[23]

The religious covenant was a tripartite compact between the king and people before God to uphold the purity of 'the true reformed religion' as expressed not only in the Negative Confession, but in the enlarged confession of faith established from the Reformation 'by sundry acts of lawful generall assemblies, and of Parliament' as by the catechisms, all being grounded exclusively in scripture. Whereas obedience to God was unconditional and irresistible, the people's obligations to the king were limited and conditional. The people stood surety for the king in defence of the true religion. But, if the king betrayed his people to God, the people were bound to hold the kingdom to its obligations: indeed, they had a positive duty to resist in order to avoid divine retribution. In short, the religious covenant placed the Scots, like the Israelites, in the role of the chosen people. Operating within the framework of this religious covenant was a constitutional contract between the king on the one hand and the people on the other for maintenance of good and lawful government and a just political order. In return for 'maintaining the Kings Majesty, His Person and Estate', the people laid down conditions which the king was bound to fulfil. If the king failed to uphold the fundamental laws and liberties of the kingdom or sought to subvert his subjects' privileges or estates, the people were entitled to take appropriate remedial action, which again included the right to resist.

Giving force to the assumption that government existed to further the interests of the subject spiritually and materially, the National

Covenant pledged its subscribers to eradicate the 'manifold innovations and evills' mentioned in past supplications. The retrospective scope of these supplications arguably extended back beyond the petitioning of the last seven months to that associated with the coronation parliament of 1633. Certainly comprehended were the petitions condemning liturgical innovations – the Service Book and the Book of Canons – which were reaffirmed to be unscriptural, subversive of the reformed tradition in the Kirk and leading to the insinuation not just of popery but, by virtue of their unconstitutional introduction, of tyranny as well. The Court of High Commission and the prosecution of presbyterian nonconformists came within the scope of evils leading to the ruination of 'the true Reformed Religion, and of our Liberties, Lawes and Estates'. Although subscribers were obliged merely to forbear rather than condemn outright the practice of innovations in worship, final determination of the acceptability of all ceremonies, as of the current corruptions in ecclesiastical government and the exercise of civil power by kirkmen, was to be left to 'free assemblies and in Parliaments': a clear inference that the pursuit of constitutional redress should not be subject to the censorious royal management that had been evident in the coronation parliament of 1633.[24] In turn, the emphasis laid on the importance of 'lawful generall assemblies' in upholding the purity of the reformed tradition, manifestly implied that some Assemblies during the reign of James VI had been unlawful. More specifically, the Fifth Table insisted adamantly that the oath exacted from entrants to the ministry – to respect the Five Articles and episcopal government – was invalidated by 'the prelates turning Popish'. The revolutionary executive, no less resolute than James VI in his management of the general assembly in 1618 and of the parliament of 1621, had made the passage and ratification of the Five Articles 'repugnant to the fundamental lawes of the kingdom'.[25]

In calling for free Assemblies and parliaments, the intention of the Fifth Table was not just to secure the redress of pressing grievances between Charles I and his Scottish subjects, but to effect a permanent check on absentee monarchy to safeguard the religious and constitutional imperatives of covenanting. Although a lawful and free general assembly was propagated as the immediate objective in order to recover the purity of the reformed tradition, the National Covenant was concerned fundamentally with the ordering of priorities between Crown and people. Thus, its first component had prescribed that the final approval of all ecclesiastical and civil issues pertained to the king-in-parliament. The second component had stressed that the dual imperatives of covenanting took precedence over the dictates of absentee monarchy. That the National Covenant was to be established as the reference point for Scottish society, necessitating constitutional monarchy in perpetuity, was underscored by the third and most revolutionary component – the oath of allegiance and mutual association.[26]

Allegiance to monarchy followed allegiance to God; the former was conditional, the latter unconditional and irresistible. The oath required subscribers to swear that they would 'to the uttermost of our power, with our meanes and lives, stand to the defence of our dread Soveraigne, the Kings Majesty, his Person and Authority, in the defence and preservation of the foresaid true Religion, Liberties and Lawes of the Kingdome'; that is, the king's person and royal authority were to be defended in the course of the people's defence and preservation of religion, liberties and laws. Therefore, the king was to be defended in so far as he accepted the religious and constitutional imperatives of the National Covenant. The oath then went on to require mutual assistance among subscribers 'in the same cause of maintaining the true Religion and his Majesty's Authority, with our best counsel, our bodies, meanes and whole power, against all sorts of persons whatsoever'. The oath was thus a positive act of defiance in reserving loyalty to a covenanted king.[27]

Despite the apparent ambiguity in the attestation of the subscribers that 'we have no intention nor desire to attempt anything that may turne to the dishonour of God or the diminution of the Kings greatness and authority', there was no necessary incompatibility in promising to defend royal authority while simultaneously promoting policies contrary to the professed interests of Charles I.[28] Nor were subscribers in a hapless position because the National Covenant seemingly ignored the potential conflict of interests in swearing to uphold the true religion and at the same time defend the person and authority of the king.[29] For the revolutionary essence of the National Covenant was its ordering of priorities: 'the true worship of God, the Majesty of our King, and peace of the Kingdome, for the common happiness of our selves, and the posterity'.

Integral to the permanent achievement of constitutionalism in Kirk and State was the crucial distinction between the office of monarchy and the personal conduct of the king. Resistance to Charles I was in the long-term interests of monarchy and people if the kingdom was to be restored to godly rule.[30] In making this crucial distinction, the revolutionary executive had manifestly learned the

## The Scottish Constitution

lesson of the Revocation Scheme when Charles, from 1626, had threatened private legal means to effect the professed public ends of monarchy.[31] Within a broader European perspective, the propagation of this distinction by the Fifth Table avoided recourse to republicanism in resisting absentee monarchy.[32]

Because Charles I was no usurper but the legitimate heir of the long-established house of Stewart, there was no question of the right of resistance vindicating tyrannicide by the private citizen. Instead, the oath of allegiance and mutual assistance upheld the right of the people as a corporate body to resist a lawful king who threatened to become tyrannical. Such resistance was to be exercised by the natural leaders of society, not the nobles exclusively but the Tables as the corporate embodiment of the inferior magistrate. In effect, therefore, the revolutionary oath required the subscribers to recognise the Tables as not just the provisional government, but as the divinely-warranted custodians of the national interest.[33]

As well as equipping the Tables with the rhetoric of defiance, the National Covenant provided the political will to effect a revolution. This political will found initial expression in the presbyterian reformation accomplished at Glasgow between 21 November and 20 December 1638, in an assembly whose composition, agenda and procedures were stage-managed by the Fifth Table.[34] The accomplishment of presbyterianism by constitutional defiance made inevitable the Bishops' Wars of 1639-40, which provided a practical demonstration of the coactive power that justified resistance to Charles I. According to Samuel Rutherford, the Tables were obliged to hold the Crown to the dual imperatives of the National Covenant in the interests of the monarchy if not of Charles personally: that is, the king *in abstracto* if not *in concreto*.[35]

The coactive power of the covenanting movement was maintained consistently by the radical mainstream to justify resistance in both the First and Second Bishops' Wars. The king was portrayed as a misinformed absentee prepared to deploy papists, rebels and mercenaries to invade Scotland. Ministers in the spring of 1639 advocated recourse to arms from the pulpit following precepts drawn up by Alexander Henderson on behalf of the revolutionary executive. An essential distinction was drawn between, on the one hand, subjects rising or standing out against law and reason that they may be freed from their obedience to their king and, on the other, the Scottish people, 'holding fast their alledgence to their soveraine and in all humilitie supplicating for Religoun and justice', obliged 'to defend themselves against extreame violence and oppression bringing utter ruin and desolation upon the kirk and kingdome, upon themselves and their posteritie'.[36]

The coactive power to resist the Crown was part of the covenanting ideology exported in the Solemn League and Covenant of 17 August 1643, which specifically incorporated the conditional oath of allegiance and mutual association (clause 3).[37] That no dilution of this coactive power was tolerable was also evident in the reaction of the radical mainstream to the Engagement implemented in 1648 between the conservative element within the movement and Charles I. The Engagers were reputedly 'so taken up with a king that they prefer a king's interest to Christ's interest'. Thus, in the move towards a patriotic accommodation with conservative and royalist forces when faced by the threat of Cromwellian occupation, the radical mainstream insisted that Charles II receive the Covenants at his coronation on 1 January 1651. As Robert Douglas pointedly remarked in his sermon at the coronation, the taking of the Covenants was to deny absolutism, for 'total government is not upon a king'.[38]

Because the coactive power entailed permanent checks on monarchy, the radical mainstream interpreted the role of the political Estates as not just to participate in but to control central government. The political Estates were the trustees of the national interest on behalf of the people. The king was merely the trustee of the political Estates, who executed their power to make law. In the eyes of Archibald Campbell, marquis of Argyle, the foremost and most formidable Scottish politician of the 1640s, limited monarchy was a constitutional imperative.[39] More immediately, the central participation of the Estates in the political process, 'when religion, laws, liberties, invasion of foreign enemies necessitateth the subjects to convene', justified the formation of the Tables in 1637, their holding of conventions throughout 1638 and 1639 and, ultimately, the formal establishment of the committee of estates as the executive arm of government in the parliament of 1640.[40]

The parliament of 2 to 11 June 1640 confirmed the rise of oligarchic centralism. Its legislative programme to reform the judicatories – in effect, to restructure central and local government – was a pragmatic necessity as well as the ideological implementation of limited monarchy. Parliament's first step was to validate past proceedings of the covenanting movement. The presbyterian reformation implemented by the General Assembly at Glasgow in 1638 and endorsed by that at Edinburgh in 1639 was ratified. In keeping with the self-denying ordinance excluding kirkmen from civil office, the clerical estate in parliament was abolished. In recognition of the stalwart service of the gentry on the Tables, the voting powers of the shires was effectively doubled. Instead of one composite vote being cast for each shire, gentry summoned as shire commissioners were accorded individual votes. Following the directives to burgesses in the convention of royal burghs of 1638 and to ministers in the General Assembly of 1639, subscription of the National Covenant was made compulsory for all holding public office. Parliament then asserted control over its own procedures. A triennial act specified that parliament should meet every three years regardless of a royal summons. The committee of the articles, hitherto the managerial vehicle by which James VI and Charles controlled the parliamentary agenda, was made optional. If deployed, the committee was to be elected by and answerable to the three parliamentary Estates – the nobility, gentry and burgesses. Henceforth, business was to be initiated from the floor of the unicameral Scottish parliament.[41]

That the parliament of 1640 was intent upon constitutional revolution rather than the consolidation of feudal insurrection was borne out by the most radical category of enactments designed to legitimise, not supplant, the exercise of executive power by the Tables.[42] Ostensibly on account of the imminent danger from extraneous forces, the country adopted a posture of defence and a committee of estates was constituted with comprehensive powers to order, direct and govern the whole kingdom; to preserve and maintain the army; to appoint and hold answerable army officers as well as commissioners and overseers for civil government; to assess and levy taxes; to borrow and disburse monies; and to summon auxiliary nobles, gentry and burgess for consultation on affairs of state whenever necessary. The inherent flexibility of this latter power was emphasised by the composition of the committee of forty which, though drawn from the three assembled estates, was not confined to members of parliament. Five gentry and eight burgesses who were not members of parliament, but all active in the covenanting movement, were named on the committee. The committee was split into two sections with equal numbers of each estate either remaining in Edinburgh to sustain central government or accompanying the army whose movements were not restricted to Scotland – a clear indication that the Covenanters were prepared to move on to the offensive and, if necessary, take the war to the Royalists in England. Each section governed autonomously within its respective sphere of influence, save for the declaration of war and the conclusion of peace, which required the assent of the whole committee. In short, the committee of estates was conceived and received as an unprecedented agency which supplanted the government of an absentee monarch.[43]

The establishment of the committee of estates represented a classical, if corporate, alternative (reminiscent of the consular system of ancient Rome) to the exercise of executive power by a monarch who was patently untrustworthy, palpably reluctant to make lasting concessions and resolutely intent on reversing all constitutional restraints on the royal prerogative. Although the committee can be viewed as a 'temporary expedient' in so far as its powers were finite – until a settlement was reached with the king or until the next plenary session of parliament – the prospects of Charles I accepting the National Covenant were not even remote. Moreover, the confirmation of the committee as the country's executive by the next parliament was not specifically proscribed. The definition of its formal powers and composition was left flexible. The accompanying legislation retrospectively warranting past decisions of the Tables taken under various guises – such as 'Conventione of the estates', 'Committee of the estates' or simply 'the estates of this kingdom' – would suggest that the Covenanting leadership was intent not only upon legitimising its exercise of executive power over the past thirty months, but in settling on an authoritative designation for its future exercise.[44]

Three other aspects of the legislative programme compounded and consolidated the exercise of executive power by the committee of estates. In the first place, the scope of treason was extended to all who advised or assisted policies destructive of the covenanting movement, effectively as interpreted by the radical mainstream. This extension of the definition of leasing-making served to marginalise the political influence of the conservative element led by James Graham, fifth earl (later first marquis) of Montrose, who were indicted as the Plotters in 1641 along with those leading royalists deemed Incendiaries.[45] Secondly, the taxation of the tenth, the first national tax levied by the Covenanters from the outset of 1640, was confirmed and extended to include a further twentieth of landed and commercial income. The levying of such national taxes, justified retrospectively by Samuel Rutherford as 'given by the kingdom rather to the kingdom than to the king, for the present war, or some other necessity', served as the precedent for the subsequent levying of innovatory taxes – notably the excise from 1644 and the cess from 1645.[46] Thirdly, restructured local government was consolidated as the principal agency for the nation-wide imposition of ideological conformity, financial supply and military recruitment.

The restructuring of local government was actually based on a blueprint drawn up before the General Assembly in Glasgow that was probably approved by members of the Tables present as elders and assessors. Commencing in late January 1639, committees were established within the shires and within the bounds of every presbytery, each with a permanent convener, in order to levy, equip and train troops; to assess and uplift a compulsory contribution based on landed and commercial rents; and to propagate commitment to the cause throughout every parish. In effect, Scotland was placed on a war footing for which the linchpin in every shire was the committee of war whose convener was to receive instructions directly from, and report back to, the Fifth Table. Henceforth, two members of the committee of war were to be on call in Edinburgh in shifts of three months as commissioners for the shire. Numbers in the capital were to be supplemented from the shires at the time of parliament or General Assembly, or in the event of any national upsurge in Royalist activity. Ministers were excluded from the shire and presbytery committees though they were expected to promote military and financial as well as ideological commitment in every parish.[47]

Restructuring, in this form of a centralising reorientation of local government in Scotland, led to the formation of Europe's second professional army (after Sweden), which decisively won the Bishops' Wars. The covenanting movement was thus able to assert and retain the political initiative in Britain from the outset of the peace negotiations with Charles I which commenced at Ripon in October before transferring to London in December 1640. Having instigated the summoning of the Long Parliament in England, the committee of the estates insisted upon English parliamentary participation in the peace negotiations which were eventually brought to a conclusion in August 1641. Unity in religion and uniformity in church government were seemingly accorded priority by the Covenanters commissioned to negotiate.[48] However, the main thrust of the Covenanting agenda – in keeping with Covenanting desires to strengthen the bond of union between both kingdoms professed since the first sustained appeal to British public opinion in the prelude to the Bishops' Wars – was to secure a lasting alliance: that is, a defensive and offensive league between Scotland and England, not an incorporating parliamentary union. Henceforth, war could not be declared within the king's dominions without parliamentary approval; nor could trade be stopped pending a parliamentary declaration that peace had been breached. Neither nation was to resort to arms against a foreign power without the consent of both parliaments. In turn, mutual assistance was to be offered against foreign invasion. The only institutional innovation was to be the appointment of commissioners, in the course of triennial parliaments in both kingdoms, charged to conserve the peace and redress any breaches in the intervals between parliaments.

In ratifying the Treaty of London on 7 August 1641, the English parliament reserved its right to determine the nature of the English reformation but duly conceded that the waging of war and the stopping of trade within the king's dominions required parliamentary approval in both countries. The English parliament assented also to the appointment of conservators of the peace and agreed to refer proposals for a permanent defensive and offensive alliance to commissioners chosen from both parliaments. The ratification of the Treaty of London, and the bestowal of royal assent three days later as Charles I departed to attend the last parliamentary session of the Scottish estates in 1641, were duly interpreted as his formal recognition of the sovereign and independent power of the Scottish estates as a 'free parliament'. This was a recognition that laid to rest the spectre of provincialism which had haunted the nation since the Union of the Crowns.[49]

Diplomatic recognition that the covenanting movement was in the driving seat in British politics proclaimed the triumph of oligarchic centralism which was duly consummated by the Scottish estates between 10 August and 18 November. Although dissolved formally with the opening of the last parliamentary session of 1641, the committee of estates continued covertly to control proceedings, having ensured that all members of the Scottish Estates had accepted the National Covenant prior to their admission. The Tables were effectively reformed as revisionary committees for each parliamentary Estate to scrutinise bills and overtures. The sophisticated procedures for the sifting and overhaul of legislation pioneered in this session led subsequently to the formation of session committees which became a regular feature of covenanting parliaments over the next decade. Executive control over parliamentary business was thus preserved through various session committees for dispatches, for prosecuting the war, for burdens and pressures and for dangers.[50]

Parliament secured an effective veto over the executive and judiciary when Charles I gave a binding commitment that officers of state, privy councillors and lords of session would henceforth be chosen with the advice and consent of the Scottish Estates. This concession, which had been on the covenanting agenda since 1639, was seemingly made more palatable for Charles on the grounds that, as an absentee, he was not always informed adequately about the best-qualified candidates. In the short-term, the limited parliamentary role conceived for Charles I left him ample time for his golfing engagements prior to his return south on 17 November. In the long-term, Charles was obliged to accept permanent restrictions on the royal prerogative that fulfilled his own prophecy in the spring of 1638: that the triumph of the covenanting movement would leave him with no more power than the doge of Venice.[51]

Charles further accepted the realities of political power north of the Border when he sanctioned, prior to his departure south, the effective continuance of interval committees to exercise executive powers between parliamentary sessions. Although the committee of estates was not resuscitated, its past role as the national government was not only approved but was able to continue financially and ecclesiastically, diplomatically and judicially through the creation of diverse commissions that were to endure, if necessary, until the next parliamentary session scheduled for June 1644. The constitutional significance of these commissions has tended to be masked by the reconstitution of the privy council with parliamentary veto. The reconstituted privy council of thirty-six nobles, fourteen gentry and one burgess was certainly dominated by the nobility. Moreover, twenty-three members of the last council of the Personal Rule had their nominations as leading officials and councillors approved by the Scottish estates on 16 November. Nonetheless, the constitutional settlement of 1641 neither justifies the conclusion that 'the substance of power had been restored to the feudal classes' nor supports the contention that the government of Scotland 'was to revert to king and council' with the covenanting leadership relying on their in-built majority to preserve the revolution.[52] The apparent compromise with pragmatic Royalism in the composition of the privy council was no more than cosmetic. All leading officials and councillors, like all lords of session and members of the three Estates, were obliged under oath not only to sustain the constitutional and ecclesiastical imperatives of the National Covenant, but to acknowledge the parliament of 1641 to be 'free and lawfull' and to advance and assist the 'execution, obedience and observation' of its enactments. More dynamically, the radical mainstream, though content to accept the gloss of moderacy, was intent on maintaining revolutionary momentum through the executive commissions composed 'of all the prime covenanters', with a basic parity in membership spread among the three Estates.[53]

Financial affairs were devolved to two commissions with a common membership, fourteen from each estate, to whom were added General Alexander Leslie, the commander-in-chief of the covenanting forces, to represent the interests of the army and, as clerk, Sir Adam Hepburn of Humbie, the former clerk to the committee of estates. The commission 'for regulating the common burdings of the kingdom' was charged to bring order to the financial chaos left by the Bishops' Wars not just by uplifting all arrears of taxes and public dues and by repaying secured loans, but also by taking all requisite measures to meet outstanding public debts. Hence, valuations for the tenth and twentieth were to be completed and additional stents on the localities instituted for the relief of common burdens. The commission 'for receiving of brotherly assistance from the parliament of England' was charged to collate and disburse the chief source of income still outstanding for the relief of common burdens, the sum of £220,000 (£2,640,000 Scots) due to be paid in equal instalments over the next two years.

The parochial ramifications arising from the abolition of episcopacy served as the primary grounds for resurrecting the work of teind valuation and redistribution primarily for the benefit of the gentry as reflected in the composition of the commission 'for plantation of Kirkes and Valuatione of Teynds'. In addition to the fourteen members of each Estate, four officers of state and three lords of session were appointed – all but one of these supernumeraries being members of the gentry. Significantly, no commissioners for the Kirk were added as supernumeraries despite the remit of the commission to dispose of episcopal rights of patronage as well as titularship of the teinds. Any relevant motion from the General Assembly was to be taken cognisance of, however. The interests of the Kirk were represented by the inclusion of its procurator and clerk of the General Assembly, Sir Archibald Johnston of Wariston, on the commission 'for conserveing the Articles of the Treaty': in effect, the commission for diplomatic affairs with special responsibility for conserving the peace within the king's British dominions. Although the nobles had one less member than the eighteen drawn from the other two Estates, the inner core of eleven members seconded to the commission 'anent the Articles referred to consideration by the Treaty', had the marquis of Argyle, the leader of the radical mainstream, and his kinsman, John Campbell, the recently created first earl of Loudoun and lord chancellor, as supernumeraries. Ostensibly this latter commission, which included Wariston among the three members of the gentry, was charged to conclude the bilateral negotiations with the English parliament left unresolved by the Treaty of London. But their primary task was 'not so much for the perfecting of our Treatie, as to keep correspondence in so needful a tyme', notably with respect to 'what assistance Scotland shall give to England for suppressing of the rebellione in Ireland'. To conclude the prosecution of the leading delinquents, six from each Estate with two additional gentry in their capacity as lords of session were commissioned 'for trying the Incendiaries and Plotters'; that is, to determine the relevancy of treasonable charges for presentation before an assize. Despite the restriction of the commission's remit to the five principal Incendiaries headed by James Stewart, first earl of Traquair and the four designated Plotters led by Montrose, an institutional format had been established for the wholescale prosecution of the public enemies of the covenanting movement.[54]

The total number of people appointed to the executive and judiciary, whether as officials, councillors, lords of session or members of the parliamentary commissions was 123 – the breakdown for each Estate being 43 nobles, 51 gentry and 29 burgesses. The total composition of parliament during the final three-month session in 1641 was 160 – comprising 56 nobles, 50 gentry and 54 burgesses. Despite superficial evidence for generous representation for members of the three Estates on the executive and judiciary, only 74 of the total number of appointees – 35 nobles, 24 gentry and 15 burgesses – actually attended the final session as members of parliament. Covenanting activists account overwhelmingly for the 49 appointees to commissions not summoned to parliament. Three of the parliamentary commissions were composed exclusively of covenanting activists. Pragmatic Royalists appointed to the privy council were denied membership of the commissions for financial affairs. Though appointed to the commission for plantation of kirks and valuation of teinds out of respect for their landed interests, they were excluded from the commissions for trying the Incendiaries and Plotters. While some courtiers were nominated as conservators of the peace to enhance the diplomatic status of that office, none were admitted to the inner diplomatic circle charged to continue negotiations with the English parliament.

The statistical evidence for the relative insignificance of council membership in determining the activists who predominated on the parliamentary commissions was compounded by the actual practice of national government in the aftermath of the parliament of 1641. As borne out by the procedures deployed to promote armed Scottish intervention in Ireland, effective power continued to be vested in the covenanting oligarchy dominating the commissions. The privy council was merely a clearing-house for the delegation and approval of affairs of state. The specific terms under which the covenanting army intervened in Ireland in 1642 were referred to and resolved by the inner circle commissioned to continue negotiations with the English parliament. The financing, equipping and levying of the covenanting army was instigated under the auspices of the commission for common burdens. In turn, the covenanting oligarchy was intent not only on preserving its dominance of national government, but also on continuing its centralist demands on the localities by perpetuating and adapting the structure of local government implemented in the shires and presbyteries.[55]

The reconstituted privy council, however, did provide a forum for the regrouping of the conservative element within the covenanting movement around James Hamilton, third marquis (and later first duke) of Hamilton, a perceptive pragmatist but underestimated political operator. As the political situation in England deteriorated markedly following Charles I's return south, rival appeals for support from the Crown and the English parliament were channelled through the privy council. The endeavours of the conservative element to promote a Royalist stance in the privy council were intensified by the outbreak of civil war in England in August 1642. In the aftermath of the inconclusive engagement at Edgehill on 23 October, Covenanting overtures to mediate, though accepted hesitantly by the English parliament, were first rejected and then toyed with by Charles I. The king's intention, ably supported by Hamilton within the privy council, was to delay indefinitely Covenanting assistance to the English parliament. Drawing primarily on the support of the nobility on 20 December, Hamilton persuaded the privy council to publish a letter from the king justifying his stance towards the English parliament but not the declaration from the latter espousing religious unity and uniformity of church government. However, Argyle rallied the radical mainstream to circumvent Hamilton and the conservative element. The in-built radical majority on the council was mobilised to secure the publication of the letter from the English parliament on 10 January 1643. More significantly, the solid bedrock of support among the gentry and burgesses was deployed through the radical mainstream's interlocking control of interval committees, most notably the conservators of the peace and the commissioners for common burdens. Radical control was further reinforced by the mainstream's dominance over the commission for the public affairs of the kirk, constituted formally as the interval committee for the general assembly on 5 August 1642, which promoted solidarity with the English parliament. A joint meeting of the privy council, the conservators of the peace and the commission for the common burdens on 12 May 1643, was duly persuaded of the necessity to summon a convention of estates as an effective substitute for the parliament which Charles I resolutely refused to countenance before June 1644 (as prescribed by the triennial act).[56] As Hamilton regretfully informed the court, institutional dominance of the radical mainstream had resulted in 'the firm resolution of the Judicatories to be actors and no longer spectators in the English civil war'.[57]

Ostensibly required to supply the Scots army in Ireland and review the arrears of the brotherly assistance, the convention of estates which met from 22 June to 28 August was an adroitly managed platform for the radical mainstream. Papers recovered from Randal MacDonnell, second earl of Antrim, following his capture in Ulster by the covenanting army, implicated prominent Scottish royalists in fomenting insurrection at home while an Irish Catholic force was brought across to assist the king against the English parliament. On 19 August, the General Assembly had accepted an invitation from the English parliament to send commissioners to an assembly of divines at Westminster to observe, advise and direct discussions on the presbyterian reformation of the Church of England. Suitably conditioned, the convention of estates on 26 August cemented a formal alliance with the English parliament for armed assistance on the basis of the Solemn League and Covenant.[58] In response to accusations of disobedience and of slighting his prerogative from Charles I, Chancellor Loudoun, on 19 October, justified the summoning of the convention of estates, the implementation of the Solemn League and Covenant and the placing of the kingdom in a posture of defence. The convention of estates lacked neither royal authority nor constitutional warrant, 'since whole proclamations and citations given out by any of the king's judicatories are by law and inviolable practice united in the king's name and therefore warranted by the king'.[59]

Notwithstanding the political incompatibilities of the alliance between the covenanting movement and the English parliament, there is a temptation to view the professed religious union as the first step towards closer parliamentary union, perhaps federalism.[60] Conversely, the Solemn League and Covenant can be deemed the single most important diplomatic transaction between the regal union of 1603 and the parliamentary union of 1707 because negotiations were founded not on religious revelation but on political pragmatism and military expediency.[61] In strategic terms, British unity entailed uniformity of public policy rather than institutional restructuring or incorporation. But the immediate political price of armed intervention in England, coupled with a nation-wide compulsory subscription of the Solemn League and Covenant, was the outbreak of civil war at home. Moreover, intensified demands for financial and military commitment created a climate of resistance to oligarchic centralism within the covenanting movement. Despite the virtual eradication of Royalist resistance in the course of 1647, reprisals and purgings within the movement in the aftermath of the covenanting army's withdrawal from England ushered in a five-year constitutional phase dominated by the politics of exclusion and marked by a high turnover in membership of the central oligarchy.

On 26 August 1643, the same day that the treaty of mutual assistance was concluded with the English parliament, the committee of estates was restored; it was renewed periodically over the next eight years – in 1644, 1647, 1648, 1649 and 1651. Although executive power was devolved upon such specialist interval committees as the commission of exchequer for financial affairs, the commission for the plantation of kirks and valuation of teinds for ecclesiastical affairs, and the conservators of the articles for diplomatic affairs, the committee of estates remained the national nucleus of oligarchic centralism. Thus, the periodic reinvigoration of local government – in 1643, 1644, 1646, 1648 and 1649 – underscored the accountability of the shire committees of war to the committee of estates. Databases would have to be constructed before the interrelation of membership, attendance and radical dominance of interval committees could be demonstrated conclusively. However, quantitative analysis of the membership of the committee of estates and comparison with that of the commission for the public affairs of the Kirk suggests that beneath the mask of aristocratic dominance of the covenanting movement, there was an oligarchic inner core able to draw on a reservoir of support among the gentry and burgesses to replenish rather than diminish the radical mainstream.

In total, 318 members from the three parliamentary Estates – 78 nobles, 157 gentry and 103 burgesses – served on the seven committees of estates whose membership rose from 40 in 1640 to 129 in 1651. Of this total membership, 170 (53 per cent) – 34 nobles, 87 gentry and 49 burgesses – served on only one committee. Loudoun headed the three members (all nobles) who served on every committee. More revealingly, no Estate had an absolute majority amongst the inner core of 48 members – 23 nobles, 8 gentry and 17 burgesses – who served on at least four committees.[62] All but twelve members of this inner core – two nobles, four gentry and six burgesses – served on the commission for the public affairs of the Kirk. Renewed annually by general assemblies from 1642 and 1651, the commission of the Kirk functioned as an ideological watchdog, monitoring agency and supplicant for the radical mainstream in affairs of State. The commission compounded its radical posturing by its espousal of exclusion politics from 1646 to purge conservative elements from public office. A total of 314 ministers and 249 ruling elders drawn from the three parliamentary Estates served on the ten commissions, whose membership fluctuated from 48 to 105. Of the total membership, 126 ministers (40 per cent) and 150 elders (60 per cent), served on only one commission. In addition to three ministers – including Robert Douglas – and the two nobles headed by Argyle who served on every commission, the public affairs of the Kirk were controlled by an inner core of 35 ministers and 19 elders – eight nobles, seven gentry and four burgesses – who served on at least six commissions. All 19 elders served on the committee of estates, albeit no more than ten – seven nobles, two gentry and one burgess – can be associated with the inner core of the latter.[63]

The purging of public offices in the wake of civil war was designed to consolidate the oligarchic control of the radical mainstream. The Act of Proscription of 1646 also imposed swingeing fines up to the equivalent of six years' rents on all deemed delinquent or malignant. Punitive fining compounded by sequestration was entrusted to a special interval committee – the commission for monies – drawn from seven members of each parliamentary Estate and accountable to the committee of estates. The impact of proscription was to destroy all prospect of re-establishing the national consensus behind the covenanting movement.[64] The transfer of the king from the custody of the covenanting army to the English parliament for a fee of £400,000 (£4.8 million Scots) in January 1647 revived the conservative element who covertly concluded by the end of that year the Engagement with Charles I to defend and restore monarchical authority. The tentative move from federalism towards the contemplation of an incorporating union by the Engagers not only signposted that the covenanting movement was no longer making the political running throughout the British Isles, but also represented a desperate aristocratic effort to reassert their dominance over Scottish affairs.[65] Oligarchic centralism was manipulated not only to carry parliament and a renewed committee of estates but to compel local government to support armed Scottish intervention in the second English civil war during 1648. The response from the localities, particularly in the west of Scotland, was the recrudescence of petitioning on a scale unprecedented since 1637 against ungodly deviations from the fundamental religious and constitutional imperatives of covenanting. The reaction of the conservative element was to extend the scope of treason to party advantage and impose martial law on recalcitrant localities. A rising of the predominantly unfranchised but disaffected in the shires of Ayr and Lanark was vigorously suppressed on Mauchline Moor on 12 June.[66]

The Engagers, headed by the duke of Hamilton, can be identified from Gaelic sources as the first Scottish Tories.[67] Although their radical opponents were in the majority on the commission for the public affairs of the Kirk, Hamilton and other leading Engagers, even as their 'tragecomediall' adventure began to unravel, continued to differentiate between Argyle's followers among the parliamentary estates and the presbyterian zealots among the ministry. Complementing the Gaelic derivation of 'Tory', the radical opponents of the Engagement took their party label from the Scots appellation of 'Whig', applied to participants in the Whiggamore Raid launched from the west of Scotland on news of the Engagers' defeat at Preston in August 1648.[68] The Whiggamore Raid and the resultant *coup d'état* supported by Oliver Cromwell, in which the Engagers were obliged to disband their army and withdraw from public life on assurance of their lives and property, culminated in a reconvened parliament passing the Act of Classes on 23 January 1649. Cromwell's contrived execution of Charles I on 30 January, the subsequent reaction of outrage in Scotland and the British ramifications of the Covenanters' proclamation of Charles II as king on 5 February, have tended to obscure the radical nature of the political programme pushed through the Scottish parliament in 1649.[69] In particular, the parliamentary Estates attempted to impose from below the social engineering implicit in the Revocation Scheme which did so much to prejudice the Personal Rule of Charles I.[70]

However, the purging of the conservative element from public office did mark the downfall of oligarchic centralism. The rigorous application of the Act of Classes militated against nationwide commitment. Even though those excluded from public office were not directly subjected to the punitive fining which marked the Act of Proscription of 1646, all comprehended within the four-fold classification of malignancy were excluded from public office from one year to life. Those excluded in 1646 had been offered the general prospect of a return to public life on the eradication of Royalist resistance. Those excluded in 1649 were not only liable to strict ecclesiastical censure, but their eventual readmission to office was conditional on their public repentance in the Kirk and their unequivocal repudiation of their involvement in 'the late unlawful engagement against England'. The Kirk thereby gained a right of veto over office-holding. But in the shaping of public policy, the Kirk remained a supplicant, not a director. The constitutional principle underlying the Act of Classes was that acquiescence in the political directives of the covenanting movement was insufficient. Those seeking to hold public office had to demonstrate a positive commitment towards radicalism. In reality, however, the territorial influence of the radical regime installed in 1649 was largely confined to Scotland south of the Tay.[71]

The drive for radical purity in the wake of the Act of Classes led to the internally damaging split between the Remonstrants (later the Protestors) and the Resolutioners which came to a head in 1650. The Remonstrants were certainly correct in deeming Charles II unreliable and untrustworthy. Their insistence that their duty to support a covenanted king did not commit them unconditionally to a patently sinful Charles II was constitutionally valid and ideologically consistent with the distinction between the person and the office of monarchy in the Covenants. But the Resolutioners, the radical majority who claimed with equal validity to adhere to mainstream principles, countered with the curse of Meroz: that the pursuit of radical purity carried the danger of undefiled inactivity in the face of the external threat from Oliver Cromwell. More culpably, the drive for radical purity in the army fatally weakened the maintenance of national independence, as was borne out by the Covenanters snatching defeat from the jaws of victory at Dunbar on 3 September. Ideological division, translated into military weakness, duly resulted in the loss of Scotland south of the Forth and Clyde by the close of 1650.[72]

The Cromwellian advance and occupation expedited the patriotic accommodation with Royalists as well as the purging of the conservative element for their complicity in the Engagement. The ongoing Protestor–Resolutioner controversy delayed the formal repeal of the Act of Classes and the opening up of membership of the committee of estates until the summer of 1651. However, conservatives and Royalists did predominate on an executive body from 1 April 1651 – the committee for managing the affairs of the army. Arguably, executive authority was not so much duplicated as divided pragmatically with the committee of estates to accord with respective spheres of territorial interest. Nonetheless, the considerable energy expended in raising and supplying forces over the next two months was critically undermined by the manifest failure of radicals, conservatives and Royalists to pull together – the committee for managing the affairs of the army sat at Perth while the committee of estates remained in Stirling.[73]

No less critical to the fall of oligarchic centralism was the state of exhaustion endemic throughout the Scottish localities after thirteen years of continuous demands for ideological, financial and military commitment, aggravated by civil war and the three-year visitation of bubonic plague between 1644 and 1647. Indeed, the radical legislative programme of 1649 was as much a reaction against unremitting centralism as it was against aristocratic leadership of the Engagement. An act of 5 July, for 'Redress of Complaints and grievances of the People, against Masters, Collectors, Officers and Souldiers', devolved power in local government to presbytery committees which were to liaise directly with the committee of estates. The presbytery committees were to act as local commissions of grievance taking special cognisance of complaints arising from the mustering and quartering of troops as well as fiscal levies in town and country. In the meantime, members of shire committees were to accord priority to their collective role as justices of peace rather than as administrators of war.[74] Defeat at Worcester on 3 September 1651 formally laid to rest oligarchic centralism – like national independence, a victim of military and financial, if not ideological, exhaustion.

NOTES
1. P. Calvert, *Revolution* (London, 1970), pp.132–36, 140–44; J. Urry, *Reference Groups and the Theory of Revolution* (London, 1973), pp.127–31.
2. The growing awareness of the British significance of the Scottish revolution is manifest in A. J. Fletcher, *The Outbreak of the English Civil War* (London, 1981), pp.17–22, 408 and C. Russell, 'Why did Charles I call the Long Parliament?', *History*, LIX (1984), 375–83; but still generally underplayed as in T. K. Rabb and D. Hirst, 'Revisionism Revised: Early Stuart Parliamentary History', *Past & Present*, 92 (1981), 51–99.
3. National Library of Scotland [NLS], Wodrow MSS, quarto, xxiv, fos 163–9; S. Rutherford, *Lex Rex or The Law and the Prince*

(Edinburgh, 1848); *The Covenants and the Covenanters*, ed. J. Kerr (Edinburgh, 1896), pp.348-98.
4. D. Stevenson, *Revolution and Counter-Revolution in Scotland, 1644-1651* (London, 1977), pp.115-22.
5. D. Stevenson, *The Scottish Revolution, 1637-44* (Newton Abbot, 1973), pp.64-79.
6. A. I. Macinnes, 'The Origin and Organization of the Covenanting Movement during the reign of Charles I, 1626-41; with a particular reference to the west of Scotland', 2 vols (University of Glasgow, Ph.D. thesis, 1987), II, 201-64.
7. R. Mitchison, *Lordship to Patronage: Scotland, 1603-1745* (London, 1983), pp.42-3; W. Makey, *The Church of the Covenant 1637-1651* (Edinburgh, 1979), pp.27-30.
8. *A Source Book of Scottish History*, vol. III, ed. W. C. Dickinson and G. Donaldson (Edinburgh, 1961), p.104.
9. I. B. Cowan, 'The Covenanters: A revision article', *Scottish Historical Review* [*SHR*], XLVII (1968), 38-9.
10. *A Source Book of Scottish History*, III, 104; G. D. Henderson, *The Burning Bush: Studies in Scottish Church History* (Edinburgh, 1957), p.64.
11. J. Leslie, earl of Rothes, *A Relation of Proceedings Concerning the Affairs of the Kirk of Scotland, from August 1637 to July 1638*, ed. J. Nairne (Bannatyne Club, Edinburgh, 1830), appendix 211 [hereafter Rothes, *A Relation of Proceedings*]; *Acts of the Parliament of Scotland*, vols III-VI(ii), (1567-1660), ed. T. Thomson and C. Innes (Edinburgh, 1814-72), III, 376-7, c. 64 [hereafter *APS*].
12. G. Donaldson, *Scotland: James V to James VII* (Edinburgh, 1965), p.316; W. Ferguson, *Scotland's Relations with England: a Survey to 1707* (Edinburgh, 1977), p.116; D. Stevenson, *The Covenanters: The National Covenant and Scotland* (Saltire Pamphlets, Edinburgh, 1988), pp.35-44.
13. Rothes, *A Relation of Proceedings*, 90.
14. *APS*, V, 272-76; *A Source Book of Scottish History*, III, 95-104.
15. *Ibid.*, 95-100; Makey, *The Church of the Covenant*, p.26.
16. Ferguson, *Scotland's Relations with England*, pp.114-15; J. H. S. Burleigh, *A Church History of Scotland* (London, 1973), p.218.
17. D. Mathew, *Scotland under Charles I* (London, 1955), p.256; Makey, *The Church of the Covenant*, pp.29, 31.
18. Donaldson, *James V to James VII*, p.314.
19. Stevenson, *The Scottish Revolution*, p.85; D. G. Mullan, *Episcopacy in Scotland: The History of an Idea, 1560-1638* (Edinburgh, 1986), pp.179-83.
20. A. H. Williamson, *Scottish National Consciousness in the Age of James VI* (Edinburgh, 1979), pp.140-41. To claim that the Covenanters founded their case on this article underplays the

other two components of the National Covenant – the dual imperatives and public banding – which upheld the importance of fundamental laws, and overstates the significance of the proposed act of union which warned against breaches of fundamental laws but did not actually constitute or implement fundamental law (*APS*, IV, 263-4, c. 1).
21. *A Source Book of Scottish History*, III, 98-100.
22. J. B. Torrance, 'The Covenant Concept in Scottish Theology and Politics and its Legacy', *Scottish Journal of Theology*, XXXIV (1981), 232-6; G. H. Sabine, *A History of Political Theory* (London, 1968), pp.375-85.
23. J. K. Hewison, *The Covenanters*, 2 vols (Glasgow, 1908), I, 19-20, 24-9, 75, 129, 135-8, 481-3; J. Gordon, *A History of Scots Affairs, 1637-41*, 3 vols, ed. J. Robertson and G. Grub (Spalding Club, Aberdeen, 1841), I, 39-42.
24. *A Source Book of Scottish History*, III, 100-2; W. Scott, *An Apologetical Narration of the State and Government of the Kirk of Scotland since the Reformation*, ed. D. Laing (Wodrow Society, Edinburgh, 1846), pp.330-42; J. Row, *The History of the Kirk of Scotland*, ed. D. Laing (Wodrow Society, Edinburgh, 1842), 357-66, 376-81.
25. Rothes, *A Relation of Proceedings*, pp.90-2.
26. *Ibid.*, 96-8, 100-102; *A Source Book of Scottish History*, III, 102-104.
27. *Ibid.*, 102; Makey, *The Church of the Covenant*, p.28; Mathew, *Scotland under Charles I*, p.256.
28. Cowan, *SHR*, XLVII, 40; E. J. Cowan, *Montrose: For Covenant and King* (London, 1977), pp.46-7.
29. Donaldson, *James V to James VII*, p.315; Stevenson, *The Scottish Revolution*, p.85.
30. *A Source Book of Scottish History*, III, 103; A. Campbell, marquis of Argyle, *Instructions to a Son, containing rules of conduct in public and private life* (London, 1661), pp.30-6 [hereafter Argyle, *Instructions to a Son*].
31. Macinnes, 'The Origin and Organization of the Covenanting Movement', I, 160-94.
32. H. Kamen, *The Iron Century, Social Change in Europe, 1550-1660* (London, 1968), pp.326-30, 362-7.
33. Sabine, *A History of Political Theory*, pp.382-3; Makey, *The Church of the Covenant*, p.28.
34. Stevenson, *The Scottish Revolution*, pp.102-6; *Records of the Kirk of Scotland, containing the Acts and Proceedings of the General Assemblies, 1638-54*, ed. A. Peterkin (Edinburgh, 1853), pp.81-193 [hereafter *Records of the Kirk*].
35. Rutherford, *Lex Rex*, pp.56, 143-8, 199.
36. NLS, Wodrow MSS, quarto xxiv, fo. 165. The arguments to defend Scotland in 1639 were reiterated in 1640 to justify the covenanting army's invasion of England – an offensive posture

## The Scottish Constitution

   for defensive purposes (Edinburgh University Library [EUL], Instructions of the Committee of Estates of Scotland, 1640-1, Dc.4.16, fo. 1).
37. *APS*, VI (i), 41-3; *A Source Book of Scottish History*, III, 122-5.
38. *The Covenants and the Covenanters*, pp.355, 362-8.
39. Argyle, *Instructions to a Son*, pp.134-43.
40. Rutherford, *Lex Rex*, pp.98-9, 222-3.
41. *APS*, V. 258-300.
42. Makey, *The Church of the Covenant*, pp.55-6; Ferguson, *Scotland's Relations with England*, pp.117-18.
43. *APS*, V, 282-4, c. 24; Gordon, *A History of Scots Affairs*, III, 181-4. To maintain a constant correspondence between the sections, Adam Hepburn of Humbie was appointed clerk to the committee, and in the likelihood of his opting to accompany the army, was empowered to employ deputies to remain in Edinburgh. Archibald Johnston of Wariston was also to reside at camp where, as clerk and procurator for the Kirk, he was to oversee the preparation of treaties, consultations and publications. The officers of the general staff were eligible to attend all meetings of the committee.
44. *The Government of Scotland under the Covenanters 1637-1651*, ed. D. Stevenson (Scottish History Society [SHS], Edinburgh, 1982), xvii-xxvii [hereafter *Government under the Covenanters*]; *APS*, V, 280-2, c. 23; 285-6, c. 26-7, 29-32.
45. *Ibid.*, 286-7, c. 33; Cowan, *Montrose*, pp.113-22.
46. Rutherford, *Lex Rex*, 223-4; *APS*, V, 280-2, c. 23; D. Stevenson, 'The financing of the cause of the Covenants, 1638-51', *SHR*, LI (1972), 90-2, 103-107.
47. NLS, Salt & Coal: Events, 1635-62, MS.2263, fos 73-78; *Calendar of States Papers, Domestic Series, of the reign of Charles I (1638-39)*, ed. J. Bruce and W. D. Hamilton (London, 1871), pp.114-16.
48. B. P. Levack, *The formation of the British State: England, Scotland, and the Union 1603-1707* (Oxford, 1987), pp.110, 130-1; C. L. Hamilton, 'The Anglo-Scottish Negotiations of 1640-41', *SHR*, XLI (1962), 84-6.
49. EUL, Instructions of the Committee of Estates, Dc.4.16, fos 101, 105; NLS, Wodrow MSS, folio lxxiii, fo. 63; *APS*, V, 335-45, c. 8; Sir J. Balfour, *Historical Works*, 4 vols, ed. J. Haig (Edinburgh, 1824), III, 33, 40-1; J. Spalding, *The History of the Troubles and Memorable Transaction in Scotland and England, 1624-45*, 2 vols, ed. J. Skene (Bannatyne Club, Edinburgh, 1828-29), I, 293-4 [hereafter, Spalding, *History of the Troubles*]; *The Memoirs of Henry Guthry* (Glasgow, 1747), pp.96-7. The covenanting movement was not exclusively concerned with a bipartisan approach to internationalism. At the same time as the Scottish commissioners were presenting their proposals for union to their English counterparts, the committee

of estates at Edinburgh was actively promoting a tripartite alliance involving not only the Scottish Estates and the English parliament, but also the Estates General of the United Provinces: a confederation which never came to fruition.

50. *Government under the Covenanters*, xxxv, appendices, pp.176-9, 183-8.
51. G. Burnet, *The Memoirs of the Lives and Actions of James and Willian, Dukes of Hamilton and Castleherald* (London, 1687), pp.46, 184-7 [hereafter Burnet, *Memoirs of the Dukes of Hamilton*]; *The Letters and Journals of Robert Baillie, 1637-62*, 3 vols, ed. D. Laing (Bannatyne Club, Edinburgh, 1841-42), I, 389-98; Balfour, *Historical Works*, III, 44-165; Spalding, *History of the Troubles*, I, 336-8, 352-9; *The Memoirs of Henry Guthry*, 99-109; *A Declaration of the Proceedings of the Parliament of Scotland* (London, 1641).
52. Makey, *The Church of the Covenant*, pp.56-8; *Government under the Covenanters*, pp.xxvii-xxxix; *APS*, V, 505-507, c. 89; *Records of the Privy Council of Scotland*, second series, vols VI-VII (1635-43), ed. P. H. Brown (Edinburgh, 1905-1906), VI, viii-ix [hereafter *RPCS*, second series].
53. Hull University Library, Maxwell-Constable of Everingham MSS, DDEV/76/10; *The Dissolution of the Parliament in Scotland* (Edinburgh, 1641); *The Memoirs of Henry Guthry*, pp.104-105.
54. *APS*, V, 391-6, c. 76-7; 400-403, c. 85; 404-405, c. 87-8; 408-409, c. 92; Scottish Record Office [SRO], Supplementary Parliamentary Papers, PA 16/3/5/3; *The Letters and Journals of Robert Baillie*, I, 397; Burnet, *Memoirs of the Dukes of Hamilton*, 187.
55. SRO, Supplementary Parliamentary Papers, PA 14/1, fo. 12; SRO, Hamilton Papers, TD 75/100/26/1458, /1472, /1488; *RPCS*, second series, VII, 149-55, 163-4, 170-2.
56. SRO, Hamilton Papers, TD 75/100/26/1688, /1742-43, /1782, /1808, /1846, /1887; Stevenson, *The Scottish Revolution*, 248-75.
57. SRO, Hamilton Papers, TD 75/100/26/1828.
58. *APS*, VI (i), 47-9; SRO, Hamilton Papers, TD 75/100/26/1840; Stevenson, *The Scottish Revolution*, 275-90; L. Kaplan, *Politics and Religion During the English Revolution: The Scots and the Long Parliament, 1643-1645* (New York, 1976), xv-xxi.
59. SRO, Hamilton Papers, TD 75/100/26/1916.
60. D. Stevenson, 'The Early Covenanters and the Federal Union of Britain' in *Scotland and England 1286-1815*, ed. R. A. Mason (Edinburgh, 1987), 163-81; Levack, *The Formation of the British State*, pp.198-9.
61. E. J. Cowan, 'The Solemn League and Covenant' in *Scotland and England 1286-1815*, pp.182-202.
62. *APS*, V, 282, c. 24: VI (i), 52-9; 99, c. 11; 199-204, c. 202-203; 211, c. 217; 235-6, c. 258; 246, c. 266; 45, c. 7; 303-304, c. 49; 394, c. 184; 433, 460; 559-63, c. 183-4; 766, c. 345;

778, c. 362; 780, c. 366: VI (ii), 30-9, c. 69; 102, c. 199; 114, c. 217; 186-95, c. 111; 290, c. 288; 300, c. 274; 321, c. 310; 573, 679, 685.
63. *Records of the Kirk*, pp.330-1, 359-60, 399, 427-8, 449-50, 477-8, 514-15, 549-50; *The Records of the Commissions of the General Assemblies, 1650-52*, ed. J. Christie (SHS, Edinburgh, 1909), pp.3-4, 499-502; D. Stevenson, 'The General Assembly and the Commission of the Kirk, 1638-51', *Records of the Scottish Church History Society*, XIX (1975), pp.59-79; Makey, *The Church of the Covenant*, pp.85-93.
64. *APS*, VI (i), 503-505, c. 102; 549-50, c. 160; 567-70, c. 195; 580, c. 210; SRO, Supplementary Parliamentary Papers, PA 14/3, fo. 501-507; SRO, Hamilton Papers, TD 75/100/26/2108, /2145; *Government under the Covenanters*, pp.8-9, 15, 17-18.
65. Stevenson, 'The Early Covenanters and the Federal Union of Britain', pp.175-6; *A Source Book of Scottish History*, III, 134-9.
66. *APS*, VI (ii), 17, c. 39; 86, c. 155; 93, c. 185; 106-107, c. 204-205; 108, c. 208; 691-2; *Government under the Covenanters*, 62-81; EUL, Laing MSS, La.I.308; SRO, Hamilton Papers, TD 75/100/26/2284, /2291, /2389; *The Memoirs of Henry Guthry*, pp.276-83; *The Letters and Journals of Robert Baillie*, III, 444-50; Sir J. Turner, *Memoirs of His Own Life and Times*, ed. T. Thomson (Bannatyne Club, Edinburgh, 1829), pp.49-57.
67. A. I. Macinnes, 'The First Scottish Tories?', *SHR*, LXVII (1988), 56-66.
68. SRO, Hamilton Papers, TD 75/100/26/2156, /2408, /2442: TD 76/100/3/10806; Burnet, *Memoirs of the Dukes of Hamilton*, pp.365-78; *The Memoirs of Henry Guthry*, pp. 283-304.
69. Stevenson, *Revolution and Counter-Revolution*, pp.115-34; Makey, *The Church of the Covenant*, pp.75-84.
70. Macinnes, 'The Origin and Organization of the Covenanting Movement', I, 247-9.
71. *APS*, VI (ii), 129, c. 13; 133, c. 18-19; 143, c. 30; 150, c. 38; 153, c. 47; 172, c. 90; 174-81, c. 98-102; 195-9, c. 112-15; 225, c. 171; 436, 446; 486, c. 237; Glasgow University Archives, Beith Parish MSS, P/CN, vol. II, no. 139; SRO, Hamilton Papers, TD 75/100/26/4044; *Government under the Covenanters*, pp.85-103.
72. *A Source Book of Scottish History*, III, 144-6; Balfour, *Historical Works*, IV, 92-109, 141-60, 174-8; *The Covenants and the Covenanters*, pp.370-2.
73. *Government under the Covenanters*, pp.105-73.
74. *APS*, VI (ii), 268, c. 215; 449, c. 159; 464-7, c. 194; 502, c. 282. Shire and presbytery committees seem to have coalesced as committees of war from 1643 to 1649 (*Ibid*., VI (i), 622-3, c. 21-3: VI (ii), 172, c. 91; 539, c. 379).

# Six

## SCOTLAND TURNED SWEDEN: THE SCOTTISH COVENANTERS AND THE MILITARY REVOLUTION, 1638–1651

### Edward M. Furgol

When the Covenanters decided, in mid-1638, that resistance to Charles I must change from the presentation of petitions to the raising of troops they showed great faith in their cause. Scotland was a country singularly unsuited for military defiance of the king of Great Britain and Ireland, who possessed a fleet capable of blockading its ports, friends within who could tie down large numbers of covenanting soldiers and the potential to invade with armies from England and Ireland. The last war in Scotland had occurred over sixty years previously. What foundations had the Jacobean and Caroline regimes provided the Covenanters with to embark on military endeavours? Was Scotland in 1638–39 an armed camp long prepared for war or a nation possessing few attributes of the military revolution which had spread across early modern continental Europe?

What were the signs of the military revolution? The major change was the replacement of the lance and pike by the musket; formerly, shock had ruled the battlefield: now, fire-power ruled. Armies mushroomed in size from a few hundred men to thousands. For instance, by the 1630s France, Spain, the Netherlands and Austria could each field 100 000 men. The new way of warfare also placed a greater burden on rulers and civilians as the cost of soldiers rose, the number of administrative problems grew and the scale of militarily created damage soared. War-making became a primary function of governments wishing to exercise control over their own destinies. As countries brought their armies in line with the innovations of the military revolution, the incidence of war became more common. In the seventeenth century, the Ottoman Empire, Austria and Sweden

## Scotland turned Sweden

undertook military operations in two out of every three years; Spain was at war three of every four years; Poland and Russia had only one year's peace in five.[1] How then did Scotland fit into the European military picture in 1638?

Traditionally, Scotland's first line of defence had been its reserves of large numbers of men trained for war. That situation had altered after the Union of the Crowns when the auld enemie had become the new friend and the necessity of training men for imminent war vanished. Between 1603 and 1638 the privy council authorised few musters or wapinschaws for the shires. When Charles was at war with France and Spain the council had ordered one national muster by shires and burghs in 1625 and two further ones in 1627.[2] While Edinburgh held annual musters from 1607 to 1637 (and some other burghs may have followed suit), the majority of the population living in the rural areas of the shires and the landwards of the burghs probably had little or no regular training. Even the Edinburgh musters had little military significance, for one finds no reference to her militia as an important element in the covenanting war machine. This differed from the situation in her sister capital where the trained bands formed the backbone of the Parliamentarian army in 1642. Therefore, one can dispense with any notion that the Covenanters had a body of trained military forces ready.

Military skills may also be gained by field service and it behoves us to see whether the Scots had a large pool of domestic manpower with this experience. After 1603 the privy council had authorised a number of expeditions for pacifying parts of the kingdom. The western Isles witnessed four main periods of military activity covering ten of the years between 1605 and 1628.[3] There had been official incursions into the western Highlands in eight of the years between 1613 and 1625.[4] Expeditions had also been mounted against the northern Isles, the clan Macgregor, Caithness, the central Highlands and the northeastern Highlands.[5] These campaigns, however, were of little use in providing Scotland with large military resources, since the numbers involved consisted of hundreds, not thousands, of men. Three further points must be made about these campaigns. They were not annual events which would have allowed many different men to gain military experience. Their occurrence was sporadic, with none occurring in sixteen of the years between 1610 and 1638. This meant that by 1639 those Lowlanders who had served probably had only vague memories of military discipline. Only the Campbells and their allies, the MacAulays, Lamonts, Malcolms, MacDougalls, Macleans and Camerons, who had served on the expeditions, were supporters of the Covenanters. These clans also possessed reserves of trained manpower, because military training remained an essential part of a Highland man's upbringing. Consequently, the importance of the decision taken by the eighth earl of Argyll (chief of the Campbells) to join the Covenanters can be appreciated in military terms. Nevertheless, these Gaelic-speaking supporters of the Covenant could have done little to impart their military knowledge (which may have been antiquated and unsuitable for resisting men trained in the Swedish and Dutch methods) to the Scots speakers of the Lowlands.

For training men to be soldiers the Covenanters by necessity relied upon Scotland's 'military reserve' – the mercenary veterans of the continental wars. The poverty of Scotland, combined with the foreign policies of James and Charles, had created vast numbers of these men. From 1620 to 1637 the kings had permitted a large exportation of surplus Scottish males to serve in the armies of the Netherlands, France, Denmark, Sweden and Russia. In the years 1624, 1626–29, 1631–33 and 1637, royal warrants had permitted the levying of 41 400 Scots for continental armies.[6] It would have been remarkable if all of these troops had been raised. However, 25 000 or ten per cent of the adult male population had departed from Scotland to serve in either the Danish or Swedish armies in the 1625–32 period.[7] Those who served in the Swedish army gained military training and combat experience in the most advanced practices of warfare. To ensure that their armies in the First Bishops' War had some chance of success, the covenanting government required that the lieutenant colonels and majors of each regiment, and the ensign and the two sergeants of each company be veteran Scottish soldiers. Thus, thirty-two of a regiment's seventy commissioned and non-commissioned officers were to be veterans. The recall of these men occurred in late 1638. They came in sufficient numbers to provide the covenanting forces with enough military training to convince Charles that 1639 was not the year in which to fight, and enough to conquer Northumberland and Durham in a few days' campaigning in 1640. At this stage the two men most responsible for bringing Swedish military practices and experience to the covenanting forces were Field Marshal Alexander Leslie, the Lord General, and Alexander Hamilton, General of Artillery. Initially, however, the covenanting forces were really unprepared for a modern large-scale action such as Lutzen or Rocroi; the military neglect of the previous thirty-six years had seen to that.

The post-union state could have provided the Covenanters with stockpiles of arms and ammunition and with artillery fortresses from which to defy the king. Unfortunately, the Covenanters received no valuable legacies in these commodities. The last massive importation and manufacture of muskets, pikes, swords, pistols, armour, gunpowder, cannon, projectiles and matches had occurred in the invasion scare of 1625-27.[8] Most of these items were subject to decay and the evidence does not suggest that they were imported in sufficient quantities to arm a force of thousands such as was required in 1639. Instead, the Covenanters relied almost entirely upon the massive importation of armaments from the Netherlands in the autumn of 1638 and ensuing months before taking the field in spring 1639. Throughout the 1640s the Covenanters 'always seem[ed] to have been able to secure enough munitions to keep on fighting.' Between 1639 and 1644 the factor at Vere, Zeeland sent 31 673 muskets, 29 000 swords, 8 000 pikes, 500 pairs of pistols and 12 field pieces to Scotland.[9] These figures suggest that sources outside of the Netherlands also must have provided pikes, pistols and cannons for the armies.

Turning to fortifications once again, one sees that Scotland was in a sorry condition. For example, in 1608 the Border castle of Annan was transformed into a kirk. While the privy council had taken measures to ensure the defensibility of Edinburgh and Dumbarton castles after 1603, their royal garrisons initially put them outwith Covenanter control. Of the burghs, which were ideological bastions of the movement, not one was defended by bastioned artillery defences. In 1627 Anstruther had actually been fortified against naval attack, but it was of little significance. The fortification of Montrose, Leith, Burntisland, Inchgarvie and Aberdeen had been proposed,[10] but it is uncertain whether the works had been constructed and if so whether they had been maintained after the invasion scare. The Covenanters fortified Leith and Burntisland in 1639 and they could have used the earlier plans; that may have been their sole inheritance from previous efforts. In 1638-39 Scotland was not militarily prepared; lacking resident reserves of men trained in the latest military techniques; deficient in the materials of war; and without any citadels or burghs capable of withstanding an early modern army.

Having demonstrated that the Covenanters had to propel Scotland into the military revolution from a standing start, we now turn to their military achievements in the 1639-1651 period. Recruitment, the size of armies, the size and weapons of different types of units, uniforms, strategy and tactics will each be considered.

The mechanism for the levying of a Covenanter army was established in 1639 and adhered to with only minor exceptions until 1651. What was the inspiration for this system? Did the Covenanters rely on the feudal, kinship, mercenary or another method? An analysis of the situation in Sweden suggests that the Swedish system was adopted by the Scots.

Of all European countries only Sweden possessed a working system of national conscription in the 1600s. The Vasa kings merged feudal obligation with the ancient duty of general military service. By the early 1600s lists of all men over fifteen were being kept. By 1620, one out of every ten eligible males (nobles, clergymen, widows' only sons, miners, arms workers and the inhabitants of certain towns were exempted) was called up annually for twenty years' service. The country was split into eight military districts for the raising of regiments. The selection of recruits lay with the local communities. (Those not called paid taxes.) The annual number of recruits varied from as many as 13 500 in 1627 to as few as 6600 in 1646. By this method Sweden fielded three per cent of her population, or at least 43 000 men.[11]

That Scotland followed Sweden is not remarkable when one recalls that Alexander Leslie, a famous Swedish general, modelled the covenanting forces. As in Sweden, the central government organised the levy. Although the Covenanters did not control the *de jure* central government in 1638–39, they had established an alternative *de facto* body, the Tables, which proposed and implemented policies at the national level. Later, the Covenanters utilised the privy council and parliament and created the committee of estates through which they preferred to control the country. From 1639 to 1651, with the exception of the Whiggamore Raid, all armies levied by the Covenanters had their origins at the national level, as in the Swedish model. The Covenanter central government nominated colonels, authorised the levying of troops and established the quotas each shire would provide. The Covenanters exempted the nobles and clergy. These quotas were rigid, unlike those in the Swedish system, which directly reflected demographic trends. Nevertheless, after the 1644–5 plague visitation the government reduced the number of men for certain shires and burghs in the levies of 1648–50. Again on the Swedish model, the Covenanters established military districts – approximately twenty in seven military regions.[12]

Effective central-local coordination was an innovation of the Covenanters. They created the committee of war or the committee of the shire, which had the mission of carrying out commands received from the national government. These committees, which consisted of men nominated by the parliament, were extremely competent. In military matters they arranged the quarterings of regiments and determined the numbers of soldiers that each burgh or rural parish would raise to meet the shire quota.

The fact that recruits were selected by their own communities also reflected the Swedish example. In the burghs the councils functioned as the recruiting agencies. In the rural parishes, the clergy and church elders had the responsibility of listing the fencible men (eligible recruits) and selecting them with the assistance of local landowners. The clergy played a special role in both urban and rural areas by publicising the levies and encouraging men to join the regiments.[14]

Another factor vital to the success of a levy by the Covenanters was the support of the landowners, who could bring out their kinsmen, tenantry and servants. For this reason the colonels of regiments were predominantly nobles or lairds. Captains of companies or troops were often from the same classes. The commissioning of men from these classes strengthened their ties with the covenanting cause and stimulated the recruiting process in areas where they held land or had kinship ties. The forces raised in this manner were not hampered by the localism that characterised English levies before the establishment of the New Model Army. Scots campaigned south to the Gloucester–Newark line, north to the Orkneys, west to the shores of Lough Foyle and along the shores of the North Sea. Loyalty to the cause and the acceptance of mobility may go far to explain the difference. (On certain occasions, principally in the Highlands and the northeast Lowlands, heads of families and their cadets raised forces without recourse to the three-tiered system outlined above.[15] Almost always, these retinues served for a short time and usually remained within the region in which they were raised.)

Sometimes the system failed. In 1648, the Kirk opposed the Engagement and did all in its power to obstruct the levy. In addition to massive resistance to the levy from the clergy, most of the burghs and the shire committees in East Lothian, Fife, Ayr, Kirkcudbright, Wigtown, Lanark and Renfrew, given a quota of nearly 8000 of the 22000-man total, balked at raising men. As a consequence, army officers resorted to quartering troops on resisters and to kidnapping recruits. The strong support for the Engagement from the landed classes produced troops in 1648, but probably no more than two-thirds of the quota were levied.[16] Following the Act of Classes in 1649 and subsequent acts for preparing the army, these landed supporters of the Engagers found themselves forbidden public employment. The functioning of the shire committees suffered from the absence of their support and experience. The levy of 1651 for the Army of the Kingdom suffered opposition from the southwestern Lowland clergy and minor lairds and from a general war-weariness. Before the summer campaign, several units of the army were quartered on those who had not provided their quotas.[17] The forces of the Whiggamores (1648) and Western Association (1650) differed from the normal pattern in that the local clergy played a primary role in bringing men out. However, some members of the landed classes (principally minor lairds) seconded their efforts.[18] For the successful levy of a regiment the cooperation of all three levels of the recruiting system was essential, as was the whole-hearted support of the clergy and the landowners.

Between 1639 and 1651 the Covenanters raised over a dozen armies ranging in size from 2000 to 24000 men. In 1639 the Covenanters occupied Aberdeen four times. The first army consisted of 9000–11000 men; the second, 4000; the third, 7000; and the fourth, 4000. Meanwhile, on the eastern border General Alexander Leslie commanded between 12000 and 20000 men.[19] An unknown number served in the defence of the Forth coastline against Hamilton's 5000 royal troops and in the subjugation of the royalists in the southwest.

Leslie invaded England in 1640 with an army of 17775 foot and horse, while Argyll devastated the lands of royalist nobles and clans with 4000 men. In the southwest a regiment was sufficient to capture Caerlaverock and Threave castles. A slightly stronger force was necessary to subdue the royalist Gordons and their allies in the northeast Lowlands.[20] Thus, the Covenanters fielded approximately 24000 men or roughly 24 per 1000 of the population. In 1630 Sweden's army was at the ratio of 50 soldiers per 1000 of the inhabitants. However, 43 per cent were foreigners and excluding them the figure would be 29 per 1000. Sweden had been militarily active from the mid-1500s, was wealthier than Scotland, and had large French subsidies – all of which shows that the Covenanters did wonders in raising so many men.

Following the Irish rebellion of October 1641 the Covenanters arranged with the English parliament to send an army of 10000 men to Ulster to help crush the Irish. However, by autumn 1642 they had sent over 11371 officers and men. As a result of wastage from military activity, lack of supplies, disease and evacuation to Scotland, this army shrank to about 4000 soldiers in 1647. The shipping of

2100 men to Scotland to aid the Engagers in 1648 halved this number.[21]

The Army of the Solemn League and Covenant (also subsidised by the English parliament) entered England in January 1644 with 18 000 foot, 3000 horse and 500–600 dragoons. In June a second army with 6800–8000 men crossed the border to recover strongholds recaptured by the royalists.[22] The Covenanter forces in 1644 may have exceeded 30 000 men or 30 per 1000 inhabitants, their greatest strength. Although this was less than half the size and magnitude of the comparable 1630 Swedish army, it was a remarkable achievement for a country which had only experienced the military revolution in 1639.

By summer 1645, Leven's field army had only 9000 foot and 5500 horse; casualties, the plague, evacuation to Scotland, garrisons in northern England and, probably, a poor supply system reduced its effectiveness substantially. Similar trends occurred on the Continent.[23] Still, about 25 000 men were under arms that year. In January 1646 at the siege of Newark the army mustered only 6943 men, the retention of men in garrisons and evacuation of regiments to Scotland having contributed to this low figure.[24] Meanwhile, in Scotland between 1644 and 1646, the Covenanters mustered several armies against the royalists, which ranged in size from 2000 to 7000 men.

Following the cessation of hostilities in England and the return of the Army of the Solemn League and Covenant in February 1647, a New Model Army of 7200 men was created from elements of the old regiments. By then over 12 000 men had died in battle. The new army served as the nucleus of the Engager Army of 14 000–15 000 troops, which crossed into England in July 1648. The Engagers also kept troops in Scotland to suppress the kirk party. In September this force of New Model units, new levies, Ulster Army men and refugees from the English campaign consisted of about 8000 men. It was opposed by over 7000 from Argyll, the southwest Lowlands and Fife.[25] Casualties in the campaigns of 1648 removed over 8000 men from the pool of manpower. Fortunately for the levies of 1649–50, these men were tainted with unacceptably strong royalist sentiments.

The Army of the Covenant was for most of its existence a small force. In July 1649 it mustered only 5300 foot and horse. On the eve of the English invasion in 1650 there had been no increase in numbers. Yet, at Dunbar, Lieutenant-General David Leslie commanded 23 000 foot and horse. However, between 2000 and 5000 men had been purged from the army for failing to meet the requirements of the Act of Classes. After Dunbar, where Leslie lost

14000 troops, the field army shrank to 4000–5000 men. In autumn 1650 the radical officers commanded 2000 horse and dragoons. Four of Leslie's former regiments formed the basis of this Western Association Army, so not all were new recruits.[26]

The Army of the Kingdom, for which no levying restrictions existed, managed to field 15000 foot and 4000–5000 horse by May 1651. In mid-July it contained 19943 foot alone, but by late July when the army headed south towards England it consisted of no more than 21000 and possibly as few as 12000 men.[27] More than 2000 soldiers were lost in the Inverkeithing débâcle, but desertion was the main cause of decline in numbers. During the rest of the campaign season, the forces in Scotland and England suffered shattering defeats with losses reaching more than 13000 men, bringing the total number of casualties for the period to more than 47000 men – a horrific figure for a nation of a million souls – and destroying the last of the Covenanter's armies.

The lack of reliable population figures for Scotland in the 1639-1651 period precludes an accurate assessment of the magnitude of the Covenanters' success in creating armies. Even assuming that Scotland possessed a large surplus male population in 1639, this surplus could no longer have remained following the more than 22000 war casualties by 1649 and the loss of 4000–5000 potential recruits in the plague of 1644–45 and of an unknown number in the famine of 1648–49. The Covenanters' facility for raising armies is remarkable, particularly in view of the fact that Scotland had not engaged in prolonged military activity since 1573 and had no established system of levying large numbers of troops before 1639. In other words, the three-tiered system of levying worked extremely well.

Turning to the type of units which made up the armies, one finds much that is similar to other early modern armies. Following continental practice,[28] the backbone of all covenanting armies, save that of the Western Association, was the foot or infantry regiment. These units were commanded by a colonel and usually had ten companies.[29] The size of infantry regiments varied enormously – from 300 men to over 1200. However, their ten foot companies ran to more standard sizes. The Ulster Army in 1642 had companies varying in strength from 93 to 121 officers and men. The Army of the Solemn League and Covenant's companies had between 100 and 120 men at full strength. On 9 December 1646 parliament set the minimum size of a company at 80 soldiers. At the creation of the New Model Army the strength of a company rose to 125 foot. On 21

June 1650 the Estates put the number at 108 men. After Dunbar many companies had fallen below this level: whereas in 1651 a company had to field only 70 foot in order to maintain its integrity, some regiments had as few as 150 men.[30]

The weapons of foot regiments were fairly standard throughout the period. All men carried swords regardless of their primary weapon. On the Continent in the 1630s Gustavus Adolphus' forces had a ratio of one musketeer per 1.2 pikemen, while the Dutch had an equal number of both. By the 1650s the continental armies had three to four musketeers for every pikeman.[31] The Covenanters followed the trend towards increasing firepower. Their infantry regiments initially had 20 per cent more musketeers than the Swedish or Dutch, but 20–25 per cent fewer than the 1650s armies. Lack of funds to buy the more expensive muskets, inadequate munitions and tactical conservatism possibly account for the situation in Scotland. In 1640, Leslie's Life Guard of Foot had just over three musketeers for every two pikemen. This ratio was, presumably, general throughout the army. The Ulster Army contained 6000 musketeers and 4000 pikemen, fitting the 3:2 ratio exactly. In April 1644 the Estates provided two regiments with two muskets for each pike, marking a 10 per cent increase in the former. Until December 1650 the covenanting forces preserved the predominance of firepower over shock. The act of levy on 23 December 1650 authorised the raising of infantry regiments with only two musketeers for every three pikemen.[32] This reversal in Scottish and continental trends probably arose from the difficulty of obtaining muskets, powder and match through the English blockade as well as from the impoverished regime's inability to obtain credit for them. With the exception of the 1651 army, the Covenanter foot regiment relied principally upon its musket fire to decide the issue. This was tactically sound, except against the Highland charge, where counter-shock, whether by pikemen or cavalry, was the only suitable response.

Regiments of horse in the covenanting armies came to the fore only with the raising of the Army of the Solemn League and Covenant. It is probably no accident that this development transpired when David Leslie, a cavalry officer in the Swedish army who became the Covenanters' best general, returned to Scotland in 1643. Previously, horse units were brigaded with the foot or served as independent troops; only rarely did they serve as regiments. Horse regiments (commanded by colonels) and troops (led by routmasters, *ex Reitermeister*) varied greatly in strength. The Army of the Solemn League and Covenant's standard horse regiment should have contained eight troops of seventy-five men each, but many were one or two troops short. In 1644 troop strength varied from fifty-four to sixty-seven officers and men. On 9 December 1646 the Estates fixed the minimum troop size within Scotland at fifty horse. On 29 January 1647 the standard size of a New Model troop was set at eighty men, which parliament later reduced to seventy-five in order to provide another troop. A cavalry regiment of the Engager Army was to contain 180 horse. In 1650 the Estates contrived to establish a standard regiment, only to deviate from it immediately. Each regiment was to contain six troops of seventy-five man each or 450 troopers. However, two regiments were to have nine troops each (for 685 men) and one was to have only five (375 troopers). Troop strength, too, fluctuated from as few as thirty-four horse to as many as ninety-five. In winter 1650–51 seven horse regiments averaged 330 men, which suggests that the levies of 1650 had been deficient because the cavalry suffered few casualties at Dunbar. In spring 1651 ten horse regiments averaged 439 horse, indicating an increase in size of older regiments as a result of recruiting.[33]

The arms and armour of horsemen changed somewhat during the wars. In 1640, horsemen were protected by a jack and armed with either a lance, carbine or pair of pistols in addition to a sword. Later, buff coats with breast and back armour over them replaced the jacks. Broadswords were universal, but they were not the sole weapon of attack. In Ulster the lance was the primary weapon against the Irish, and at Marston Moor Leven's mounted force charged the English royalists with lances. The last mention of covenanting horse using the lance relates to Dunbar, where the front rank of the Ministers' Horse was armed with lances. As late as December 1650 the government authorised cavalry regiments to be armed with either lances or pistols in addition to swords. However, in 1651 the only offensive weapons referred to in official documents were swords, pistols and carbines.[34] The precise tactical arrangements of the Covenanter cavalry is unknown. Nevertheless, we know that they charged in the Swedish manner with swords and pistols.[35]

The last type of regular unit in the armies to be considered is the artillery. That the Covenanters followed Sweden's example is hardly surprising, since the generals of artillery were former officers in the Swedish army. As in the Swedish army, regular officers and gunners (but not civilian contractors, as was the practice in some armies) transported and manned the cannon. The Covenanters purchased some guns from the Continent. They also possessed a cannon foundry for three-pounders in Potter Row, Edinburgh, until September 1650.

These were neither the leather guns nor the frames that Parker has misidentified and correctly called useless,[36] but excellent iron field pieces. The three-pounder was the main field gun of all of the major Covenanter armies; each regiment probably deployed two in formal battles. (The Swedes assigned four three-pounders to each regiment. Yet it must be remembered she was the chief producer of iron cannons in the mid-1600s.)[37] The Covenanters also possessed 24-, 18-, 12-, 9- and 6-pounders. There was no standard number of guns for an army. For instance, the armies of the Second Bishops' War and Solemn League and Covenant had trains of over sixty pieces, or 1:300 and 1:360 men respectively, while the army at Duns in 1639 had forty cannon and that at Dunbar in 1650 possessed between thirty-two and twenty-two pieces. The Engager Army lacked artillery, because the General of Artillery was too disorganised to make up a train. The cannon-rich Swedish armies had, between 1630 and 1645, trains varying from sixty to eighty guns. Certain forces such as the Ulster Army and David Leslie's army in Argyll (1647) found that the terrain immobilised cannon. The Covenanters frequently used cannon during sieges, in garrisons and in some battles.[38]

The clan forces and family retinues fielded by the Covenanters contrast with the regular Swedish-style units and indicate continuity with Scotland's past. Rarely is any mention made in surviving records of the numbers serving under a particular clan leader or noble or laird. In the cases of units consisting of several hundred men one may assume that there was some sort of company organisation. In clan regiments, for instance, the chief and his close relatives served as the staff officers and the cadets acted as captains of the men from their districts. But in neither clan nor retinue is there any suggestion of a standard size for companies. Highland units were primarily infantry. A well-armed clansman possessed a musket, sword, dirk, skean-dhu and targe. Some might have only had polearms – a pike, Lochaber-axe or halberd – and others, probably officers, carried pistols and swords.

The retinues fielded from the northeast Lowlands probably contained some cavalry. It is possible that the mounted leaders had some armour, a sword and pistols. The better-armed infantry would have had muskets or pikes, but some certainly took the field with only sharpened agricultural implements. The non-regular units of the Covenanters varied from men who fought to the last gasp to those who ran at the first sign of serious action; from war-trained Highlanders to semi-skilled Lowland militia.

To state that the Covenanters possessed standard uniforms would be anachronistic. In early modern armies, armour or buff coats obscured the view of any clothing and soldiers replaced their worn-out clothing with anything that came to hand. Instead of uniforms, armies used coloured materials – sashes, ribbons or plumes – as distinguishing marks.[39] The retinues and mass levies appeared in the field wearing their usual clothing. Until the Covenanters retained several regiments in August 1641, it appears that troops wore their normal clothing. However, from the time of the Ulster Army onward clothing was issued. The regular Lowland infantry units possessed suits of woollen cloth, hodden grey in colour. Yet this was not the only colour of coat worn by the foot regiments, because in 1651 Lord Lorne requested that his regiment be provided with coats of one colour only. The characteristic headgear of both Lowland and Highland foot was the flat round blue bonnet. Highland infantry wore either belted plaid or, in the case of Ross of Balnagowan's foot, tartan trews in the red Ross pattern. The Highlanders also wore shirts, some with cravats. Among cavalry units, buff coats may have been universal either as an undercoat for armour or as a substitute for it. The lack of a standard uniform presented the immediate problems of identification and of fostering *esprit de corps*. On 30 March 1639 the earl of Montrose devised the solution of issuing blue ribbons to his men. The infantry sash was worn from the neck to under the left arm. Blue ribbons were also attached to the infantry bonnets and to the spanners of cavalry pistols. Captains sported scarves from blue ribbons as a rank badge.[40] Thereafter it was blue bonnets or blue ribbons that served as the identifying mark of the regular forces. (The Army of the Solemn League and Covenant supplemented the blue field marks by wearing white tokens, as did its Parliamentarian allies.)[41]

The strategy of the Covenanters tends to reflect the continental preoccupation with fortresses and garrisons, but national variations were also present. The strategy of 'fire and sword', that is, the burning of crops, food stocks and houses and the killing of any supporters of the enemy (often without regard to sex or age) had a long tradition in Scottish history, particularly as an instrument of policy against royal opponents. Thus, it should not be surprising to see the Covenanters following this strategy as early as 1639. In Ulster, from the beginning, the policy of fire and sword aimed to destroy the rebels' subsistence and their will to resist and was allied with the establishment of garrisons to protect the friendly Protestant population and to serve as bases for expeditions against the Irish. The alliance with the British forces in the province may be likened to the Swedes' alliance with German Protestant princes during the Thirty Years War. In Scotland, the devastation of the royalists' home bases was not united with a garrisoning policy until 1644. (Before then, garrisons were limited to traditional locations such as Dumbarton, Edinburgh and Stirling Castles and to the new fortified centres at Leith, Burntisland and Aberdeen.)

From 1644 to 1647, however, the Covenanters established a large number of garrisons within both their own and enemy areas. These were instrumental in the protection of various Covenanter families and in the pacification of royalists. In 1650, Lieutenant General David Leslie varied the policy outlined above. He established a number of garrisons in Berwickshire and East Lothian athwart Cromwell's overland line of supply and created a fortified line stretching from Edinburgh Castle to Holyroodhouse to Leith (on the present line of Leith Walk). In addition, his men stripped the abandoned shires of food and fodder, forcing the English to rely on seaborne supplies. Finally, he employed Fabian tactics in the field and by 2 September 1650 had won the campaign (only to disastrously lose the battle).

In England, the key strategy of covenanting intervention was the capture and garrisoning of important towns. In 1640 Leslie took Newcastle, which supplied London's coal, and Durham, which was an important symbol of Laudian religious policy. In 1644 Leven's sights were again on Newcastle and Durham, but York was the key to the north and he willingly cooperated in its capture. That December, the siege of Carlisle began; its capture provided the southwest Lowlands with security from royalist incursions and hindered the linking of English royalist forces with Montrose's army. The other activities of the Army of the Solemn League and Covenant were dictated by the conflicting demands of the Committee of Both Kingdoms, which required the army to serve south of the Trent, and by Leven's fears about a juncture between Montrose and the English royalists, which dictated retention of the army north of the Tyne. The Covenanter-Parliamentarian alliance closely parallels the Swedish-French league of the 1630s and 1640s, the latter partner in each case providing subsidies to the former. In 1648 the incompetent duke of Hamilton desired to capture Manchester and London, but proceeded with such sloth that disaster overtook him. The 1651 campaign into England was aimed at London; however, the fortifying of Worcester was seen as necessary to provide a mustering place for western English and Welsh recruits.

The tactics of the Covenanters followed the continental example.

The ideal formation for an army equipped like the Covenanters' was as follows: two lines, one regiment each in depth, with the second line covering the gaps between the regiments in the first line. (A reserve was also permitted which acted as third line.) The flanks of the first and second lines were covered by cavalry. The infantry formed the centre and in front or beside each regiment these would have been (ideally) two three-pounders. An individual infantry regiment was arranged with pikemen in the centre and musketeers equally divided on their flanks. It was usual to post a forlorn hope several hundred feet in advance of the infantry to soften up the opposing enemy forces. This was the ideal deployment. The Covenanters did not always try to achieve it, often because the terrain prohibited it or because artillery was lacking. The Covenanters were not timid about advancing against their enemies. They also stood to receive enemy attack. The Covenanters were not ignorant of the contemporary military strategies and tactics, but adapted them to fit the situation. Defeat arose more often from the exceptional skill of the opposition, the lack of trained men and leaders, and from sheer bad luck. Incidentally, Geoffrey Parker cannot have it both ways in the matter of Montrose's campaigns. Either the Irish regiments of Alastair MacColla MacDonald were veterans raised from the Spanish Army of Flanders or they were 'undisciplined clansmen armed with traditional weapons. . . .' Parker also overstates the case when he calls *all* the Covenanter forces that faced Montrose, 'regular troops, equipped with all the tools of the military revolution.'[42]

The preceding has shown how the Covenanters pulled Scotland from military incoherence into the military revolution. That Scotland became a significant military state was owing to the importation of Swedish practices by Scottish officers who had served with that army. The Covenanters' willingness to innovate in military matters secured and maintained the political and religious goals of the movement until the impoverished regime faced the onslaught of the Commonwealth's superior armies.

NOTES
1. G. Parker, *The military revolution: Military innovation and the rise of the West, 1500–1800* (New York, 1988), pp.1–2, 43.
2. *The Acts of Parliament of Scotland* [hereafter *APS*], 12 vols, ed. Thomas Thomson and Cosmo Innes (Edinburgh, 1814–75), vol.

5, pp.177, 180-1; *The Register of the Privy Council of Scotland, 1625-1660* [hereafter *RPCS*], 8 vols (Edinburgh, 1899-1908), 2nd ser., vol. 1, pp.158-9, 180-1, 185-6, 197-8, 213-15, 379, 418-20, 502-5; *Ibid.*, vol. 2, pp.30-1, 61-2, 88-90, 93-5, 114, 168-71.
3. *Ibid.*, 1st ser., vol. 7, pp.68-70, 74, 76, 87-8, 91-2, 115, 255, 435; *Ibid.*, vol. 8, pp.60, 72-3, 79, 94-5, 106, 113, 126-7, 173-5, 281, 521-4, 738, 740; *Ibid.*, vol. 9, pp.380-1; *Ibid.*, vol. 10, pp.279-80, 303, 346-8, 350, 389, 488-9, 513, 561, 577, 609-11, 692, 697, 738-40, 742-70; *Ibid.*, vol. 13, pp.83-6; *Ibid.*, 2nd ser., vol. 1, pp.403-5, 450-1.
4. *Ibid.*, 1st ser., vol. 10, pp.185-6, 189-91, 270-1; *Ibid.*, vol. 11, pp.403; *Ibid.*, vol. 12, pp.539-43, 742-5; *Ibid.*, 2nd ser., vol. 1, pp.18-24, 26-7, 31-6, 38-40, 43-4, 97, 100-110, 188-9.
5. *Ibid.*, 1st ser., vol. 9, pp.124-6, 129, 134, 166-70, 178-80, 211, 255, 281, 462, 626; *Ibid.*, vol. 10, pp.47, 289-91, 695, 697, 700-17; *Ibid.*, vol. 13, pp.142-8, 280-4, 332-3, 351, 391, 394-5, 477, 591, 609, 657-8; *Ibid.*, 2nd ser., vol. 5, pp.362-4, 465, 507-9, 522.
6. *Ibid.*, 1st ser., vol. 12, pp.257-60, 272-3, 431, 453, 730-1, 739, 781; *Ibid.*, vol. 12, pp.137, 146, 478; *Ibid.*, 2nd ser., vol. 1, pp.49, 67, 83-4, 244-5, 247, 295, 310-11, 313, 315-16, 320-1, 329-30, 347-8, 354-5, 363-4, 381-2, 385, 389, 523, 531-2, 539-40, 542-3, 546, 550-2, 556-7, 580, 585, 603-4, 608-9, 611-13, 627-8; *Ibid.*, vol. 2, pp.7-8, 31-7, 40, 55-6, 71, 77-8, 84, 97, 105-6, 113-14, 147-8, 162, 241, 295-7, 303-4, 308-9, 325-6, 332-3, 397-8, 405-6, 456-7, 472, 600, 608; *Ibid.*, vol. 3, pp.48, 99, 120-1, 124, 136-8, 142-3, 147, 152, 167, 169, 197, 208, 214-15, 282, 288-9, 313; *Ibid.*, vol. 4, pp.193-4, 219, 318-20, 342-3, 349-51, 360-1, 482-4, 525, 531-2; *Ibid.*, vol. 5, pp.65-6, 79-81; *Ibid.*, vol. 6, pp.28-9, 65-6, 140-1, 157, 225-6, 401-2, 458-9, 484-5, 526-7, 533; *Ibid.*, vol. 7, pp.84-5, 103-4, 106-7.
7. Parker, *The military revolution*, pp.49, 174 n.18.
8. *RPCS*, 1st ser., vol. 12, pp.191-2, 308, 377, 379, 527, 639.
9. Parker, *The military revolution*, pp.69, 74.
10. *APS*, vol. 4, pp.441; *RPCS*, 1st ser., vol. 10, pp.261, 328, 477-8, 612-15; *Ibid.*, vol. 12, pp.646, 721; *Ibid.*, 2nd ser., vol. 1, pp.337; *Ibid.*, vol. 2, pp.44, 52-3, 67-8, 70, 74-5, 125-8, 131-2, 159-61, 174-5, 184-8; *Ibid.*, vol. 3, pp.125; *Ibid.*, vol. 5, pp.27.
11. G. Clark, *War and Society in the seventeenth century* (Cambridge, 1958), p.59; A. Corvisier, *Armies and Societies in Europe, 1494-1789*, trans. A. T. Sidda (Bloomington, Indiana, 1976, 1979), p.52; M. Howard, *War in European history* (Oxford, 1976), pp.57-8; Parker, *The military revolution*, pp.52-3, 177 n.30.

12. Borders: Merse/Berwickshire and Teviotdale/Roxboroughshire-Selkirkshire; Lothian: East Lothian/Haddingtonshire, Midlothian, Edinburgh and West Lothian-Tweeddale; Southwest: Dumfriesshire (east and west), Galloway (Kirkcudbright-Wigtonshire), Ayrshire (north and south), Clydesdale/Lanarkshire; Central: Stirlingshire, Perthshire-Clackmannanshire (north and south), Fife-Kinross-shire (east and west), Angus; Northeast: Aberdeenshire-Mearns/Kincardineshire, Aberdeenshire-Banffshire, Moray; Northern: Inverness-shire, Sutherland, Caithness; and Western Military Reserve: Dunbartonshire, Argyll, Bute and marquis of Argyll's part of Inverness-shire.

13. S[cottish] R[ecord] O[ffice], GD. 16. Sec. 50.5, 6; GD. 26.12.5, 7; K[irk] S[ession] R[ecords] Holy Rude, Stirling, 24 June 1639; N[ational] L[ibrary of] S[cotland], Lee Papers 3496 (KSR Lasswade), 26 April 1639; G. Burnet, *The Memoirs of the Lives and actions of James and William dukes of Hamilton and Castle-Herald*, 2nd edn. (Oxford, 1852), p.146; *Extracts from the Burgh Records of Dunfermline in the Sixteenth and Seventeenth Centuries*, ed. A. Shearer (Dunfermline, 1951), p.217.

14. N[ew] R[egister] H[ouse], KSR Carnock, 24 December 1643; KSR Largo, 20 February, 8 March, 29 August 1644; SRO, P[resbytery] R[ecords] Brechin, 24 August 1643; PR Dunoon, vol. 2 f. 10; PR Elgin, vol. 1, fo. 30; PR Haddington, 26 October 1643, 3 April 1644; PR Jedburgh and Kelso, 2 March 1645; PR Lanark, 25 June, 9 July, 1 October 1640; PR Linlithgow, 23 July 1645; PR Perth, vol. 2, pp.800, 802; PR Stranraer, vol. 1, fo. 51v; KSR Ceres, vol. 1, fo. 7; KSR Holy Rude, Stirling, 29 June 1640; KSR Humbie, vol. 1, fo. 24v; KSR Kilconquhar, vol. 1, fo. 62v; KSR Livingston, 21 July, 29 September 1640, 10 January 1641, 27 August 1643; KSR Old Kelso, 24 September 1643; KSR St Cuthberts, Edinburgh, vol. 5, fo. 343v; KSR Slains, 17 December 1643, 29 August 1646; KSR Tyninghame, vol. 1, fos 139v-40, 151v, 154v; GD. 158.390.1; PA. 16.1 (Fencible Men East Lothian 1645); *The Memoirs of Henry Guthry, late Bishop of Dunkeld*, ed. G. Crawford (Glasgow, 1748), p.72; *Minutes of the Synod of Argyll, i, 1639-1651*, ed. C. MacTavish, Scottish History Society, 3rd ser., vol. 37 (1943), pp.80-1; *Selections from the Registers of the Presbytery of Lanark, 1623-1709*, ed. R. Robertson, Abbotsford Club, vol. 16 (1839), pp.20-2; *South Leith Records*, ed. D. Robertson (Edinburgh, 1911), pp.45, 47, 50; J. Spalding, *The History of the Troubles and Memorable Transactions in Scotland from the year 1624 to 1645*, ed. J. Stuart (Spalding Club 1850-1), I, pp.255, II, pp.59, 196, 226, 276, 284, 293, 321-2; *Unpublished papers of John, Seventh Lord Sinclair*, ed. J. A. Fairley, reprinted from *Transactions of the Buchan Field Club* (1905), pp.42-3.

15. SRO, GD. 112/39.754, 762, 766, 774; PA. 7.24, fos 109v-110; PA. 11.11; *APS*, vol. 6, part 2, pp.217-18, 598-9 for nobles

and lairds without previous military commands who received them in 1649-50; *Correspondence of Sir Robert Kerr, First Earl of Ancram and his son William, Third Earl of Lothian*, ed. D. Laing, Bannatyne Club, XCVI (1876), II, pp.330-1; J. Thurloe, *A collection of papers, containing authentic memorials of English affairs, i, 1638-1653* (London, 1742), pp.170, 172; *Unpublished papers of Sinclair*, pp.25-6; C. V. Wedgwood, *The King's Peace* (London, 1973), p.236.

16. The following civil and ecclesiastical judicatories petitioned against the Engagement: the burghs of Glasgow, *Extracts of the Records of the Burgh of Glasgow*, ed. J. Marwick, Scottish Burgh Record society (XII), pp.133-4; and Dumfries, D. Stevenson, *The Battle of Mauchline Moor*, Ayrshire Collections, vol. 11, no. 1, p.4; as well as the committees of war of the shires of Haddington, *APS*, vol. 6, part 2, p.691; Fife, Hist. MSS. Comm., report 72, p.235; Ayr, NLS, Wodrow MS. Folio 20, fo. 59; Kirkcudbright, Wigton, Lanark and Renfrew, Stevenson, *Mauchline*, p.4; NLS, KSR Anstruther Easter, 30 May 1648; SRO, S[ynod] R[ecords] Moray, vol. 2, fo. 84; SR Perth and Stirling, vol. 1, fos 79-89; PR Ayr, 17 May 1648; PR Biggar, vol. 1, fos 177-8, 196; PR Dumbarton, 16 May 1648; PR Dunfermline, vol. 1, fo. 40; PR Haddington, 7 June 1648; PR Linlithgow, 24 May 1648; PR Paisley, 25 May 1648; PR Peebles, 29 May, 1 June 1648; PR Perth, vol. 3, fo. 18; PR Stranraer, vol. 1, fo. 136; all the kirk sessions of Paisley presbytery, PR Paisley, 25 May 1648; and others: KSR Corstorphine, vol. 1, fo. 17; KSR Falkland, vol. 1, fo. 74; KSR Kingsbarns, vol. 1, fo. 18; KSR Liberton, vol. 1, fo. 40; KSR Livingston, vol. 2, fo. 15; KSR Newburn, 28 May 1648; S[trathclyde] R[egional] A[rchives], PR Glasgow, vol. 3, fos 106-8, also the petitions of Rutherglen, Barony kirk, Lequham, Cader, Govan, Monydie and Carank are recorded on fos 101-5; *APS*, vol. 6, part 2, p.691 (a joint petition of the presbyteries of Dunbar and Haddington); Hist. MSS. Comm., report 72, synods of Angus and Mearns, p.229; Merse and Teviotdale, p.228, Dumfries, p.231, Lothian and Tweeddale, pp.240-2, presbyteries of Lanark, p.234 and Kirkcaldy, 236; *Extracts from the Presbytery Book of Strathbogie, 1631-1654*, ed. J. Stuart, Spalding Club, vii (1843), p.89; *Extracts from the Records of the Burgh of Edinburgh*, ed. M. Wood (Edinburgh, 1938), pp.403-4 (Edinburgh presbytery) *Selections from the minutes of the Presbyteries of St. Andrews and Cupar, 1641-48*, ed. G. R. Linloch, Abbotsford Club, vii (1837), p.41; Linlithgowshire committee of war presented one of the few pro-Engager petitions, Hist. MSS. Comm., report 72, p.235. For further details about the levy see: NLS, Gordon Cummings Papers 67, fos 609, 639; SRO, PR Dingwall, vol. 1, fo. 35; PR Garioch, 17 July 1650; PR Linlithgow, 21 March 1649; PR Perth, vol. 3, pp.66, 71, 75, 123, 126, 153, 171; GD.

38.1, fo. 193; GD. 75.654-5, 657, 658; Burnet, *Lives*, p.451 (who estimated the strength of horse at 4000, or 1900 more than specified in the act of levy); *The Diplomatic Correspondence of Jean de Montereul and the brothers de Bellievre, French Ambassadors to England and Scotland, 1645-48*, 2 vols., ed. J. G. Fotheringham, Scottish History Society, 1st ser., XXIX-XXX (1898), II, pp.482, 492, 524; *Lanark*, pp.60-1; *The Letters and Journals of Robert Baillie, Principal of the University of Glasgow, 1637-1662*, ed. D. Laing, Bannatyne Club, LXXII, parts 1 and 2, LXXVII (1841-2), III, pp.47-8; *Memoirs of Guthry*, p.274; *St. Andrews and Cupar*, pp.128-9, 136; Turner, James, *Memoirs of His Own Life and Times, 1632-1670*, ed. T. Thomson, Bannatyne Club, XXVIII (1829), pp.53-5.

17. SRO, PR Fordyce, 29 January 1651; PR Paisley, 9-10 January 1651; GD. 16.50.62; PA. 11.11, fo. 35v; *The Presbyterie Book of Kirkcaldie*, ed. W. Stevenson (Kirkcaldy, 1900), p.367; E. M. Furgol, 'The Religious Aspects of the Scottish Covenanting Armies, 1639-1651', Oxford University D.Phil. thesis (1983), pp.239-45, 288-94.

18. SRO, PR Paisley, 10, 25 September 1650; PR Stranraer, vol. 1, fos 206v-207, 210v-211v; PA. 11.11, fos 79-9v; Hist. MSS. Comm., report 72, p.251; *Baillie*, III, pp.112, 118, 120; Nicoll, John, *A Diary of Public Transactions*, ed. D. Laing, Bannatyne Club, LII (1836), p.36; Peterson, John (1847), *History of the county of Ayr*, 2 vols (Edinburgh, 1847), vol. 1, p.127n.

19. Northeastern armies: *Aberdeen Council Letters*, 3 vols, ed. L. B. Taylor (London, 1950), vol. 2, p.130, vol. 3, p.117; *Extracts from the Council Register of the Burgh of Aberdeen, 1625-1747*, 2 vols, ed. J. Stuart, Scottish Burgh Record Society, vol. 8-9 (1881-82), vol. 1, p.159; Spalding, *History*, vol. 1, p.107; Leslie's army: 10000-12000 men, 'The Journal of John Aston', *North Country Diaries*, ed. J. C. Hodgson, Surtees Society, CXVIII (1910), p.28; 20000, *Baillie*, I, p.210; 23000, Burnet, *Lives*, p.175; 26000-30000, Balfour, James, *The Annales of Scotland*, 4 vols (Edinburgh, 1823-25), II, p.324; and 30000, Hist. MSS. Comm., re[port] III, p.77, rest of Scotland: Gordon, James, *History of Scottish Affairs from 1637-1641*, 3 vols, ed. B. Robertson and G. Grub, Spalding Club (1841), II, p.205.

20. Forces in Scotland: SRO, RH. 13.18; *Baillie*, I, p.260; Gordon, *History*, III, pp.163-5; *Memorials of Montrose*, ed. M. Napier, Maitland club, LXVI, part 1 (1848), I, p.259; Spalding, *History*, I, pp.198, 204, 217; Leslie's army – the English wildly inflated the figures: 32000, Hist. MSS. Comm., report 4, p.295; 37000, *Calendar of State Papers, Domestic, 1639-1649*, 8 vols, ed. W. D. Hamilton (London, 1873-93), 1640-41, p.31. Scottish estimates were: 26500, Gordon, *History*, III, p.257; 25000,

*Baillie*, I, p.247; 16000, Spalding, *History*, I, p.214. One English guess put the figure at 22500, J. Rushworth, *Historical Collections* (London, 1680), III, p.1222. My estimate is based on P[ublic] R[ecord] O[ffice], SP 16/464/59II, fo. 134, which gave the total of 15250, plus the following additions: Life Guard of Foot, 425 men (SRO, E100/1/1; E100/1/112; PA. 16.2 Account of Ld Register's regt.); Elcho's, 400 (Fraser, William (1888), *Memorials of Wemyss of Wemyss*, Edinburgh, I, p.242); Erskine's, 400 (PRO, SP 16/461/57II, fo. 121), Lothian's, 400 (Kennedy, John W. (1903), 'The Teviotdale Regiment', *Hawick Archaeological Society*, XXXV, p.59); Montrose's, 900 (Gordon, *History*, III, p.257).

21. D. Stevenson, *Scottish Covenanters and Irish Confederates* (Belfast, 1981), pp.68, 230.
22. C. S. Terry, *The Life and Campaigns of Alexander Leslie, first earl of Leven* (London, 1899), pp.176, 180.
23. Furgol, 'Aspects', p.26; Parker, *The military revolution*, pp.53–8.
24. Furgol, 'Aspects', p.26.
25. Scots' New Model Army: *APS*, vol. 6, part 1, pp.674, 684–5; *Memoirs of Guthry*, p.240; Turner, *Memoirs*, pp.43–4; *The Army of the Covenant*, 2 vols, ed. C. S. Terry, Scottish History Society, 2nd ser., XVI–XVII (1917), I, pp.civ-cvi. Engager forces: 'Lt. Gen. Cromwell's Letter to the Honourable William Lenthall', *Tracts relating to the military proceedings in Lancashire*, ed. G. Ormerod, Chetham Society, II (1844), p.266; *The Scottish Army Advanced into England* (1648), London, p.11. Estimates of numbers of Scots army in England ranged from 7000 foot and 3500 horse, *Scottish Army*, pp.10–11; 10000 foot and 4000 horse, Burnet, *Lives*, p.451; 12000 foot and 5000 horse, 'Cromwell's Letter', pp.265–6. Anti-Engager forces: SRO, PR Ayr, 27 September 1648; PR Stranraer, vol. 1, fo. 141; KSR Ceres, 10 September 1648; KSR Colmonell, vol. 1, p.131; Burnet, *Lives*, pp.265, 465, 469–71; *Memoirs of Guthry*, pp. 285–6, 292; Rushworth, *Historical Collections*, VIII, pp.1264, 1273.
26. NLS, Adv. MS. 23.7.12, fo. 96v, 107, 108, 111v; *APS*, vol. 6, part 2, pp.217–18, 489–91; Wishart, George, *The Memoirs of James, Marquis of Montrose, 1639-1650*, ed. A. D. Murdoch and H. F. M. Simpson (London, 1893), p.291. For the purging of the army see Furgol, 'Aspects', pp.239–45, 288–94. Western Association Army: *Baillie*, vol. 3, pp.112, 118; Nicoll, *Diary*, p.36.
27. May: Bod[elian] Lib[rary], MS Carte XXIX, fos 438, 443; Balfour, *Annales*, IV, p.397; July: SRO, PA. 16.5; invasion: 'Several Proceedings in Parliament', *Tracts*, Ormerod, p.292, lists 6000–7000 foot and 5000–6000 horse; Turner, *Memoirs*, p.94, gives the totals of 9000 foot and 4000 horse; E. Robinson, *A*

*discourse of the war in Lancashire*, ed. W. Beaumont, Chetham Society, LXII (1842), p.69, puts the Scots at 16 000 strong; Bod. Lib., MS Tanner 54, fo. 142, estimates the army's strength at 14 000-15 000 foot and 6000 horse. Given the casualty lists of 12 000 dead and captured and the difficulty of reaching Scotland from Worcester a lower figure may be preferred.

28. Parker, *The military revolution*, pp.69, 185 n.78.
29. *APS*, vol. 6, part 1, pp.708-9.
30. SRO, PA. 11.11, fo. 6; *APS*, vol. 6, part 1, pp.631, 672; *Ibid.*, vol. 6, part 2, p.586; E. M. Furgol, *A Regimental History of the Scottish Covenanting Armies, 1639-1651* (Edinburgh, 1990), ch. 4, Ulster Army.
31. Parker, *The military revolution*, p.18.
32. *APS*, vol. 6, part 2, pp.599, 625; *The Journal of Thomas Cunningham of Campvere*, ed. E. J. Courthope, Scottish History Society, 3rd ser., XI (1928), pp.62, 95; Furgol, *Regimental* [pp.149, 154].
33. SRO, PA. 11.11, fo. 6; *APS*, vol. 6, part 1, pp.631, 672; *Ibid.*, VI, part 2, pp.587, 590; Furgol, *Regimental* [pp.108, 114-18, 129, 134, 145-8, 150, 154, 156, 159, 184, 186-7].
34. SRO, PA. 11.11, fo. 19; Committee of Parliament (1640), *Act Anent the out comming of Horses*, Edinburgh, s.s.; *APS*, vol. 6, part 2, pp.599, 625; C. Lawson, *A history of the uniforms of the British Army*, 2 vols (London, 1940), vol. 1, pp.83-4; Furgol, *Regimental* [pp.159, 341].
35. Parker, *The military revolution*, p.23.
36. *Ibid.*, pp.33-5.
37. *Ibid.*, p.23.
38. *Baillie*, vol. 1, p.210; Stevenson, *Covenanters*, pp.72, 109; Furgol, *Regimental* [pp.42, 83, 112-3, 248, 297-8, 360-1].
39. Parker, *The military revolution*, pp.71-2.
40. Spalding, *History*, I, p.108; Gordon, *History*, III, pp.260-1; E. J. Cowan, *Montrose: for Covenant and King* (London, 1977), p.66; J. Aiton, *The Life and Times of Alexander Henderson* (Edinburgh, 1836), p.387; J. Buchan, *Montrose* (London, 1928), p.119; Lawson, *Uniforms*, I, pp.57, 67, 69, 136; Furgol, *Regimental* [pp.11, 32, 102, 116, 299].
41. Parker, *The military revolution*, p.185 n.88.
42. *Ibid.*, pp.51, 35.

# *Seven*

## COURTIERS AND CAVALIERS
## SERVICE, ANGLICISATION AND LOYALTY
## AMONG THE ROYALIST NOBILITY

### Keith M. Brown

In June 1641 Robert Baillie commented on the favour being shown at court by Charles I to John Leslie, sixth earl of Rothes, one of the leading Covenanter noblemen. This, he wrote,

> is lyke to change all the Court; that the King and Queen begin muche to affect him; and if they goe on, he is lyke to be the greatest courteour either of Scotts or English. Lyklie he will take a place in the bed-chamber, and be little more Scottish man.[1]

Baillie clearly took the common view that any Scot holding court office could not possibly be patriotic. The equation was a simple one: courtiers were anglicised supporters of the king. Clarendon has reinforced this picture with his commonly quoted assertion that those Scots who 'shined most at the Court of England [*sic*] had the least influence in their own country'. He went on to dismiss the Scottish courtiers as useless in the king's cause in spite of the enormous sums of money and other forms of patronage lavished on them by James VI and I and Charles I.[2] Underlying this is the common English view of parasitical, redundant Scots cluttering up *their* court. In fact, few characters have as bad a press in the early seventeenth century as the Scottish courtier. From Scotland he was attacked as a traitorous absentee, in England he was seen as a foreign liability, and both images have stuck. The reasons behind the success of this myth are not difficult to identify. The presbyterian dominance of Scottish intellectual life for the three centuries which followed the revolution has always made the Covenanters, as the heroes of the national story, the more popular subjects. It has been relatively easy to identify their opponents with a centralised and anglicised monarchy. Where the royalist story has been told, the giant figure of Montrose overshadows everything.[3] Analysis of the Scottish royalists has been further hampered by the appropriation of both the monarchy and the court by English History, leaving Scottish History with kings who have 'Scottish policies' (they *never* have English policies) and an 'English Court' in which poor, sycophantic Scottish politicians vie with one another to implement those policies. Here, too, Clarendon's legacy has been powerful, since he claimed that 'there was so little curiosity in the Court or the country to know any thing of Scotland, or what was done there'. What he should have said was that English courtiers, like most subsequent English historians, were uninterested in Scotland. Scottish courtiers, like the king himself, had a very keen interest in their native country.[4]

In 1603 the Scottish court was transported to London, and this has been commonly interpreted as a merger in which the Scots were swallowed up in the vast labyrinth of Whitehall, where they were either hastily anglicised or packed off home to their provincial backwater. Certainly the English court was much bigger than that of James VI – some ten times bigger in personnel – and some Scots were anglicised there. But thanks to the work of P. R. Seddon and Neil Cuddy we now know just how astonishingly dominant the Scots were at the Jacobean court until Buckingham's rise after 1615. Even in the 1630s Scots were still holding down a sizeable number of the most desirable offices at court.[5] We also know that court culture was not simply English, but contained a great deal that was common to all late renaissance European courts, as well as an internationally recognised Protestant ethos, and a British dimension which James VI and I had deliberately stimulated and which continued to have some influence at the court of his son.[6] To say that a Scot at Charles I's court necessarily would be anglicised is far too simplistic. In some ways this is little more than a ready-made derogation to hang on men who were unsympathetic to covenanting opinion in Scotland. After all, there were people in Yorkshire who experienced the same alienation from the court, and in this instance anglicisation is obviously inappropriate as an explanation.[7] Furthermore, the recent emphasis by Kevin Sharpe and Malcolm Smuts on the common ground between court and country in England, although exaggerated, should make us a little less eager to magnify the distance between the two in Scotland.[8] At the same time, David Stevenson's description of Scotland as virtually all country and no court is understandable. The number of Scots from the political community who had close contacts with the court in the 1630s was relatively small compared with the corresponding number before 1603 and even throughout the first decade of the Union, and the gap between court culture and Scotland's native public culture was a widening one.[9] Yet there were men who bridged that gap, or tried to bridge it, and it is these men, the Scottish court elite, which this essay seeks to identify and to understand.

In dealing with such an ill-defined figure as the courtier it is likely that there will be some uncertainty over who should be counted as one. Obviously, those holding court office had a claim to be regarded as courtiers, but most court offices were in the Household and were well below the status of those being considered here. Those offices of greater political significant and social acceptability were held by the heads of departments and the gentlemen and officers of the king's chambers. This was where the Scots were concentrated, especially in the first twenty years of the regal Union. The majority of these men were members of the aristocracy; some, like the duke of Lennox and the marquis of Hamilton, were peers but most were lesser nobility, lairds or younger sons of these social groups, and all used their court office as a springboard into the upper levels of the Scottish political elite. Court office was undoubtedly the surest and the most dramatic means of social acceleration in Britain in the early seventeenth century, bringing men like the earls of Annandale and Stirling titles, wealth and influence, and leaving them and their families with a strong sense of loyalty to the person of the king. Altogether, there were in 1638 sixteen peers: the duke of Lennox; the marquis of Hamilton; the earls of Ancram, Annandale, Belhaven, Buchan, Dunfermline (his appointment may have been after 1638), Kellie, Kinnoul, Morton, Roxburghe, Stirling and Tullibardine; Viscount Stormont; Lord Almond; and Lord Napier, who held or had held court office in England since 1603. To these one can add twelve peers who had close contact with the court either directly or through an immediate kinsman in office there: the earls of Abercorn, Airth, Atholl, Dumfries, Galloway, Haddington, Lothian, Linlithgow, Mar, Nithsdale, and Traquair and Lord Dalzell. These courtiers account for thirty-two per cent (eighty-nine) of the total adult peerage on the eve of the signing of the National Covenant. In addition, there were a number of lesser noblemen, such as Sir Robert Gordon of Gordonstoun and Sir William Anstruther of that ilk, who enjoyed court office but were never created peers. With their access to court patronage and to the king himself, these men and their families had, potentially, a political significance greater than their numbers might suggest, and their responses to the unfolding revolution in Scotland were extremely important to the king and to his enemies.

Identifying the royalist aristocracy is much more difficult, partly because of the constantly developing situation which caused men such as the earls of Southesk, Mar or Winton to change sides, and partly because prudence dictated that many noblemen sought to avoid commitment to either side. The very effective pressure which the Covenanters quickly brought to bear on the equivocal and the moderate also makes a mere head-count of those who signed the National Covenant an exercise of doubtful usefulness. Clearly, a full analysis of aristocratic attitudes towards the Covenant is necessary, and the figures here are estimates based on a straw poll. However, as a rough guide, something like thirty-two peers or twenty-eight per cent had made their opposition to the Covenant clear before the signing of the Cumbernauld Bond in August 1640 revealed a split within the Covenanters which brought moderates like the earl of Montrose and Lord Napier over to the king. The non-courtier royalists – the marquises of Huntly and Douglas; the earls of Aboyne, Airlie, Crawford, Glencairn, Seaforth, and Winton; and Lords Oliphant, Reay, Sempill, and Spynie – formed a disparate grouping which included a number of Catholics and heavily indebted lords. What is important for the present discussion is that twenty-one of the twenty-eight courtiers were found among these most intransigent of the royalists. Of the court office holders only Dunfermline, Stormont, Napier and Almond failed to support Charles I, along with the earls of Haddington, Lothian and Mar, whose families were well connected at court. The great majority of courtiers and their families remained remarkably loyal to the king throughout the troubles which followed. Naturally, there were different shades of loyalty and not all of these men had enjoyed the same degree of contact with the court, but in broad terms there was a very clear relationship between service and access to the king before 1638 and support for him in the years that followed.

Kinship with the royal house of Stewart had made the Lennox Stewarts and the Hamiltons the two most important families in the dynastic politics of sixteenth-century Scotland. Baillie described James Stewart, fourth duke of Lennox, as one of 'our three great men' (the other two were the marquis of Hamilton and the earl of Morton), and Clarendon rightly commented that he lived 'under the disadvantage of being looked upon as a Scotchman' when in fact Scotland's premier peer had scarcely a drop of Scottish blood in his veins. Lennox was born at London, and his parents were Esme Stewart, the French-born third duke, and his wife, Catherine Clifton, daughter of Lord Clifton of Leighton Bromeswold. He was bred at court, and grew up to be an archetypal Caroline courtier whose portrait by Van Dyck epitomised the age. His education included Trinity College Oxford, Gray's Inn and the Grand Tour. Lennox was elected a Knight of the Garter in 1633, inherited the English earldom of March from his father, the barony of Clifton through his mother, and was created duke of Richmond in 1641. The estates in Scotland were small and unprofitable, and Lennox was content to cooperate with the king in the transfer of the priory of St Andrews to the new bishopric of Edinburgh. His wealth lay in the south; it included a country seat at Cobham House, estates in Yorkshire, the Clifton inheritance, the riches of the Dowager Countess of Lennox, who died in 1639, and a number of pensions, gifts and patents received from the king. Lennox inherited the offices of lord chamberlain and lord high admiral in Scotland, was appointed a gentleman of the bedchamber by Charles, and he was a privy councillor in both England and Scotland. He resigned his Scottish sheriffdoms to the king, and acquired local office in England in 1635 with the lord lieutenancy of Hampshire and, more controversially, the wardenship of the Cinque Ports in 1640. It was 1637 before Lennox married, his wife being the duke of Buckingham's widowed daughter, Mary Villiers (worth a £20 000 sterling portion), and he was linked through the marriages of his sisters and brother to the houses of Arundel, Portland and Suffolk as well as to the Scottish marquis of Douglas. Lennox only ever visited Scotland on three occasions: Charles I's coronation in 1633, when he was appointed a Scottish privy councillor and sat in Parliament; his mother's funeral in the autumn of 1637 (her second husband had been the second earl of Abercorn), when the Covenanters had hoped to persuade him to present their case to the king; and, for the last time, in 1641, when as one of the king's 'evil councillors' he accompanied the defeated king, and was obliged to subscribe the Covenant. The duke was a gut royalist, but was no politician, failing to build up any clientele either at court or in Scotland, and his influence was entirely personal – he 'used to discourse with his majesty in the bedchamber rather than at the Council-board'. Lennox remained at Charles's side throughout the wars, becoming steward of the Household in 1641 (an office his uncle had held) and president of the council of the Prince of Wales in 1646. He was a commissioner at the Uxbridge negotiations in 1645 and again at Newport in 1648. He contributed huge sums of money to the royalist cause; three of his brothers were killed fighting for the king; and, after a few years' exile, he died in England in 1655.[10]

Of all Charles I's courtiers the most influential and the most enigmatic was James, third marquis of Hamilton, the man who came closest to being Buckingham's political heir. In the years immediately after the Union it was the junior branch of the family who took up residence at court, and before his death in 1618 the king had helped James Hamilton, first earl of Abercorn, to amass a huge Irish plantation. By contrast, James, second marquis of Hamilton, could not be persuaded to come to court until 1616, but was lavishly rewarded before his unexpectedly early death in 1625. His success at court was in part due to an alliance with Buckingham, whose niece, Mary Fielding, daughter of William, first Lord Denbigh, was married to Hamilton's son and heir in 1620. The young third marquis of Hamilton (and second earl of Cambridge) succeeded to Buckingham's offices as master of the horse and gentleman of the bedchamber in 1628, and was elected a Knight of the Garter in 1631; in 1631-2 he commanded the British expeditionary force in Germany, and in 1633 became a privy councillor in both kingdoms. Hamilton had vast business interests, spread throughout Britain, Ireland and even America, owned large estates in Scotland, and benefitted greatly from royal gifts, most controversially out of the Scottish tax revenue. He, too, sold lands to the crown to help endow bishoprics, but he was not another Lennox, and his roots remained firmly planted in Scotland. He was the natural figure for Charles to turn to in 1638, and Hamilton's failure as the king's commissioner at the Glasgow Assembly arose more from the impossibility of his mission than from his own incompetence. One of the remarkable phenomena of the 1640s was Hamilton's continuing ability to force himself onto centre stage as a recognised natural leader whose views mattered a great deal. For a man who had lived most of his adult life in England, married an Englishwoman, and whose sympathies were clearly with the court, this prominence, rather than his failure to save the situation for the king in 1638 is the more notable. Described by Baillie as 'a great lover both of the king and his country' Hamilton had the misfortune to lose the trust of both. He engaged in endless jockeying to find a way of reconciling an untrustworthy king with the Covenanters, and it was this which finally persuaded Charles to order his arrest in 1643, shortly after creating him duke of Hamilton. In spite of this, he and his younger brother William, who had been created earl of Lanark and appointed secretary of state in 1640, were the prime movers behind the Engagement. After his defeat and capture at Preston, Hamilton was executed in England (as an English peer) in March 1649. Lanark succeeded as second duke and while his royalist commitment was even more suspect than that of his elder brother, he fought for Charles II and died of wounds received at the Battle of Worcester in September 1651.[11]

The third of the court grandees referred to by Baillie was William Douglas, sixth earl of Morton, who had succeeded his grandfather in 1606, shortly before he was appointed one of the gentlemen of the king's privy chamber. With the effective withdrawal from political life by the crypto-Catholic and antiquarian William Douglas, eleventh earl of Angus (and from 1633 first marquis of Douglas), Morton found himself as head of the powerful Douglas family. However, his political career did not take off until after his return from a European tour in 1621 when he was appointed to the Scottish privy council and the influential committee of war. In the following year his position was greatly strengthened by the marriage of his daughter to the son and heir of the new chancellor, Sir George Hay. Staunch support of Charles I against his father's intransigent old councillors further advanced Morton's career, as did a second judicious marriage in 1627 between his eldest son Robert, Lord Dalkeith, and Anne Villiers, daughter of Sir Edward Villiers of Brokesby, a kinsman of Buckingham. The latter's patronage was obviously behind Morton's appointment to the English privy council in that same year, and his relationship with Buckingham was strengthened when he commanded a regiment under the duke at La Rochelle. Buckingham also threw his weight behind Morton in pursuit of the treasurer's office, although it was 1630 before the uncooperative old earl of Mar resigned. Having been identified with the war, Morton was now closely associated with the growing fiscal demands of the 1630s. He continued to reside chiefly at court where his son, Lord Dalkeith, was a gentleman of the privy chamber, and his son-in-law, Sir George Hay, was appointed captain of the guard in 1632. Morton himself was elected a Knight of the Garter in 1634, a highly prestigious reward, and in the following year succeeded Hay to the guard captaincy as part of a deal which paved the way for his resignation from the treasurer's office in 1636. When the revolution broke out, Morton remained unquestioningly loyal to the king, acting as one of the Scottish advisors to the English commissioners at the Treaty of Ripon in 1641. Later that year Charles tried to have him appointed chancellor, but was opposed by Argyll (another son-in-law) who called Morton 'decrepit and unable' (he would have been in his late fifties). However, his loyalty was rewarded when he was appointed one of the gentlemen of the bedchamber in 1641. He attended Charles throughout the war, spending much of his vast fortune in the king's cause, and remained with him until Newcastle. Thereafter he retired to Kirkwall in Orkney where both he and his son Robert, seventh earl of Morton, died within a few months of one another in 1649 while awaiting Montrose's arrival. Two younger sons did fight in the ensuing campaign, John Douglas being killed at Carbisdale, and his grandson, William eighth earl of Morton, followed in the family's tradition of loyal service to the crown.[12]

Within the king's household the man with the longest record of personal service to Charles was William Murray, the son of the parish minister at Dysart in Fife and nephew of Thomas Murray, tutor to Prince Charles and provost of Eton. When the latter had gone south in 1603 he took William with him, and the boy was appointed page and whipping boy to Prince Charles who was of the same age. Murray remained a member of Charles's household for the next twenty years, and following the latter's accession was appointed a groom of the bedchamber. Before the wars he had little direct political influence, but in 1626 sat in the House of Commons as M.P. for Fowey, and in 1628-9 for East Looe. Surprisingly, he married the daughter of a lesser Scottish laird, but in 1639 his status as an English gentleman was assured with the grant of Ham House and adjoining lands. Clarendon described Murray as a man in whom Charles 'singularly trusted', and the king employed him in Scotland on a number of occasions after the outbreak of the Troubles. However, while his kinship with a number of covenanting leaders made him a useful go-between, he was accused by some of double-dealing. It was also said that Murray's gossiping to Lord Digby led to the escape of the Five Members from the House of Commons in 1642. Yet Murray was one of four royal servants named as evil councillors by the committee of both houses in February 1642. Like a number of Charles's personal servants, he had to wait a long time for his peerage, but was finally created earl of Dysart in 1643. In 1645 Dysart was in attendance on the queen in Paris, and was captured on his return, but after a spell in the Tower was released and rejoined the king at Newcastle where he tried to arrange a compromise. Dysart continued to serve Charles, working to further the Engagement, and after the king's execution transferred his loyalty to Charles II, dying in exile in 1651.[13]

Charles's other surviving household officers from the days before his accession were all much older. Of these the most important was Sir William Alexander, a lesser Stirlingshire laird, dependant and tutor of the earl of Argyll. Alexander was also a man of outstanding intellectual qualities who was to become the most successful Scottish poet of the period. It was these academic skills which attracted King James's attention, and Sir William was appointed tutor to Prince Henry, a post he continued in after 1603 along with that of gentleman of the prince' bedchamber. An enthusiast for the idea of Britain, Alexander undoubtedly had a major influence in shaping Prince Henry's ideas, but he appears to have had less success when he was appointed tutor to Prince Charles on the death of his eldest brother in 1612. In the years which followed, Alexander was appointed a master of requests and a privy councillor in both kingdoms, and he used his court contacts and income to finance the outright purchase and enlargement of his Menstrie estate. At the same time he developed interests in Ulster and in North America, being appointed Governor of Nova Scotia in 1621. James's death in 1625 brought Alexander new prominence as his former pupil made him a gentleman of the bedchamber and secretary of state, an office he administered from London. Elevation to the peerage came in 1630; he was created earl of Stirling at the coronation in 1633; and another private ambition was achieved when he persuaded Archibald Alexander of Tarbert to resign to him the chieftaincy of the MacAlexander clan. However, at the outbreak of the revolution Stirling was about seventy years of age and long past his best to be of great service to the king. Besides, he had his own problems. The multifarious business interests which criss-crossed Britain and the Atlantic (for example, he owned Long Island, New York) were failing to support the ostentations lifestyle he enjoyed (exemplified by the building of an expensive new town house in Stirling in 1632). Heavy debts were compounded by the fact that the large pension of £10000 he was awarded in 1633 had never been paid. Stirling was also unpopular, having a long record of exploitive commercial dealings, which included selling worthless Nova Scotia baronetcies, taking a hand in the mismanagement of the Scottish fishery project, and, most notoriously, acquiring monopoly to mint cheap copper coins in 1631. Furthermore, he was an enthusiastic episcopalian and the binding of his translation of the Psalms along with Laud's Service Book associated him with the suspect liturgical innovations. There was personal tragedy, too, when three of his sons, including the eldest, Lord Alexander, himself a privy councillor and entrepreneur, all died in 1637-8. Crushed by these losses, pursued by a multitude of creditors, and woefully out of touch, Stirling was quite unable to deal with the unfolding crisis in Scotland, and in fact he was 'little esteemed in Court, and not at all employed in Affairs, except in matters of course'. This last Jacobean unionist died at his home in Covent Garden in February 1640. His grandson died shortly after and his remaining son, Henry, succeeded as third earl of Stirling. He resided chiefly in the south with his English wife and was forced to sell off most of the estates to pay his father's creditors. He played little part in the wars, but was classed a delinquent and fined by the covenanting government for his royalist sympathies.[14]

Similar career patterns were followed by Robert Ker of Ancram and Robert Douglas of Spott, both of whom had begun in Prince Henry's household. In spite of being a tough, hot-headed Borderer, Ancram developed an interest in poetry and literature – he was a book collector and composed his own metrical translation of the Psalms – and was a lively contributor to the exciting ideas found in Henry's circle. He was one of the Knights of the Bath at the king's coronation in 1603, and advanced to become a gentleman of the bedchamber, first of Henry and then of Charles. In 1621 Ancram married his second wife, Anne (widow of Sir Henry Portman in Somerset and eldest daughter of William Stanley, sixth earl of Derby), who later became the governess of Charles's daughters. Ancram accompanied the prince to Spain in 1623, the same year in which he received a pension for £500 sterling per annum, and when Charles became king, Ancram was given charge of the privy purse. As a loyal royal servant he sat in the House of Commons as M.P. for Aylesbury in 1625 and for Preston in 1628–9, was appointed to the English privy council in 1631, and sat on the unpopular commission on cottages. He was further rewarded for his loyalty by being created earl of Ancram in 1633. The correspondence between Ancram and his son, William Ker, third earl of Lothian, (the earldom was acquired through marriage) reveals a sustained interest in his home locality, even down to planning the precise details of improvements to Lothian's castle. At the revolution, Lothian, who had briefly attended the University of Cambridge and had served under Buckingham in 1627–8, became a committed Covenanter, a stance which may explain Ancram having to resign as keeper of the privy purse in 1639, although health was also a factor. This effectively marked his retiral from public life, and after the outbreak of war heavy debts ruined him. The last years of Ancram's life were spent in great poverty in Amsterdam where he died in 1654. Creditors seized his corpse as security, and it was only released for burial four months later after Cromwell's personal intervention.[15]

Ancram's longstanding colleague, Robert Douglas of Spott, had been a page of honour to Prince Henry before becoming his master of the horse. After 1612 he was appointed a gentleman of Prince Charles's bedchamber and master of his household, offices he continued in when Charles succeeded his father. The laird of Spott was also keeper of the king's house and park at Richmond, and though largely resident in England, he became a Scottish privy councillor in 1622. In spite of his long association with the court, Spott opposed the revocation, but Charles forgave this lapse and in 1633 he was created Viscount Belhaven. By the 1630s, however, he was going blind and appears to have retired to Scotland where he had purchased a number of properties with the proceeds of his court spoils. In 1638 Belhaven was at court and was sent back to Scotland to prepare the way for Hamilton's visit, but died in the following year.[16]

Charles also inherited a number of his father's household servants, including Patrick Maule of Panmure and James Maxwell of Innerwick, two grooms of the bedchamber. Panmure had entered the royal household as a page, and went to England with the king at the age of seventeen. His impoverished father died in 1605 leaving the young laird of Panmure with an unimpressive and indebted estate, and 'Except he had favour in Court, his house had ended'. By 1611 Panmure was a groom of the bedchamber, a much sought-after office among the younger members of the court, and in 1616 he married Frances, daughter of Sir Edward Stanhope of Grimston in Yorkshire, brother of Lord Stanhope, the vice-chamberlain. Panmure expended a good deal of energy on rebuilding and enlarging the family estate, and in 1625 James further enriched him with the grant of the manor of Collyweston in Northamptonshire. Panmure continued to enjoy royal favour under Charles who retained him as a groom of the bedchamber, appointing him keeper of the great park at Eltham for life in 1629. Following the death of his first wife, Panmure married Mary Waldrum, one of the queen's ladies-in-waiting. Yet he never lost touch with his home and friends in Scotland where he encouraged planting for enclosures, introduced a more commercial attitude to the marketing of grain, and was appointed sheriff principal of Forfarshire in 1632. His correspondence throughout the 1630s showed a detailed interest in the affairs of his neighbours, in his estates, and in his business enterprises at home (soap manufacturing) as well as in Ireland (he was surveyor general of the customs in Ireland), and African trade. Panmure was also interested in Scottish history, and wrote a manuscript account of William Wallace, although it is unknown when this work was undertaken. When trouble broke out in Scotland in 1637 Panmure was in the country, and on his return to court in October the king sought his advice. He was generally thought of as a conciliator, advising Charles to seek compromise with the Covenanters for whom he expressed some sympathy in private. Whatever his doubts about the king's policies, Panmure remained loyal to Charles, who promoted him to be a gentleman of the bedchamber, and created him earl of Panmure in 1646. He remained at his master's side, acting as privy purse, and was the very last of Charles's servants to leave him at Carisbrooke. Panmure contributed money to Charles II, his sons continued to fight on until 1651, and in spite of paying heavy fines to the Cromwellian regime he was able in his seventieth year to send Charles II a gift of £2000, congratulating him on his restoration.[17]

James Maxwell shared a similar beckground to Panmure's, being the younger son of Robert Maxwell of Kirkhouse, a lesser Dumfriesshire laird. Little is known of his career, but he was in royal service before 1603, advancing thereafter to become an usher of the Order of the Garter, and in 1620 the second marquis of Hamilton found him a place as one of the grooms of the bedchamber. Maxwell may also have been in the same circle as the hard-line Robert Maxwell, first earl of Nithsdale, and his cousin was John Maxwell, bishop of Ross, the most outspoken of the Caroline episcopate and one of the compilers of the Prayer Book. Beginning with the estate at Innerwick, Maxwell acquired considerable property in Scotland, chiefly in the southwest, and he had a share in a number of monopolies, including in 1636 a share in the lease of all minerals in Scotland. He married in England, and in 1639 one of his daughters was married to Charles Cecil, Viscount Cranbourne (the other had married William Hamilton, brother to the marquis of Hamilton, the year before). Maxwell had no political influence in Scotland, but he was a devoted loyalist who made large loans to the king, and in 1646, a few years before his death, he was created earl of Dirleton.[18]

Charles also retained James's gentlemen of the bedchamber, but men like the earls of Kellie and Annandale now found their influence had waned with the death of their old master. The man James himself described in 1604 as 'one of my oldest servants' was Sir Thomas Erskine, first earl of Kellie, one of the heroes of the Gowrie Conspiracy. After 1603 Kellie combined the immensely important offices of first gentleman of the bedchamber and groom of the stool, both of which he retained until James's death. In addition, he was captain of the yeomen of the guard from 1603–17, a member of the English privy council from 1603, and was made a Knight of the

Garter in 1615. Kellie had an estate at Englefield in Berkshire, and after the death of his first wife he remarried twice in England, both women being wealthy English widows. In spite of repeated grumblings about selling up and returning home, Kellie retained his place in the bedchamber after 1625, living at court until his death in London in 1639. His grandson, Thomas Erskine, second earl of Kellie, grew up in Scotland, and was initially a moderate Covenanter, but was involved in organising the Cross Petition at the time of his death in early 1643. His younger brothers, Alexander, third earl of Kellie, and Sir Charles Erskine of Cambo were low-key royalists throughout the 1640s, but the former was taken prisoner and exiled after Worcester, while the latter continued to fight until 1654 when he, too, was captured.[19]

John Murray, was the younger son of the Annandale laird, Sir Charles Murray of Cockpool, and he began his career as a groom of the bedchamber some twenty years before accompanying his master south in 1603. In England, Murray retained this office, and in 1608 he was appointed keeper for life of Guildford Park in Surrey, which became his country residence. In 1612 he succeeded his patron, the earl of Dunbar, as keeper of the privy purse, and began to participate in the management of Scottish affairs from London. By 1618 Murray was a gentleman usher in the bedchamber, but the step up to gentleman of the bedchamber only came in 1622, along with the title of earl of Annandale, as part of a disadvantageous marriage deal – which never took place – involving his eldest son and Buckingham's daughter. He now owned substantial property in the southwest and elsewhere in Scotland, as well as in Donegal and Cumberland. Annandale retained his bedchamber place after 1625, but not the keepership of the privy purse, and although he was employed by Charles, his influence at court had declined considerably by the 1630s. His correspondence at this time reveals a man intimately involved in Scottish affairs even at a local level where he took an active interest in the management of his Scottish estates. There was never any doubt about his Scottish roots, and he was, for example, building a house at Falkland in 1639. Annandale was one of the men Charles turned to for help in 1638, and was a signator of the King's Covenant, but he died in London in September 1640. His son James, second earl of Annandale, was a keen royalist, joining Montrose on his abortive raid into Dumfriesshire in 1644.[20]

Outside the bedchamber the next circle of royal servants were found in the privy chamber, where the proportion of Scots was never as great, nor the rewards as spectacular. The privy chamber could, nevertheless, be a useful launching place for attracting royal favour. Robert Ker, first Lord Roxburghe, was a contemporary of James VI and I, and one of the most dashing and violent border chiefs of the 1590s (he murdered Ancram's father). In 1603 he accompanied James to England, was one of the parliamentary commissioners for union in 1604, and was appointed to the privy chamber before 1608. However, it was as a privy councillor that he performed his greatest services to the king, sitting on a wide variety of committees. In 1614 he married Jean Drummond, governess of the king's younger children, and two years later James rewarded him with elevation to earl of Roxburghe. Roxburghe supported the Five Articles in 1621, and attained ever greater prominence under Charles, colluding in the gradual removal of those of James's stubborn old councillors who dared to oppose the new king. In May 1637 he was, at the age of sixty-seven, appointed lord privy seal and was admitted to the English privy council. His son, William, Lord Ker, joined the Covenanters in 1639, but Roxburghe signed the King's Covenant and was with the royal army in 1639. The death of his only son in 1643 (Lord Ker had returned to the royalist fold in 1641) appears finally to have sapped the old reiver's energies, and his last political act may have been when (allegedly) he held open the door of the House of Commons to facilitate the bungled arrest of the Five Members. He died in 1650, aged eighty.[21]

Sir Archibald Napier of Merchiston, only a few years younger than Roxburghe, was born in 1576, the same year in which his father was appointed master of the mint. Napier was among the original 1603 privy chamber staff, and was described in 1622 by the king as a man 'tied to none but oure self, with whome he hath beene bred even from his youth'. However, he spent little time at court after his appointment as a privy councillor in 1615. He served as treasurer depute from 1622–30, and was created Lord Napier in 1627, but after 1631 took less interest in public affairs following allegations of corruption from his enemies. Napier gave some early support to the Covenanters, being critical of the bishops and suspicious of the Prayer Book. However, he signed the King's Covenant, and with his brother-in-law Montrose drew up the Cumbernauld Bond in 1641, for which he was arrested; again imprisoned in 1644, he was freed after the Battle of Kilsyth. Now over seventy years of age, Napier accompanied Montrose to Philiphaugh, and died a few months after that defeat. His son Archibald, second Lord Napier, fought alongside Montrose throughout 1645, continued to serve his uncle on the Continent, and was among the most virulently disliked of the royalists in covenanting circles. He died in exile in 1658.[22]

Like the Kers and Erskines, the Murrays were extremely successful at the Jacobean and Caroline courts, although there was no direct kinship between William Murray, Annandale and the Tullibardine branch of the clan. Sir Patrick Murray was the younger son of Sir John Murray of Tullibardine, a Perthshire laird who had been master of the king's household in Scotland since 1592, and was created earl of Tullibardine in 1606. Patrick had a minor office in the household before 1603, and on James's accession to the English throne was appointed one of the gentlemen of the privy chamber and was a Knight of the Bath at the coronation. In 1605 he was created M.A. by the University of Oxford and was admitted to Gray's Inn in 1610. Sir Patrick's second wife was Elizabeth Dent, widow of Sir Francis Vere and a daughter and co-heir of a wealthy London merchant. It was as a result of this marriage that he acquired the property at Cheshunt which became the family home. He remained in favour at court, being one of the most richly rewarded of James's privy chamber gentlemen, and was appointed keeper of the royal park at Theobalds in 1617. Sir Patrick retained his privy chamber office under Charles, and was helped by the latter in 1628 to succeed his elder brother as third earl of Tullibardine after the latter had acquired the earldom of Atholl for his own son through marriage. Their younger brother, Sir Mungo Murray, had also been appointed to the privy chamber in or before 1628, and in 1631 he succeeded to the titles and estates of his cousin, David Murray, first Viscount Stormont, King James's old cupbearer. Tullibardine signed the Covenant in September 1638, but in the following spring was with the king in the north of England, and later in the year visited the royalists in the northeast of Scotland. His brother Stormont signed the Covenant in 1638, but was also a signator of the Cumbernauld Bond before dying in 1642. Tullibardine himself died and was buried at his home at Cheshunt in 1644. His eldest son and heir, James, second earl of Tullibardine, was a staunch Covenanter who commanded the centre of the army which was defeated by Montrose at Tippermuir in 1644, but he opposed the handing over of the king to the English in 1646 and subsequently supported the Engagement. Colonel Charles Murray, another of Tullibardine's sons, appears to have been killed (or otherwise died) while serving in the Army of the Covenant, but another son, William Murray, was executed in 1646 after being taken prisoner at Philiphaugh. Tullibardine's nephew, John Murray, first earl of Atholl supported the king from the outbreak of the crisis, was arrested by Argyll in 1640, signed the Cumbernauld Bond and died in 1642.[23]

Perhaps the most successful of all the Scottish courtiers of this period when one takes account of the length of his career and the wealth he accumulated, and squandered, was Sir James Hay, first earl of Carlisle who died in 1636 and was succeeded by his thoroughly anglicised son.[24] However, Carlisle had retained contacts with Scotland through his cousin, Sir George Hay, who had served in the Household before the Union, and was one of the sixteen Scots placed in the forty-eight strong privy chamber in 1603. He pursued an administrative career after becoming a privy councillor in 1616, and held a number of offices before becoming lord chancellor in 1621. Hay amassed large estates, was created Viscount Dupplin in 1630 and earl of Kinnoul in 1633, shortly before his death. His son, also Sir George Hay, remained at court where he progressed from serving in the yeomen of the guard to gentleman of the privy chamber after his father resigned in his favour. Sir George enjoyed the enormous advantages of having a powerful father in Scotland and Carlisle's patronage at court; he married Morton's daughter and served under Buckingham on the Isle of Rhe in 1627, taking over the command of Morton's regiment when he resigned. He continued in his military career until 1632 when he was appointed captain of the guard, an office he filled until 1635 when Morton replaced him. The second earl of Kinnoul showed his impeccable royalist credentials after 1637, but surprisingly took little active part in affairs; dying at Whitehall in 1644, he was buried at Waltham Abbey, the home of his kinsman, William Hay, second earl of Carlisle. His son, George, third earl of Kinnoul had been brought up at court by the first earl of Carlisle, and with his brother William fought under Montrose. He was with his grandfather, Morton, in Orkney in 1649 awaiting the arrival of Montrose from the Continent when they both fell ill and died. He was succeeded by his brother William, fourth earl of Kinnoul, who continued to fight on for Charles II long after 1651, and was the subject of a number of heroic adventures.[25]

Sir Robert Dalzell was the eldest son of Robert, first Lord Dalzell, a privy councillor and fierce opponent of the National Covenant. Sir Robert was subsequently a gentleman of the privy chamber, and it is this court connection that probably explains his second marriage to the daughter of a Gloucestershire gentleman. Like his father, who died towards the end of 1638, Dalzell signed the King's Covenant, and his brother, Sir John Dalzell of Glenae, sheriff of Dumfries, was appointed one of the commissioners to gather subscriptions. Reward for this loyalty came in the following year when Dalzell was created earl of Carnwath. In 1641 he again refused to sign the National Covenant, and his name was deleted from the list of privy councillors Charles presented to the Estates. His outspoken denunciations of the Covenanting leadership brought about an order for his arrest two years later. The Covenanters' hatred of the man Baillie described as 'that monstre of profanitie' led to the death sentence being passed against him in February 1645, but his titles and estates were transferred to his eldest son, who had not joined the king. Carnwath spent most of the war with Charles, fighting beside him at Naseby when allegedly he led the king prematurely from the field, precipitating the royalist defeat. In the following year he served under Lord Digby, and after the rout at Sherborne escaped to Ireland. In 1651 he joined Charles II on the march to Worcester, and was taken prisoner along with his brother at the battle and imprisoned in the Tower of London. He was allowed a measure of freedom in 1652 on account of ill health, and died two years later.[26]

The remaining gentlemen of the privy chamber are more difficult to identify and cannot really be classed among the court elite. However, a few examples serve to underline the picture of strong bonds of loyalty to the king and only a superficial degree of anglicisation. Sir William Stewart of Grandtully served King James from his coronation in 1567 until his death in 1625, after which he retired to his Perthshire estate, although as sheriff of Perth from 1630 he continued to act as a link between court and locality. Both he and his son, Sir Thomas Stewart, were unable to fight for Charles I, but they also avoided cooperating with the Covenanters.[27] Sir William Anstruther of that ilk and his brother Sir Robert were sons of another master of the royal Household (he was also heritable carver to the king). They were both members of the 1603 chamber; Sir William was made a Knight of the Bath at the coronation, became a burgess of Portsmouth, was admitted to Gray's Inn in 1609, and under Charles was appointed one of the gentlemen ushers of the privy chamber; Robert was knighted in 1615, he began his long and successful diplomatic career as ambassador to Norway in 1620, and he married a daughter of Sir Robert Swift of Rotherham which brought him an estate at Wheatley, near Doncaster, where he built a house. The allegiance of the Anstruthers during the civil conflict is not entirely clear, but they appears to have remained circumspectly loyal.[28] Sir Francis Henderson of Fordel, who was a member of the Caroline privy chamber by 1628, belonged to a family with three generations of Household service behind it, and while he was dead by 1637, his adventurer brother, John Henderson of Fordel, fought for Charles, serving under the earl of Newcastle.[29] Sir John Spottiswoode, son of John Spottiswoode, Archbishop of St Andrews, received part of his comprehensive education at Exeter College, Oxford, and while he too was a member of the Caroline chamber, his career was largely made in Scotland. He was appointed a privy councillor and judge in 1622, and president of the court of session in 1633, offices of which he was deprived after the revolution. He was acting secretary of state from 1643 and was with Montrose at Philiphaugh, where he was taken prisoner. (He was executed in January 1646.)[30] Sir David Murray of Stanhope was a gentleman of the privy chamber in 1641, and while his own war activities are unclear, his son, Sir William Murray, was a staunch royalist and was fined by Cromwell.[31]

There were a number of other court families with their roots in household service. Most prominent was John Stewart of Traquair who never attained court office, but whose family had a strong tradition of service in the king's guard. Traquair made his mark through county administration and in parliament as a committee man fully prepared to back the king, as in 1621 when he voted for the Five Articles. In 1627 he was given a place on the privy council, and was appointed treasurer-depute in 1630. His peerage came in 1628, and at the coronation he was created earl of Traquair. In May 1636 Charles finally appointed him lord treasurer, effectively putting him in charge of the government in Scotland. Baillie described Traquair in 1637 as 'a great couteour', but he held no court office and was more of an administrative functionary and political fixer whose power base remained in Edinburgh (he was never admitted to the English privy council and had no English kinsmen). A staunch but not uncritical royalist whom Clarendon rather generously praised as a man whose 'integrity to the King was without blemish', Traquair worked hard in the early stages of the revolution to reach some accommodation between the king and the Covenanters. Latterly his efforts were directed towards preserving his own interests and fortune by some skilful trimming, none of which saved him, and in 1641 he finally fell foul of the Covenanting government and was impeached. Fighting for the king at Preston in 1648, he was taken prisoner, to be released four years later. Traquair was forced to sell all his estates and ended his days begging for a living in the streets of Edinburgh, where he died in 1659.[32]

James Galloway was the son of one of James VI and I's chaplains. He was appointed a master of requests in Scotland in 1627, and by

1631 he had been knighted, appointed to the privy council, and had become a vigorous monopolist, working in partnership with the English entrepreneur Nathaniel Udwart. He is listed as a gentleman of the privy chamber in 1634, and had by this time married a daughter of an English gentleman, Sir Robert Norter. There is little record of his wartime sympathies, but as he was appointed master of the minerals in 1641 and was created Lord Dunkeld in 1645 it seems likely that, along with most other monopolists and courtiers, he sided with the king.[33]

Much younger than any of the above was James Livingston of Kinnaird, the son of Sir John Livingston, one of the grooms of the Jacobean bedchamber and a clerk of the market from 1626 until his death two years later. Kinnaird's mother was Jane Sproxtoune, a daughter of Richard Sproxtoune of Wakefield, steward of the star chamber, who later married Edward Gorges, first Lord Gorges. In 1638 Kinnaird matriculated at Merton College, Oxford and it was after this that he was sent by the king to 'be bred in France'. On his return in 1646 he was found a place as a groom of the bedchamber, and in the following year was created Viscount Newburgh. In 1648 he and his father-in-law, Theophilus Howard, second earl of Suffolk unsuccessfully attempted to organise the king's escape from Bagshot. Newburgh was with Charles II in Scotland in 1650-1 when he was obliged to subscribe the Covenant, but after Worcester he lived in exile where he was fortunate in that Charles found him a regiment to command. At the Restoration he joined the court in London, was raised to earldom and appointed to the command of the Scottish Life Guards.[34]

Few aristocratic families were as intimately identified with King James as the Erskines. James himself had been brought up with John Erskine, second earl of Mar by the latter's mother in Stirling Castle, and he remained one of the king's oldest and most trusted friends, amply rewarded with lands and honours in England after 1603, and serving as lord treasurer from 1617 until 1630 when he resigned, despairing of the course of royal policies. His eldest son, John, Lord Erskine had also been honoured in England, being created M.A. by the University of Oxford in 1605 and being one of Prince Henry's Knights of the Bath in 1610 (Mar himself had been the prince's governor from 1594-1604). Mar's second son, Sir James Erskine, later earl of Buchan, was a gentleman of the privy chamber from 1603, and was created a Knight of the Bath at James's coronation. He lived mostly in London, marrying as his second wife a daughter of Sir Philip Kynvett of Buckenham in Norfolk, and became one of

Charles I's select number of gentlemen of the bedchamber. Another brother, Mr Alexander Erskine, appears to have been a gentleman of the privy chamber by 1629, and yet another, William, was a cupbearer to Charles I. John Erskine, third earl of Mar, who succeeded his father in 1634, was an active privy councillor, involved in aggressive estate building, land speculation, and the operation of a monopoly patent for tanning leather. Yet when the revolution came the Erskines were reluctant royalists, and their court connections were further eroded by the deaths of Mar's cousin Kellie in 1639 and of Buchan in 1640. Mar's son and heir, John, Lord Erskine, tearfully joined the Covenanters at the Glasgow Assembly and later fought with General Leslie in England, while Mar himself was sufficiently suspect to be removed from the privy council in 1640. Later, both men gave grudging support to Montrose, but it was only with the Engagement that they, along with the second earl of Buchan and the third earl of Kellie, demonstrated a more whole-hearted support of the royalist war effort.[35]

One of the more familiar noblemen at Charles's court was William Graham, seventh earl of Menteith. Menteith was relatively unknown before his appointment to the privy council in 1626, but thereafter his rise was meteoric. In 1627 he was appointed president of the council, and in the following year became lord justice general. His success was based on a close working relationship with the king and his frequent attendance at court. Menteith was also a member of the English privy council from 1630, by which time he had become the king's leading minister in Scotland. In 1633 he was dramatically disgraced, but in spite of this he showed unstinting loyalty to the king, a loyalty which confirmed his ruin and cost the life of his eldest son, John, Lord Kilpont (who may have been the Sir John Graham listed in the privy chamber in 1637), killed while serving under Montrose in 1644.[36] Montrose himself was chief of the Graham kindred and came from a family with a long record of loyal service, his grandfather having been successively chancellor and president of the privy council. (The latter post was also briefly held by his father.) James Graham, fifth earl of Montrose, was a minor at the time of his father's death, and was abroad throughout the years immediately preceding the revolution. He was unknown at court, and in 1638 emerged as a keen Covenanter, but by 1641 had switched to the king's side, becoming in 1644 the leader of the Scottish royalists.[37]

There were a number of other noblemen whose father's administrative and political service had earned them access to court. Charles Seton, second earl of Dunfermline was the son of Chancellor

Dunfermline, and came from a family with an impeccable royalist record stretching back beyond Queen Mary. Dunfermline enjoyed Charles's favour, being a gentleman of the privy chamber, and he lived in London where he frittered away much of his inheritance. He was committed to working out a compromise between the king and the Covenanters, frequently acting as a commissioner for the latter in their dealings with the king. However, it was not until the Engagement that he openly supported the king, going into exile with Charles II, and returning in 1660 to hold government office.[38] Similarly, Thomas Hamilton, second earl of Haddington, son of James's secretary of state and a councillor himself, tried to steer a middle course before his mysterious death in 1640, but his brother, Sir James Hamilton of Priestfield, a gentleman of the privy chamber, served as a colonel of horse in the royalist army in England.[39] Thomas Bruce, third Lord Kinloss (son of Edward, first Lord Kinloss, the lawyer and diplomat who became an English privy councillor and chancellor of the exchequer) inherited English estates, married in England, and in 1641 acquired an English peerage. His visit to Scotland in 1633 may have been the only occasion he was in the country since childhood. He had a quiet war, but was generally thought to have favoured the king.[40]

Two noblemen who were closely tied to the court by gratitude and dependance were the neighbouring earls of Nithsdale and Dumfries. In 1618 Robert, tenth Lord Maxwell, was restored to the title which had been forfeited along with the family estates when his brother was executed in 1613. Royal patronage and his marriage in 1619 to Elizabeth Beaumont, daughter of Buckingham's uncle, Sir Francis Beaumont, hastened Maxwell's rehabilitation. In 1620 he was elevated to the earldom of Nithsdale and admitted to the privy council. Nithsdale repaid his political debts by becoming an ardent supporter of absolutist ideas, almost a Scottish Strafford. He supported the Five Articles in parliament in 1621, acted as collector of taxation in 1625, sat on the council of war, and raised a regiment to serve in Charles's proxy war in Denmark in 1627. An arrogant, violent man, he advised Charles from the start to employ Catholics to enforce a military solution in Scotland. He was the only royalist nobleman in the south to organise successful resistance to the Covenanters, and his castles at Carlaverock and Threave were among the last in the kingdom to surrender in September 1640. Thereafter Nithsdale continued to plot from England, participating in Montrose's abortive raid on Dumfries, and taking part in Digby's ill-fated march to Doncaster and the defeat at Sherborne in October 1645. He fled to Ireland and died on the Isle of Man a year later, ruined and with his estates and title once again forfeited.[41]

Like his neighbour, William Crichton of Ryhill succeeded (as ninth Lord Sanquhar) to the title and ruined estates of an executed murderer-criminal. Sanquhar was too poor to live at court, but he did have contacts in England. In 1618, in a double wedding, his eldest son was married to a daughter of Sir Robert Swift of Rotherham, and his eldest daughter was married to Edward Barnham Swift. Following Sir Robert Swift's death, Sanquhar himself married his widow, Ursula Barnham, heiress to a York merchant. In 1628 he was appointed steward of Doncaster where he lived much of the time. By now his political career had begun to flourish. In 1622 he was created Viscount Ayr in recognition of support for the Five Articles of Perth; admission to the privy council came in the 1620 and in 1633 he was created earl of Dumfries. In 1637 Dumfries supported the king; in consequence, his precarious finances were ruined and he was forced to sell off all his estates by 1642. He was living in exile at Doncaster when he died in the following year.[42]

It would, however, be a mistake to equate court office automatically with royalist loyalties. A surprising lack of loyalty was found within the Scottish family who could boast of the longest association with Charles I. Alexander Livingston, first earl of Linlithgow, had been an adherent of Mary Queen of Scots and, in spite of his Catholicism, was favoured by James VI and I, who appointed him keeper of his younger children, including Prince Charles. His son, Alexander, second earl of Linlithgow, was a Protestant and privy councillor, acquiring a gunpowder monopoly which allowed him to make money out of the wars of the 1620s. He initially signed the Covenant, but had changed his mind by the latter half of 1638, and was sufficiently distrusted by the Covenanters to have his name struck off the list of privy councillors in 1641. Linlithgow remained a staunch royalist until his death in 1645.[43] His younger brother, James Livingston, was a professional soldier on the Continent, but was appointed a gentleman of the privy chamber in 1631 and was created Lord Almond in 1634, probably in recognition of the king's childhood association with the Livingston family. Once the wars began both sides tried hard to attach Almond to their service, but it was the Army of the Covenant that he led into England in August 1640. In the same month he signed the Cumbernauld Bond, and Charles continued to have high hopes of detaching Almond to his side, creating him earl of Callendar in 1641. However, it was 1648 before he fought for the king alongside his nephew, George, third earl of

Linlithgow, who had been a committed Covenanter until the Engagement.[44] Sir William Balfour of Pitullo was one of the original 1603 privy chamber, and was married to Lord Napier's sister. In 1630 Charles I appointed him lieutenant of the Tower of London 'to the great and general scandal of the English nation', but surprisingly he turned against the king in 1641. Balfour commanded the parliamentary horse under the earl of Bedford at the Battle of Edgehill.[45] Robert Gordon, the younger son of the twelfth earl of Sutherland, became a gentleman of the privy chamber in 1606, and his ties with England were strengthened in 1613 when he married the only daughter and heiress of John Gordon of Longormes, dean of Salisbury, through whom he acquired lands in the south and in France. Sir Robert lived at Salisbury, but from 1615 he was increasingly drawn back to Scotland to fulfil his responsibilities as tutor to his young nephew, the thirteenth earl of Sutherland. Furthermore, he showed great enthusiasm for the schemes of Sir William Alexander, becoming the very first Nova Scotia baronet in 1625, and having a twenty-five per cent share in the copper coin project. Once Sutherland attained his majority in 1630, Sir Robert was able to take on other duties in Scotland, where he had acquired estates (in Moray and Galloway), becoming sheriff of Inverness in 1630, vice-chamberlain of Scotland in 1631, and a privy councillor and lord high commissioner in 1634. He signed the King's Covenant, and attended the king at York in 1638, but Sir Robert's allegiance was already wavering. In 1642 he brought his family up from Salisbury to Gordonstoun and threw himself into vigorous support of the Covenanters, particularly in church affairs, before dying in 1656 at the age of seventy-seven.[46] Sir James Lockhart of Lee was a Caroline appointment to the chamber who sympathised with the Covenanters from an early date, holding office in the exchequer and college of justice between 1645 and 1649, when he was ousted on account of his support for Charles II. His son, Sir William Lockhart, served Charles II as a colonel of horse, but in the 1650s was employed on a number of embassies by Oliver Cromwell, whose niece he had married. Both Sir James and his son enjoyed high office and favour after 1660.[47]

There were other Scottish royalists in 1638: Alexander Stewart, first earl of Galloway, who had strong familial ties in England;[48] Ludovick Lindsay, sixteenth earl of Crawford, the 'loyal earl' who was a drunken young mercenary;[49] the impoverished and Catholic James Ogilvy, first earl of Airlie;[50] the emigré George Gordon, second marquis of Huntly, who had been a Knight of the Bath in

1603 and whose indifference to his kindred and followers was blamed on 'his breiding in England, the habit and long custom he gott there'.[51] However, these men were only on the very fringes of the Scottish court establishment. In spite of a few exceptions, and in spite of the unease many court families shared about royal policies, the general picture is of an impressive level of loyalty among those individuals and families who had experienced long years of association with the royal family and the court. Much of this was inspired by a self-interested desire to preserve a system which had clearly benefited these noblemen and their families, but it would also be true to say that a high view of monarchy, a preference for episcopal church government, and a commitment to some idea of Great Britain was common to most. Certainly, the loyalty of the Scottish courtiers was more solid than that of their English counterparts, among whom both the lord chamberlain, Robert Devereux, second earl of Essex, and the groom of the stool, Henry Rich, first earl of Holland, joined the king's enemies from an early date.[52] Behind this lay the legacy of the dynasty's Scottish origins. In England the Crown was more of an idea, or a symbol, than a person, and this had become even more the case after 1603 with the arrival of a foreign king. Unlike the Scottish courtiers, many of whom had served King James since their youth and whose fathers had served the Crown before them, those from England could not trace their relationship with the Stewarts back more than one generation.

It is difficult, and perhaps unwise, to typify these men or their families. They covered a wide age-range, from very old men such as Kellie and Stirling to relatively young men such as Dysart and Newburgh, but most were between the age of forty-five and fifty-five by the revolution. A significant number were either old or in ill health, and between 1637 and 1641, when the revolution was lost and won, Annandale, Belhaven, Buchan, Kellie and Stirling all died, while Atholl, Kinnoul and Tullibardine were all dead by 1644. To some extent the courtiers were a party of old men whose ideas and political values were shaped under James VI and I and who were overwhelmed by something they could barely understand in 1638. It is hardly surprising that men so conspicuously successful and so at ease at court should be unsympathetic to the charge that the regal Union was not working. There were exceptions, but the tradition of service to the king and an appreciation of the benefits bestowed by the Crown ensured that most of their sons followed in the royalist tradition of their fathers. Confronting them were men like Rothes, Balmerino, Argyll and Johnston of Wariston, who all belonged to a younger generation with much less need to feel appreciative of the Crown. They had grown up and attained adulthood at a time when the Union was already demonstrably not working, and while it would be too crude to explain the Covenanting nobility simply as a frustrated country party, the almost complete absence of courtiers among them does suggest dissatisfaction with the spread of court patronage, a lack of any personal relationship with the king, and the likelihood that their world-view was narrower and more natively Scottish than that found among those familiar with court life. Provincial noblemen – the earls of Cassillis, Kinghorn and Sutherland for example, or lords Borthwick, Duffus and Rollo – had every reason to support the Covenant and none to fight for a far-away king they barely knew.

Yet it would be a mistake to contrast the provincial patriotism of the Covenanters with the courtiers' indifference to and ignorance of their native land. The great majority of Scottish noblemen were educated in Scottish schools and universities. A few courtiers had been youths in 1603, serving on the first rungs of the court ladder as grooms or pages, and they had therefore received the greater part of their informal education in England. However, only Lennox and Hamilton attended an English university, and the earl of Lothian's deeply-held covenanting principles are no more the product of the University of Cambridge than Hamilton's royalism was a fruit of his time at the University of Oxford. Nor is there any evidence to suggest any significant cultural alienation between Scots at court and those who lived at home, other than a superficial difference in lifestyle brought about by living in a large city like London and mixing with the wealthier English aristocracy. There are no grounds for believing that this aroused disapproval among the noblemen left at home, although it undoubtedly generated envy, and any contrast is in degree and not in fundamental cultural values. Among courtiers and those who visited the court there was no great enthusiasm to emulate English manners and customs or to encourage English architectural styles or farming methods at home, and the correspondence of both Ancram and Kellie shows a surprising lack of interest in life in England. A large proportion of courtiers did marry Englishwomen or sought English marriages for their children, but many of these were second and third wives, and most noblemen preferred to find a wife for their heirs in Scotland. The conservatism of many Scottish noblemen, particularly among older families with a local power network to maintain, ensured that domestic marriage alliances reinforced links between court and country. In addition, the English were reluctant to marry their daughters to Scots.

As one would expect, most courtiers were exposed to the Anglican church, and gave steady support to policies such as the Five Articles, while some, such as Stirling, were enthusiastic supporters of liturgical change. No courtier risked his place by siding with presbyterian critics, but there was sensitivity to what was going on in Scotland. An elderly and disappointed courtier like Lord Napier, who had retired to his estates a few years before 1638, was opposed to the king's ecclesiastical policies, but so too were younger men like Panmure and William Murray, who sympathised with the anger and fear those policies aroused. However, one cannot equate episcopalianism, or even liturgical reform, with anglicisation before the mid-1630s, when Archbishop Laud quite clearly was engaged on a campaign to bring the Scottish Church into line with that of England. A significant minority of courtiers were Catholics, or came from Catholic families (all the Catholic nobility supported the king), particularly among the older peerage families, and this helped to fuel mistaken popular impressions of a crypto-Catholic court in the 1630s. After 1637 it was these Catholic peers, especially Nithsdale, who took the lead in advocating a military solution to the king's problems in Scotland, and a number of them were engaged in plotting with their English counterparts and the papal agent, George Con.[53]

Only a minority of courtiers had major economic interests in England, and only a few of these were dependant for the greater part of their income upon English sources. Where an income derived from the king was essential, however, was in maintaining a court lifestyle, and while the Scots suffered from a poor exchange rate and less profitable estates, they were no different from English courtiers who were almost as needy and every bit as avaricious in seeking out patronage in order to sustain a life at court. More prolonged absenteeism was certainly a feature of the post-Union period, but most courtiers continued to take an active interest in their estates, visiting them on a regular basis and directing their management. Only a very few turned their backs on their homes, and household men like Annandale and Dirleton who made their fortune in England set about establishing themselves as landowners in Scotland. There is little doubt that, like Panmure and Stirling, they took great pride in advertising their newly-found wealth and status in localities where they had once been insignificant members of the landed community. Access to royal patronage meant that these men were involved in a wide range of economic activities besides land investment, and a large number had a hand in tax collecting, customs rates, industrial and trade monopolies, and any of the other speculative and unpopular activities which passed for Caroline economic policy in Scotland. As in England and Ireland, where some Scots such as Hamilton and Stirling also had an interest, the courtiers were seen to be benefiting from extremely unpopular fiscal expedients, and charges of corruption were rife and largely justifiable. Here the accusations had an additional sting, since the money was seen to be drained out of Scotland to satisfy the voracious appetites of courtiers who seemingly cared nothing for the effect of those policies on the rest of the population. But these men were not simply financial predators, and courtiers spent considerable sums of money in Scotland carving out new estates and building houses worthy of men who were friends of the king, thus contributing to the growing and overlapping consumer and financial markets from which the merchant community greatly profited.[54]

A number of courtiers were Scottish privy councillors and actively participated in Scottish administration, but naturally those with heavy commitments in Scotland were less likely to be members of the inner court circle. Meetings of parliament, conventions and the privy council were not well attended by courtiers, but to some extent their presence was unnecessary on bodies already well tuned to respond to Crown management. Besides, courtiers were able to give counsel to the king in London and they acted as useful intermediaries between the king and those who wished to bypass the privy council in Edinburgh. However, the physical separation of the court and the administration meant that Charles I was unable to make as effective political use of his household as kings had before 1603. Instead, he was forced to rely more on less prestigious crown officials and bishops, neither of whom could be expected to show the same level of loyalty as men intimately connected to the king.[55]

The physical distancing of the court also made courtiers less useful in representing the king's interests in the localities. This was to have some bearing on events in 1637-8 when, as in England where the royalists were far more successful, the level of support raised for the king in a locality often depended more on the standing of the king's representative than on any popular mandate.[56] Apart from the fact that courtiers were less likely to be resident and to have built up a powerful local clientele, the geographical distribution of court families was uneven. They were concentrated in two regions: in and around Stirlingshire and Perthshire where the houses of Mar, Stirling, Callendar, Newburgh, Atholl, Tullibardine and Stormont were based; and on the Borders where the houses of Roxburghe, Ancram-Lothian, Traquair, Galloway, Annandale, Dirleton, Dumfries and Nithsdale were based. By contrast, there was no significant courtier family in the covenanting stronghold of Ayrshire, while in Fife both Kellie and Dysart had no appreciable power. Even where lay courtiers had taken an active interest in a locality, absenteeism exacerbated the observable decline in lordship itself and contributed to the increasingly fluid dynamic in local politics provided by a rising gentry. Furthermore, the effect of royal policies, particularly over the previous decade, was primarily to undermine the influence of lords identified with the court, fostering habits of disobedience and an attitude of dissent difficult to overcome even by lords intimately known in their localities. It was this above all else that accounted for the astonishing success in 1638 of Archibald Johnston of Wariston and David Calderwood in persuading people that 'Such Noblemen as are not joyned in Covenant with us, whether they favour our cause or not, are not to be attended at this tyme'.[57]

The complete failure of the Scottish royalists between 1637 and 1641 contrasts with the situation in England in 1642, where the king's propaganda was better prepared and the royalist nobility were better organised.[58] Yet it is too easy to be fooled by the Covenanters' success and to dismiss the royalists in Scotland. Certainly Robert Baillie saw reasons to be afraid as he contemplated the strength of the king's supporters when surveying the scene in the spring of 1639.[59] The sociopolitical background of the royalists may have put them at a disadvantage, but their failure to counter the Covenanters' challenge was more directly a result of political incompetence on the part of the king, who failed to make proper use of these natural supporters either in their localities, or to form the nucleus of a royalist party in parliament. Certainly the courtiers themselves were aware of what was going on – Roxburghe, Traquair, Panmure, Nithsdale and Lennox were all in Scotland during the early stages of the revolution – and their advice to Charles was both informed and reasonable (Nithsdale excepted). The king himself contributed to the failure of his servants in Scotland in 1637 by his slowness to summon his advisors south, or to listen to what they had to say.[60] This was followed by his failure to send the courtiers home to secure their localities. It was the spring of 1638 before Hamilton went north, and it was Hamilton himself who insisted that other courtiers, such as Morton, Linlithgow, Kellie, Mar, Kinnoul, Haddington, Belhaven and Almond, be dispatched before him to prepare the way.[61] Thereafter, the courtiers remained at the core of royalist activity in Scotland until Montrose exploded onto the scene in 1644. Thus in September 1639 'our Scottishmen were dismissed from

Court to come home' to strengthen the king's party in the country; it was the courtiers who bore the brunt of the king's defeat in 1641; they were prominent among the many Scottish noblemen at York in the spring of 1642; the same men were sent from Oxford in 1643 'to advance the King's affairs among us'; and when parliament finally got around to the forfeiture of the leading royalists in November 1643 the courtiers took heavy losses.[62] Significantly, Charles surrendered control over his privy council and over parliament in the summer of 1641, but the Household remained beyond the reach of his enemies, and neither Rothes or Loudoun ever was granted the place in the bedchamber which rumour had associated with them.[63] Instead, at a time when Covenanters were being rewarded with peerages and offices, and Carnwath was bitterly criticising the king's lack of gratitude,[64] Morton joined the bedchamber, Lennox became lord steward of the household, and the influence of the master of the horse, Hamilton, appeared to be unchallengeable. The link between loyalty, personal service and counsel remained. But in Scotland the Covenant was in the ascendant, and had staked a claim for the monopoly of patriotic loyalties. The court had been marginalised, and those identified with it found that what had once been an advantage had become a huge liability. The Scottish cavaliers, now widely and unfairly perceived as anglicised agents of a tyrannous and popish monarchy, were consigned to play out the rest of the British wars as broken and uprooted emigrés.

NOTES
1. R. Baillie, *The letters and journals*, ed. D. Laing (3 vols, Bannatyne Club, Edinburgh, 1841–2), I, 354.
2. E. Hyde, Earl of Clarendon, *The history of the rebellion in England and Wales began in the year 1641* (6 vols, Oxford, 1888), I, 108. The difficulty with this analysis is in identifying whether the problem is structural or personal.
3. The best of the many biographies of Montrose is E. J. Cowan, *Montrose, for Covenant and King* (London, 1977). In England there used to be the same unhealthy concentration on Prince Rupert, but the last decade has seen some important new studies of the royalists, especially R. Hutton, *The royalist war effort 1642–1646* (Harlow, 1982), and J. L. Malcolm, *Caesar's due: Loyalty and King Charles 1642–1646* (London and New Jersey, 1983). Unfortunately both studies concentrate exclusively on England.
4. Clarendon, *Rebellion*, I, 145–6.

5. P. R. Seddon, 'Patronage and officers in the reign of James I', (unpublished University of Manchester Ph.D. thesis, 1967); N. Cuddy, 'The king's chambers, the bedchamber of James I in administration and politics 1603-1625' (unpublished University of Oxford D.Phil. thesis, 1987); N. Cuddy, 'The revival of the entourage: the bedchamber of James I, 1603-1625', and K. Sharpe, 'The image of virtue: the court and household of Charles I' in D. Starkey, ed., *The English Court from the Wars of the Roses to the Civil War* (Harlow, 1987), pp.173-225, 226-60.
6. G. Parry, *The Golden Age: the culture of the Stuart court, 1603-42* (Manchester, 1981); G. Parry, *The seventeenth century, the intellectual and cultural context of English literature* (Harlow, 1989), pp.9-41; R. Strong, *Henry, Prince of Wales and England's lost renaissance* (London, 1986); R. M. Smuts, *Court culture and the origins of a royalist tradition in early Stuart England* (Philadelphia, 1987); S. Orgel, *The illusion of power* (Berkeley and London, 1975); S. Orgel, ed., *Ben Jonson: The complete masques* (New Haven and London, 1975); S. Orgel and R. Strong, *Inigo Jones: the theatre of the Stuart court* (2 vols, Berkeley, 1973); R. Strong, *Britannia Triumphans: Inigo Jones, Rubens and Whitehall Palace* (London, 1980); J. Goldberg, *James I and the politics of literature* (Baltimore, 1983); K. Sharpe, *Criticism and compliment: the politics of literature in the England of Charles I* (London, 1986).
7. J. T. Cliffe, *The Yorkshire gentry from the Reformation to the Civil War* (London, 1969), pp.282-308.
8. Smuts, *Court culture*; Sharpe, *Criticism and compliment*.
9. D. Stevenson, *The Scottish Revolution 1637-44* (Newton Abbot, 1973), p.324, where he argues that because the court was in England, the court-country polarity was magnified. At the time of writing Stevenson was clearly influenced by P. Zagorin, *The court and the country: The beginning of the English revolution* (London, 1969). In Scotland there was a very powerful public culture which fed the national consciousness: see A. H. Williamson, *Scottish national consciousness in the reign of James VI* (Edinburgh, 1979).
10. In this and all succeeding biographical notes I have included the major printed secondary sources as well as specific references. D. Mathew, *Scotland under Charles I* (London, 1955), pp.236-42; J. B. Paul, ed., *The Scots peerage* (9 vols, Edinburgh, 1904-14), V, 356-60; G. E. Cockayne, ed., *The Complete peerage* (13 vols, London, 1910-59), VII, 604-10; IX, 831-3; J. E. Doyle, *The official baronage of England* (3 vols, London, 1886), II, 472-3; III, 121-5; *D.N.B.*, IV, 85-6; Baillie, *Letters and journals*, II, 383, 393; Clarendon, *Rebellion*, I, 160-1, 207, 409-12, 281, 544-8; II, 327, 527-8; III, 46-7; IV, 393; Sir J. Balfour, *Historical works* (4 vols, Edinburgh, 1824-5), III, 46 and 66ff, for his active participation in the 1641 parliament. In

1654 Baillie wrote that Lennox was living 'as a man buried, in his house of Cobhame', *Letters and journals*, III, 249.
11. J. Burnet, *Memoirs of the lives and actions of James and William Duke of Hamilton and Castleherald* (London, 1677); H. L. Rubinstein, *Captain Luckless: James, First Duke of Hamilton, 1606-1649* (Edinburgh, 1975); Mathew, *Scotland under Charles I*, pp.234-6; *Scots peerage*, IV, 373-80; *Complete peerage*, VI, 258-64; *D.N.B.*, XXIV, 178-83, 218-20; Baillie, *Letters and journals*, I, 115. Hamilton's well-known comment in a letter to the king from Scotland that 'next Hell I hate this place' arose from the difficult circumstances of his visit there in 1638; Stevenson, *Scottish Revolution*, p.122. Hamilton is currently the subject of a Ph.D. thesis being researched by John Scally at Selwyn College, Cambridge, which should at last reveal his full significance in the politics of the 1630s and 1640s. Hamilton's Abercorn cousins were predominantly Catholic and had settled in Ireland. The second earl of Abercorn himself was involved in a number of Catholic plots and was banished from Scotland. Of his uncles, Sir Claud Hamilton of Shawfield had been a gentleman of the privy chamber, but died in 1614, and Sir Frederick Hamilton was also of the chamber, had a career as a mercenary on the Continent, and married a daughter of Sir John Vaughan, governor of Londonderry. Abercorn's brother, Sir George Hamilton of Donalong, fought for Charles throughout the wars and was rewarded after the Restoration: *Scots peerage*, I, 46-9, 52-3; *Complete peerage*, I, 2-5. Hamilton's brother-in-law, Denbigh, was killed fighting for the king in 1643.
12. W. Fraser, *The Douglas Book* (4 vols, Edinburgh, 1885), II, 412-23; *Scots peerage*, VI, 375-8; *Complete peerage*, IX, 294-6; *D.N.B.*, XV, 367-8. For the marquis of Douglas: Fraser, *Douglas Book*, II, 412-41; *Scots peerage*, I, 202-4; *D.N.B.*, XV, 368-70.
13. Mathew, *Scotland under Charles I*, pp.233-4; *Scots peerage*, III, 401-5; *Complete peerage*, IV, 562; *D.N.B.*, XXXIX, 407-8; Clarendon, *Rebellion*, I, 389, n.1, 527; Baillie, *Letters and journals*, I, 393. In 1643 one minister told the General Assembly that William Murray 'had done manie good offices, and none evill, to the Church', *ibid.*, II, 48. In 1646 Dysart tried to persuade the king to escape, but after Charles had been handed over to the English he was forbidden to see him. In 1648 the queen sent him to Scotland to drum up support for the Engagement, and he was involved in the murky dealings between Charles II and the Covenanters which effectively sealed Montrose's fate in 1650.
14. C. Rogers, *Memorials of the earl of Stirling and the house of Alexander* (2 vols, Edinburgh, 1877), I, 32-204; C. Rogers, ed., *The earl of Stirling's register of royal letters relative to the affairs of Scotland* (2 vols, Edinburgh, 1885); Sir William Alexander,

Earl of Stirling, *Poetical Works*, ed. L. E. Kastner and H. B. Charlton (Scottish Text Society, Edinburgh and London, 1921-2); *Sir William Alexander and American colonization* (Prince Society, Boston, 1873); A. H. Williamson, 'Scotland, Antichrist and the invention of Great Britain', in J. Dwyer, R. A. Mason, A. Murdoch, eds, *New perspectives on the politics and culture of early modern Scotland* (Edinburgh, 1980), pp.50-2; *Scots peerage*, VIII, 170-81; *Complete peerage*, XII, prt 1, 277-83; *D.N.B.*, I, 275-80; Burnet, *Memoirs of Hamilton*, 2. Among Stirling's remaining children Anthony was the king's joint master of the works from 1629, John of Gartmore was joint master of the minerals and metals along with his father and until 1641 was also master of the mint. Both his daughters were married in Kensington Church in the early 1620s, one to the Scots-Irish peer Viscount Montgomery of the Ards, the other to one of the court Murrays. A Henry Alexander, possibly the future 3rd earl, was a server in Prince Charles's household in 1638; B.L. HL. 7623. He married a daughter of Sir Peter Vanlore of Tilehurst in 1637. Following Lord Alexander's death, Baillie wrote that Stirling 'is old, and extreamely hated of all the countrey for his alledged briberie, urgeing of the Psalmes, and the Books for them, overwhelming us with his Black money': Baillie, *Letters and journals*, I, 77. See, too, Sir James Balfour's scurrilous poem celebrating the earl's death: Rogers, *Memorials*, I, 189-90 and 202-3 for Sir Thomas Urquhart's description of him, 'The purity of this gentleman's vein was quite spoiled by the corruption of his courtiership.... He was born a poet, and aimed to be a king; therefore, would he have his royal title from King James, who was born a king and aimed to be a poet'. A biography of Stirling is long overdue.

15. D. Laing, ed., *Correspondence of Sir Robert Kerr, First Earl of Ancrum, and his son William, third Earl of Lothian* (2 vols, Edinburgh, 1875); Newbattle Collection S.R.O. G.D. 40/2; *Scots peerage*, V, 464-73; *Complete peerage*, I, 131-2; *D.N.B.*, XI, 56-7. Ancram was among the chief beneficiaries of Charles's generosity; for example, in January 1635 he was gifted a share of the tax levied on starch imported into England, and in March 1639 had a pension of £2000 sterling to be paid out of the English exchequer. Mathew, *Scotland under Charles I*, pp.232-3, notes. He also had a reversion of the keepership of Marylebone Park: B.L. Eg. 2553 fo. 82. Commenting on Ancram's loss of the privy purse, Baillie wrote that he was removed 'whether for the zeale of the Earle of Lothian, his son, in the countrie's cause, or for his long and evident infirmity, which made him very unmeet to ly in a prince's chamber, we doe not yet know', *Letters and journals*, I, 116. However, he was still a gentleman of the bedchamber in 1644.

16. *Scots peerage*, II, 36-7; *Complete peerage*, II, 92; *D.N.B.*, V,

345-61; Belhaven Muniments S.R.O. G.D. 162. Belhaven had a pension of £666 13s 4d sterling, and among the larger gifts he received from the king was £7000 sterling for keeping Richmond, £2000 sterling in 1625 and £5000 in 1630. For his activities in 1638, see Baillie, I, *Letters and journals*, I, 107.

17. J. Stuart, *Registrum de Panmure* (2 vols, Edinburgh, 1874), I, pp.XXXVIII-XLIV; II, 317-39; Inventory of Dalhousie Muniments S.R.O. G.D. 45/14/1-115; *Scots peerage*, VII, 19-21; *Complete peerage*, IX, 298-300; *D.N.B.*, XXXVII, 87-8; *Report of the royal commission on historical manuscripts* [hereafter *H.M.C.*] Vth Report, 637-8; I. Whyte, *Agriculture and society in seventeenth century Scotland* (Edinburgh, 1979), pp.120, 179, 231. Panmure was still a groom in 1629, and in 1643 a passport simply describes him as 'of his Majesties bedchamber': B.L. Add. MSS 23,206 fo. 22. Sometime between 1650 and 1653 he petitioned against the loss of his Irish office: B.L. St. 152 fo. 74. A Robert Maule, possibly a relative, was described as a groom of the privy chamber in 1618: B.L. Add. MSS 5750 fo. 17.

18. *Scots peerage*, III, 128-30; *Complete peerage*, IV, 386. Dirleton was still alive in 1649: G.D. 45/14/62. He does not appear to have been the same James Maxwell who held the office of Black Rod and who arrested Strafford in 1642: e.g., Baillie, *Letters and journals*, I, 272.

19. *Report of the historical manuscripts commission on the manuscripts of the earl of Mar and Kellie*, ed. H. Paton (2 vols, London, 1904, 1930), I, 202-3; II, 52, 125, 227 and *passim*; *Scots peerage*, II, 271-3; V, 84-7; 615-25; *Complete peerage*, II, 380; VII, 100-1; VIII, 420-5; *D.N.B.*, XVII, 434-5; Baillie, *Letters and journals*, I, 64 for Cross Petition.

20. *Scots peerage*, I, 227-8; *Complete peerage*, I, 265; *D.N.B.*, XXXIX, 380; *HMC*, VI, 324 describes him as a gentleman usher in 1618; VII, 668-9 for Guildford; *Report of the historical manuscripts commission on the Laing manuscripts preserved in Edinburgh University Library* (London, 1914, 1925), I, 160-1, 169-72, 184. In January 1631 Annandale wrote telling Haddington that he had no more influence in the bedchamber than the latter had in the session, indicating just how much times had changed since James's death. Like most courtiers, Annandale was actively interested in the practical running of his estates; see Inventory of the Murrays of Murraythwaite S.R.O. G.D. 219/281 for correspondence with his chamberlain between 1636 and 1642.

21. *Scots peerage*, VII, 341-8; *Complete peerage*, XI, 215-19; *D.N.B.*, XXXI, 53-5. At the outbreak of the war in England the parliament there seized Roxburghe's jewellery, including a diamond-studded picture of Queen Anne and another piece with the duke of York's name on it. Here was material evidence of a lifetime of service to the royal family: Newbattle Collection

S.R.O. G.D. 40/5/25/3. For privy chamber lists see N. Carlyle, *An inquiry into the place and quality of the gentlemen of his majesty's most honourable privy chamber* (London, 1829), 126-44.

22. *Scots peerage*, VI, 422-6; *Complete peerage*, IX, 453-6; *D.N.B.*, XL, 35-8.
23. *Scots peerage*, VIII, 411-12; *Complete peerage*, XII, pt 2, 66-7; John Murray, seventh duke of Atholl, *Chronicles of the Atholl and Tullibardine families* (5 vols, Edinburgh, 1908), I, 94; Clarendon, *Rebellion*, I, 66-7; *Mar and Kellie*, I, 117, where he is described as being in the privy chamber in 1623. Like most courtiers, Tullibardine was kept well informed of local affairs; see, for example, Breadalbane muniments S.R.O. G.D. 112/39/361 ff. on his plans to develop Glenalmond Forest.
24. R. E. Schreiber, *The first Carlisle, Sir James Hay, First Earl of Carlisle as courtier, diplomat and entrepreneur, 1580-1636* (Transactions of the American Philosophical Society 74, pt 7, 1984); *Complete peerage*, III, 32-3; Doyle, *Complete peerage*, I, 327-8. Carlisle was the only Scottish courtier mentioned by Clarendon in his review of James's court in 1625. Clarendon, *Rebellion*, I, 77.
25. *Scots peerage*, V, 222-8; *Complete peerage*, IV, 557; VII, 318-19; J. Ferguson, *The papers illustrating the history of the Scots Brigade in the services of the United Netherlands* (3 vols, Edinburgh, 1899, 1901), I, 311. The deaths of the third earl of Kinnoul and his grandfather, Morton, appear to have followed a bitter quarrel over the command of the expedition.
26. *Scots peerage*, III, 409-13; *D.N.B.*, XIII, 442-3; Balfour, *Works*, III, 109; Baillie, *Letters and journals*, II, 78.
27. W. Fraser, *The red book of Grandtully* (2 vols, Edinburgh, 1868), I, XXXIX-XLIX; Sir R. Douglas, *The complete baronage of Scotland* (Edinburgh, 1798), p.486. However, Sir Thomas did cooperate with the Cromwellian regime and was heavily fined after the Restoration.
28. A. W. Anstruther, *History of the family of Anstruther* (Edinburgh and London, 1923); Douglas, *Baronage*, pp.314-15.
29. Douglas, *Baronage*, p.519.
30. Douglas, *Baronage*, p.448; *D.N.B.*, LIII, 416-17.
31. Douglas, *Baronage*, p.108.
32. *Scots peerage*, VIII, 402-5; *Complete peerage*, XII, pt 2, 6-9; *D.N.B.*, LIV, 326-8; Baillie, *Letters and journals*, I, 11; Clarendon, *Rebellion*, I, 143.
33. *Scots peerage*, III, 376-9.
34. *Scots peerage*, VI, 451-3; *Complete peerage*, IX, 511-14; *D.N.B.*, XXXIII, 398; Clarendon, *Rebellion*, IV, 477-8; V, 19-20, 239-40, 242. Of Newburgh's uncles, Alexander had letters of denization, married a daughter of Mathew Chubbe of Dorchester and had a pension from the king, while James was a

groom in King Charles's bedchamber. Newburgh's wife, Lady d'Aubigny, was herself a fanatical royalist. For evidence of his activities in Scotland on Charles II's behalf in 1650: Inventory of Airlie Muniments S.R.O. G.D. 16/50/50.

35. *Mar and Kellie, passim*; *Scots peerage*, II, 271-3; 615-25; *Complete peerage*, II, 380; VIII, 420-5; Another Erskine, Sir Thomas Erskine, brother to the laird of Balgonie, was a gentleman of Prince Charles's privy chamber in 1616; Mar and Kellie Muniments S.R.O. G.D. 124/3/23. Mar and Lord Erskine were very leniently treated by the Covenanters following their episode with Montrose, and were given a good deal of help by General David Leslie. Sir Arthur Erskine, Mar's brother, was killed at Worcester.

36. W. Fraser, *The red book of Menteith* (2 vols, Edinburgh, 1880), I, 331-94; *Scots peerage*, I, 133-9; VI, 164-5; *Complete peerage*, VIII, 673-5; *D.N.B.*, XXII, 363-4. For an exaggerated account of Airth's importance see M. Lee, *The Road to Revolution: Scotland under Charles I, 1625-37* (Urbana and Chicago, 1985), pp.43-118. Lord Kilpont was killed in 1644 in a brawl with a fellow-officer in Montrose's army. Airth himself lived to see the Restoration, but neither he nor his family was ever compensated for their losses.

37. Cowan, *Covenant and King; Scots peerage*, VI, 231-42; *Complete peerage*, IX, 148-9.

38. G. Seton, *A history of the family of Seton* (2 vols, Edinburgh, 1896), I, 658-64; *Scots peerage*, III, 373-4; *Complete peerage*, IV, 582-3; Stevenson, *Revolution*, 151-2, 181, 212, 223, 250; Baillie, *Letters and journals*, I, 205.

39. W. Fraser, *Memorials of the earls of Haddington* (2 vols, Edinburgh, 1889), I, 189-200; *Scots peerage*, IV, 314-17; *Complete peerage*, IV, 582-3; P. R. Newman, *Royalist officers in England and Wales 1642-1660* (New York and London, 1981), p.174; Baillie, *Letters and journals*, I, 205. Haddington was at court in 1637-8 and was approached to act as an intermediary between the Covenanters and the king.

40. *Scots peerage*, III, 474-8; *Complete peerage*, I, 58-9; II, 350-1; V, 41-2. The highlight of Elgin's war appears to have been a quarrel with the residents of Gillingham forest in Dorset, where his enclosures and deforestation sparked off a riot in 1643: *H.M.C.*, VI, 40; VII, 42.

41. W. Fraser, *The Book of Carlaverock* (2 vols, Edinburgh, 1873), I, 5-18; II, 325-72; *Scots peerage*, VI, 485-6; *Complete peerage*, VIII, 599; Balfour, *Works*, II, 263; Baillie, *Letters and journals*, I, 194, 260; II, 74, 116, 164; Stevenson, *Revolution*, pp.270, 273; Clarendon, *Rebellion*, III, 120-1, n. 4; IV, 120-1; C. Hibbard, *Charles I and the Popish Plot* (Chapel Hill, North Carolina, 1983), pp.43, 96, 115, 152-3, 158, 180. His eldest son and heir, Robert, second earl of Nithsdale was a royalist, but

the 'Philosopher', as he was called, was more interested in astrology than politics. His kinsman, John Maxwell, seventh Lord Herries joined Montrose in 1644: *Scots peerage*, IV, 416-17; *Complete peerage*, IX, 562.
42. *Scots peerage*, I, 232-5; *Complete peerage*, I, 68-9. B.L. Eg. 2552 fo. 31. Dumfries sold most of his estates, including the barony of Sanquhar, to the first earl of Queensberry.
43. E. B. Livingston, *The Livingstons of Callendar* (Edinburgh, 1920), 111-13; *Scots peerage*, V, 443-7.
44. Livingston, *Livingstons of Callendar*, 143-75; *Scots peerage*, II, 360-3; *Complete peerage*, II, 488-9; *D.N.B.*, XXXIII, 399-400; Baillie, *Letters and journals*, I, 212; Clarendon, *Rebellion*, II, 384; Balfour, *Works*, IV, 371. In the 1650s Callendar made his peace with the occupying regime, received some compensation for his services from Charles II and died in 1674.
45. *Scots peerage*, VI, 417; Baillie, *Letters and journals*, I, 447-8, 477-8; II, 354-5.
46. Sir R. Gordon, *A genealogical history of the earldom of Sutherland* (Edinburgh, 1813); W. Fraser, *The Sutherland book* (3 vols, Edinburgh, 1893), I, 192-205; Douglas, *Baronage*, pp.2-5.
47. Douglas, *Baronage*, pp.325-6.
48. *Scots peerage*, IV, 159-61. Galloway's eldest son, Lord Garleis, was married to a daughter of the earl of Nottingham, and a younger son, Sir James Stewart, was married to a daughter of Sir Richard Houghton. Garleis died in 1638.
49. *Scots peerage*, III, 34-5; *Complete peerage*, III, 518-19; Newman, *Royalist Officers*, 233; Baillie, *Letters and journals*, I, 391. Crawford had been a professional soldier in Spain and only succeeded his brother to the impoverished estates in 1639. He allegedly offered to murder Argyll, Hamilton and Lanark in 1641. In 1642 he joined the king in England, was appointed a colonel of horse, fought at Edgehill, Marston Moor and was captured at Newcastle.
50. *Scots peerage*, I, 123-5; *Complete peerage*, I, 71-2. Airlie and his sons fought under Montrose, Sir Thomas Ogilvy being killed at Inverlochy.
51. J. Spalding, *Memorialls of the trubles in Scotland and in England, AD 1624-AD 1645*, ed. J. Stuart (2 vols, Spalding Club, Aberdeen, 1850-1); P. Gordon of Ruthven, *A short abridgement of Britain's distemper* (Spalding Club, Aberdeen, 1844), pp.229-30 and *passim*; Gordon, *Earldom of Sutherland*; Mathew, *Scotland under Charles I*, 135-51; *Scots peerage*, IV, 545-7; *Complete peerage*, VI, 681; *D.N.B.*, XII, 190-4. Huntly was executed by the Covenanters in 1649, and of his sons George, Lord Gordon, was killed fighting under Montrose at Alford in 1645; James, Viscount Aboyne, died in exile in 1648; and Lewis, third marquis of Huntly also died in exile.

52. Charles demanded their resignations: Clarendon, *Rebellion*, II, 59-61, n. 1.
53. Hibbard, *Popish Plot*, pp.42-3, 92-3 identifies Douglas, Winton, Nithsdale, Abercorn, Semple and Herries as the leading Catholic peers. For Scottish involvement in Catholic plots see pp.96-7, 115.
54. On the general background to this see K. M. Brown, 'Aristocratic finances and the origins of the Scottish Revolution', *EHR*, CIV No 140 (1989), 46-87; K. M. Brown, 'Noble indebtedness from the Reformation to the Revolution', *Historical Research*, LXII No 149 (1989), 260-75.
55. At the 1633 parliament a large number of courtiers were present, viz. Lennox, Hamilton, Nithsdale, Dunfermline, Abercorn, Tullibardine, Annandale, Stormont, Ayr, Napier, Morton and Stirling, while Buchan, Galloway, Kellie, Kinloss and Newburgh sent proxies. However, at the 1625 convention only Morton, Buchan, Galloway and Stormont attended, and in 1630 only Morton, Buchan, Tullibardine, Annandale, Ayr and Napier were there: *The acts of the parliaments of Scotland*, ed. T. Thomson and C. Innes (Edinburgh, 1814-75), V, 8, 166, 208. At meetings of the privy council between April 1635 and December 1637 the highest attendance was by Archbishop Spottiswoode who was there on 179 occasions. Of the courtiers who attended, Dumfries was there 107 times, Sir Robert Gordon 23, Belhaven 19, Annandale 13, Stirling 7 (although Lord Alexander attended 105 meetings), Tullibardine 6, Morton 4, Lennox and Hamilton 1 each: *The register of the privy council of Scotland*, 2nd series, ed. D. Mason and P. H. Brown (Edinburgh, 1899-1908), VI, pp.VIII-IX.
56. Malcolm, *Caesar's due*, pp.54-5.
57. J. Leslie, earl of Rothes, *A relation of proceedings concerning the affairs of the Kirk of Scotland, from August 1637 to July 1638*, ed. D. Laing (Bannatyne Club, Edinburgh, 1830), pp.130-1. This was a direct response to the sending-down of the courtiers, especially Hamilton, whose efforts to gather his friends and dependants at Dalkeith was frustrated by Rothes' appeal that 'none of the subscryvers, no not of his dearest friends and vassals should goe', Burnet, *Hamilton*, pp.45, 52.
58. Hutton, *Royalist war effort*, pp.3-32. Compare this with Scotland, where the Covenanters did nearly all the running: Stevenson, *Scottish Revolution*, chs 2-3.
59. Baillie, *Letters and journals*, I, 194.
60. See P. H. Donald, 'The King and the Scottish Troubles, 1637-1641' (unpublished University of Cambridge Ph.D. thesis, 1987), pp.15-79. However, I am not suggesting that a more astute use of his supporters in Scotland in 1637-8 would necessarily have saved the day for the king. The widespread nature of opposition

to Charles could not simply be resolved by old-fashioned baronial politics; see A. I. Macinnes, 'The Origin and Organization of the Covenanting Movement during the reign of Charles I, 1626-41; with a particular reference to the west of Scotland', (2 vols, University of Glasgow, Ph.D. thesis, 1987).

61. Hamilton 'would not stirr from the King, till he saw all our countreymen, which the Court any way might spare, sent home before him, to do for the King's service all the good offices they were able, at least to do him no evill offices with his prince by their misinformations in his absence', Baillie, *Letters and journals*, I, 74-5, 78.
62. Baillie, *Letters and journals*, I, 194; II, 67; Clarendon, *Rebellion*, II, 384; Stevenson, *Scottish Revolution*, pp.63-4. Those forfeited were Hamilton, Lennox, Morton, Kinnoul, Lanark, Crawford, Tullibardine, Traquair, Dumfries, Sir James Galloway and William Murray: Stevenson, *Scottish Revolution*, pp.291-2.
63. Baillie, *Letters and journals*, I, 305. In 1641 the privy council was purged of Huntly, Airth, Linlithgow, Home, Tullibardine, Galloway, Dumfries and Carnwath, leaving Lennox, Hamilton, Morton, Perth, Roxburghe and Sir James Galloway as the only royalists: Stevenson, *Scottish Revolution*, pp.239-40. In Parliament, Lords were prevented from taking their seats until they subscribed the Covenant and Lennox, Hamilton, Morton, Perth, Roxburghe, Lanark, Annandale and Dumfries were among those who did, but Linlithgow, Carnwath and Tullibardine remained under a summons to appear and answer charges against them: *ibid.*, p.234.
64. H. Guthry, *Memoirs* (Glasgow, 1747), pp.108-9. Carnwath said that in order to receive royal favour he would have to go to Ireland and join the rebels.

# *Eight*

## IRELAND AND SCOTLAND 1638 TO 1648

M. Perceval-Maxwell

The period of 1638 to 1648 stands among the more formative decades in the histories of both Ireland and Scotland. In recent years David Stevenson has written four books about the period, two of which are directly concerned with the subject of this article. Any consideration of the topic, therefore, must begin by recognising the contribution his work has made to our understanding of this period in Irish and Scottish history.[1] What follows leans heavily upon Stevenson's account of the political and military aspects of the relations between these two kingdoms, but an attempt is made here to look in a more general way at the interaction between these two countries, and particularly at the way in which English interests influenced this interaction.

Relations between Ireland and Scotland during this decade fall into three periods: first, that between 1638 and the outbreak of the rebellion in Ireland in October 1641; second, the period between 1641 and the swearing of the Solemn League and Covenant in Scotland and parts of Ireland; and finally, the period covering the last four years of the decade, from the adoption of the Solemn League and Covenant to the defeat of the duke of Hamilton's army in England.

It is generally recognised that the opening of Ulster to Scottish settlement in the reign of James VI and I led to a strong Scottish interest in Ireland. Nevertheless, the extent of Scottish penetration into Ireland by 1638 is often not fully appreciated. This is because there is virtually no reliable statistical data about the Scottish presence in Ireland after 1630. What estimates we possess about the size of the Scottish population in Ireland at this time come from Thomas Wentworth and Archbishop Laud, neither of whom had access to reliable sources of information on the subject, and both of whom tended to exaggerate the threat posed to the Dublin government by the Scottish presence in the north of Ireland. Such estimates put the Scottish population of Ulster at between 40000 men and 150000 'of that nation'.[2] It is likely that there were no more than 8000 Scottish males in Ulster in 1630.[3] However, considerable migration took place after this date up to 1638, and in the absence of famine, pestilence and war there must have been some natural increase. Just how quickly the Scottish population of Ulster grew at this time is a matter for speculation. In 1644 it was reported that 40000 males had taken the Solemn League and Covenant, and Lord Castlehaven, who served the Irish Catholics as a general, claimed that Sir Robert Stewart, who commanded the British forces in the west of Ulster, led 5000 to 6000 'old Scots', a term used to distinguish them from the Scots who landed in or after 1642. If we double this number to get total males, and this assumes a very high participation rate in the army, we reach a figure of about 10000 males for this part of the province alone, which implies that the rest of the province contained a similar number – at least.[4]

If statistical information on migration during the 1630s is scarce, other evidence on the active presence of the Scots in Ireland during the decade is abundant. Such was the flow of people between the two countries at this time, that when an inn which could house sixty 'horse and foot at once' burned down at Portpatrick, the owner had no difficulty in borrowing money to rebuild it.[5] George Monk, who conducted a survey of Ulster ports in 1637, made frequent reference to the Scottish presence. He mentioned, for instance, that near Carrickfergus Scottish peddlers swarmed 'about the country in great numbers'. The ports in Donegal, he remarked, were so dominated by Scots that it was useless to appoint an Englishman to collect customs there as the traders would ignore him.[6]

The strength of the Scottish presence in the west of Ulster is confirmed by the request of the Catholic bishop of Rapho to be transferred to the diocese of Derry because Donegal was so heavily planted with Protestants, both English and Scots, that he had 'scarcely enough to live decently on, nor can he have a single family to receive him.'[7] Moreover, this Scottish penetration extended beyond Ulster. From a variety of sources, but particularly the depositions taken from the British refugees after the rebellion had broken out, we can detect a Scottish presence in 1641 in the counties outside Ulster of Wexford, Cork, Limerick, Longford, Roscommon, Mayo and Sligo.[8]

The Scottish interest in Ireland was based essentially upon the desire for land. Under Thomas Wentworth, the policy of plantation in Ireland was extended to Connacht. As early as 1636, Scots, including the marquis of Hamilton, showed strong interest in participating in the project. The scheme was never implemented, because the necessary legislation had not passed through the Irish parliament before Wentworth's enemies had him killed, but Wentworth made it clear long before he faced his personal crisis that the Scots would not be allowed to participate in the development of Connacht; as a consequence, he told William Laud, 'the whole nation bear me the ill will of it.'[9] The next year Hamilton embarked on a bizarre scheme to drain Strangford lough and to plant the lands so recovered. This, too, Wentworth opposed.[10] We can imagine his reaction when he discovered that, just as the Scots were signing their National Covenant, Hamilton was leading another Scottish consortium to plant the lands in Londonderry recently forfeited from the city of London because of its failure to fulfil the original plantation conditions. When he heard of this venture, he warned Laud that if the project was approved, it would 'turn the English wholly out of Ulster', and 'you shall see' the Scots 'here in the very same rebellion against the clergy and discipline of the church as they are now in Scotland.'[11] Laud's agent in Ireland, John Bramhall, bishop of Derry, was even more outspoken. Hitherto, he noted, non-conformity had been restricted to the diocese of Down and Connor. Now, however, the 'contagion' had spread to his own diocese, with 'anabaptistical prophetesses . . . gadding up and down' and the doors of the churches barricaded for three months. Hamilton's agent in Ireland, a Robert Barr, he reported, was 'a maintainer of secret conventicles' and had only narrowly escaped being brought before the Irish court of high commission.[12]

Hamilton, of course, was not a Covenanter, and he subsequently allied himself with the Catholic earl of Antrim in his campaign to secure County Londonderry; Wentworth's and Bramhall's reaction to the scheme, however, shows how Scottish territorial ambitions in Ireland were linked in men's minds to the ideological struggle taking place, not only in Scotland, but also in England and Ireland.[13] Samuel Rutherford had to resort to sexual imagery to convey his sense of the religious bond that he saw linking the three countries together. In responding to Wentworth's persecution of the Scots in Ulster, he wrote to his fellow countrymen there:

> We do welcome Ireland and England to our well-beloved. We invite you, O daughters of Jerusalem, to come down to our Lord's garden, and seek our well-beloved with us; for his love

will suffice both you and us. We do send you love-letters over the seas, to request you to come to marry our King, and take part in our bed.[14]

If Rutherford saw the struggle in terms of all three countries, so too did the authorities in both England and Ireland. Once the Scots had taken the National Covenant, these officials quickly moved to the offensive, in Ireland even earlier than in England. It is perhaps significant that it was Hamilton rather than Wentworth who initiated this policy for Ireland, again reflecting the strong Scottish interest in Ireland. It was Hamilton who told Charles in June 1638 that the earl of Antrim 'may be of great use to you in this business.' He suggested that Antrim, who 'hath some pretensions to lands' in Kintyre, the Isles and the Highlands, would be pleased to attack the Covenanters on their flank.[15] In making this proposal, Hamilton was attempting to harness to Charles's cause the same territorial drive that had brought the Scots to Ireland, but was now trying to turn it in the opposite direction.

Wentworth had utter contempt for this exercise in military private enterprise; it was, he declared, 'vast, vain and childish' and he was proved right by events.[16] He was, however, happy for the state to launch a similar expedition. He thus embarked on a dual policy, first to neutralise the Covenanters' potential allies in Ulster by the imposition of an oath that dissociated those who took it from the National Covenant, and second, by the formation in 1640 of an army of 8000 men, made up largely of Catholic Irish, who could be depended on to fight loyally in Protestant Scotland. By the end of the summer, this army was poised in Ulster, ready to be launched against the Covenanters' flank.

No Irish Catholic forces landed in Scotland till 1644. The Covenanters' success at Newburn spared them the challenge of having to deal with a well-trained Irish army in the west while they confronted their king in the south. This military success relieved them of an immediate threat, but if their security was to last, they had to unseat the regime they confronted, and to do this they needed political allies in Ireland as well as England. They had already used John Livingstone, a Scottish minister who, after being forced out of Ireland in 1636, had established links with puritan leaders in England. Soon after the Covenant had been subscribed, Livingstone was sent down to London to renew these contacts.[17] More important, however, was the role of Sir John Clotworthy, an English settler in Ulster who had tried to help Livingstone while he was in Ireland, and who also had strong family ties with leading English puritans, being, for instance, related by marriage to John Pym.[18] Clotworthy, who had land interests in both Antrim and Londonderry, had quarrelled with Wentworth over both economic and religious issues. He was also connected with a group of planters in Ireland whose territorial ambitions had been curbed by Wentworth and who sought to control the Irish executive for their own interests.[19] In 1638, Clotworthy requested permission to go to England to represent those who had leased land from the city of London in Londonderry before it had been forfeited and whose leases were put in jeopardy by the proposed reorganisation of the city's land. By June 1638 he had gone to Edinburgh, where he established a method of communicating with the leading Covenanters. His next major appearance on the political scene was in November 1641, after his election to the Long Parliament, when he delivered a swingeing condemnation of Wentworth's Ireland in preparation for the impeachment proceedings.[20]

The demographic effects upon Ireland of the covenanting movement are much easier to document than the political ties between the two countries. As early as January 1639, Antrim reported to Hamilton a reverse migration inspired by the fear that the Irish court of high commission would persecute those in Ireland who sympathised with their Covenanter compatriots.[21] After Wentworth had imposed the anti-Covenanter oath, the flow of refugees to Scotland began seriously to jeopardise the economy as crops lay unharvested for want of labour.[22] This flow of population, however, also had political implications. One of the companies in the covenanting army that occupied Newcastle consisted of Scots who had fled Ireland and it was this group that submitted the first, formal set of Scottish accusations against the lord lieutenant on 2 December. This complaint echoed the charges made by Clotworthy in November to the Long Parliament. It complained of the 'great growth of popery and Arminianism' in Ireland during Wentworth's administration, but it also vented bitterness at the way that the Scots had been treated in Ireland in general.[23] This may have contributed to the Scottish desire, expressed during the treaty negotiations, for unity of religion in all the king's dominions. Such unity, on Scottish terms, would have given assurance against persecution, but such unity also meant, in effect, the imposition of the presbyterian form of worship, not only upon England, but upon Catholic Ireland. Edward Furgol has, with justice, described the effort to impose the Scottish form of worship by force as presbyterian imperialism, but, as in many other instances of imperialism, it was as defensive as it was aggressive.[24]

The 'Information of the Irish company at Newcastle' and the subsequent charges drawn up by the Scottish commissioners against Wentworth on 16 December 1640 reveal the extent to which Ireland under Wentworth was perceived as a threat to Scotland.[25]

The Scots had to drop the demand for unity of religion, though the treaty gave assurance that Scots in both England and Ireland would be 'free from censure' for subscribing the Covenant. Yet the treaty went further than this in trying to ensure that Scotland would not have to face a strategic threat again from the west. It declared 'that the kingdom of England nor Ireland shall not devise nor make war against the kingdom of Scotland without the consent of the parliament of England.'[26] Here the Scots found themselves in a contradictory position. This clause attempted to put Ireland under the jurisdiction of the English parliament, but Strafford had shown that the king could raise an army in Ireland against Scotland without reference to the English parliament. They therefore demanded that the treaty be ratified, not only by the king and the parliaments of England and Scotland, but also by the parliament of Ireland.[27] In so doing, however, they recognised that, until Ireland ratified the treaty, the English parliament had no jurisdiction in Ireland on the matter. As Sir Simonds D'Ewes explained to the English commons, the Scots wanted the articles confirmed in Ireland because the parliament there had declared its readiness 'to assist his majesty with their persons and purses against the Scots.'[28] The Scots were, in effect, asking the Irish parliament to legislate the end of its autonomy in matters of war, something it never did, for it never ratified the treaty.

Within two months of the Scottish ratification of the treaty the northern Irish had risen in rebellion on 22 October, and by the new year they had been joined by Catholics throughout Ireland.[29] In going into rebellion, the Irish were both reacting to the Scottish challenge to royal authority and copying it. Charles had pursued a moderate policy towards the religion of the majority in Ireland. Anti-Catholic legislation remained on the statute book but was seldom enforced. The rhetoric employed by the covenanting Scots and their allies in the English parliament suggested that a very different type of policy would be followed in Ireland if the Covenanters and their friends began to determine Charles's policy. Richard Bellings, the confederate Catholic historian, blamed the Scots in Ulster for forcing the Irish into rebellion. These Scots, he wrote, 'puffed up with the success of their bretheren in Scotland . . . prevailed with [the king] to approve their covenant' and had petitioned the English commons, not only for the suppression of prelacy and papists, but for their 'extirpation'.[30] At the same time, it was supposed in Ireland that if the Scots could assert their local autonomy so could the Irish. These two elements of animosity and example were brought together in the report of a statement made by the mayor of Limerick, who joined the confederate Irish. 'The Scots,' he was reported to have said, 'have mightily abused his majesty and they in this kingdom would see him righted,' but then he went on to add that, in the same way that the Scots 'took up arms for the maintenance of their religion[,] or rather [its] profanation, so we have done for the main because of ours being the true religion.'[31]

The rebellion in Ireland immediately raised the question of whether Scottish troops should be sent to Ireland, just as the Covenanters' challenge to Charles had raised the possibility of using Irish troops in Scotland. Many, including historians writing in our own era, have suspected Charles's complicity in the plotting that preceded the Irish rebellion.[32] However, it has recently been shown, using new evidence, that the earl of Antrim, on whose word this suspicion chiefly depends, must have been lying about the king's involvement when he made the allegation to Cromwell's government during the early 1650s.[33] This suggests that Charles was sincere when, on 28 October, and again on 1 November, he urged the Scottish parliament to send assistance to the British in Ulster, and specifically to reinforce Carrickfergus and Londonderry.[34]

The committee of the Scottish Estates which looked into the matter reported that nothing could be done until more information about what was happening in Ireland was available 'and our assistance be required by the parliament of England.'[35] There was no treaty obligation upon the Scots to consult the English parliament, but it is understandable why such approval was thought necessary, particularly as the Scots could not have expected reimbursement for any costs incurred in the absence of consultation. There remained a number of outstanding issues between Scotland and England that had not been settled in the treaty, including free trade among the three kingdoms and a common coinage. Thus, when the Scots sent commissioners south to deal with these issues, they added to the commissioners' mandate the question of 'what assistance Scotland shall give to England for the suppressing of the rebellion in Ireland.'[36]

Essentially, the Scots proposed that an army of 10 000 Scots be sent to Ireland, with England bearing the operational costs, such as pay and supply, once they had landed in Ulster. In return, the Scots wanted the right to govern three Ulster towns – Carrickfergus,

Coleraine and Londonderry – to be transferred to the Scottish army for the duration of the war and a share in any plantations that followed the confiscation of Irish lands.[37] The tripartite negotiations between the Scots, the king and the English lords and commons that preceded the launching of the Scottish military expedition were complex and stretched over several months. It was not until April 1642 that the first contingents of the army stepped ashore in Ireland, and another four months passed before it reached its full strength.[38] The Scots expressed considerable impatience at the delay. The earl of Loudoun, for instance, wrote to Wariston early in January 1642 saying, 'I believe if 5000 men had gone tymouslie to Ireland it might have kept life in the play and in many thousands of British who has lost their lives for want of tymous assistance.'[39] There was also the tendency to blame the growing quarrel between the king and his English parliament for the delay. Undoubtedly, this rift did complicate the negotiations, but if, as David Stevenson has shown, it was the English lords who offered the strongest resistance to the scheme of sending a Scottish expeditionary force to Ulster, the Scots must bear some responsibility for this resistance. The earl of Leicester and other lords informed the Scottish commissioners in the new year that their demands were of a 'hard digestion' for three principal reasons: the insistence by the Scots on the control over the Irish towns; the recompence desired in the form of post-war plantation land; and the proposed nature of the command over the Scottish forces, which gave the Scottish army a very high measure of autonomy while serving in Ireland.[40] As late as mid-February 1642, the Scottish council was still insisting on 'plantations and other recompenses' and control over Londonderry.[41] In the end, the Scots had to forgo both, though they were permitted to participate in the English adventurers' scheme that traded the promise of Irish land in the future in return for money to help suppress the rebellion.[42] Clearly, along with a genuine desire to help their compatriots in Ireland and protect their own shores from possible Irish penetration, the Scots saw in the rebellion the possibility for further expansion into Ireland. What Leicester and other lords feared was precisely what Wentworth had resisted before the war: the growth of Scottish influence in Ireland. As the Venetian ambassador observed, the majority of the lords suspected the Scots of 'cherishing ambitious designs' to take advantage of the rebellion in Ireland in order 'to become masters of that island'.[43]

This fear of Scottish encroachment on Ireland contributed to the difficulties the army faced when it arrived there. During 1642, the

Scots proved fairly effective in clearing the Irish forces from Counties Antrim and Down, and they brought some parts of Armagh under British control. Moreover, they ensured that the Irish did not continue to succeed in the way they had at the start of the rebellion. Thus they contributed to the stabilisation of the British position even in those areas, such as the west of Ulster, where they had no physical presence.[44] Nevertheless, the Scottish army failed to destroy the Irish military capacity even though the Irish were equipped with inferior arms. Much of the responsibility for this failure, however, lay with the English parliament, for once it had succeeded in persuading the Scots to send an army into Ireland, it failed to provide the necessary supplies. Stevenson has calculated that by the end of 1643 the English parliament should have spent £312 000 sterling on the Scottish army in Ireland, but that 'only a tiny part of this was ever received.'[45] Given the outbreak of the civil war in England, it is easy to accept that the parliament there had few resources to spare to maintain an army remote from the central struggle; yet there are grounds to suspect that it was not simply the lack of resources in England that led to the neglect of the Scottish army in Ireland. Sir John Clotworthy appears to have worked strenuously in England to frustrate any effort on the part of the English parliament to live up to its obligations. Just as he had formerly opposed the attempt of the Dublin government under Wentworth to assert its authority in Ulster, and had used Edinburgh to reinforce his efforts, now he opposed the influence of Edinburgh in the province and manipulated Westminster to achieve his ends.

Clotworthy was associated with a group of planters in Ireland who sought to gain control of the Irish executive in order to add to their already substantial estates. Until 1629, this group had looked to Lord Falkland, the lord deputy, for leadership. After he left office in that year, they tended to be associated with the earl of Cork. The group included such men as Roger Jones, first Viscount Ranelagh, president of Connacht, whose son had married one of Cork's daughters, and who was Clotworthy's father-in-law; Sir William Parsons, master of the Irish court of wards and a justice when the rebellion broke out, who was referred to in Cork's will as the earl's 'credible and constant friend'; and Sir Adam Loftus, vice-treasurer of Ireland, two of whose daughters married into the Parsons family. Wentworth's appointment as lord deputy undermined the ambitions of this group, although several of its members continued to serve on the Irish council during his administration.[46] Once the Scottish crisis rendered Wentworth's position insecure, this group linked up with his enemies in England, such as the earls of Arundel and Holland, and Sir Henry Vane, to remove him from office. We find Clotworthy, for instance, pressing for the appointment of the earl of Holland to succeed Wentworth as governor of Ireland during February and March 1641; almost certainly, having acquired control of the highest office in Ireland, this group planned to implement the plantation of Connacht to its own advantage.

The rebellion ended the prospects for the plantation of Connacht, but opened the possibility for the acquisition of more substantial tracts of land once the rebellion had been crushed. However, if the Scots, or worse still, the Scottish state, established a firm foothold in Ulster, Clotworthy and his friends would face competition both for land and political influence in Ireland.

As early as December 1641, one Scot reported a rumour that Clotworthy was secretly feeding information to the king, but he was, nevertheless, sufficiently trusted to be a member of the committee of both houses involved in the negotiations to send a Scottish army to Ireland. At the end of January 1642, he, along with such peers as Hamilton, Bedford, and Saye and Sele, visited the Scottish commissioners at their lodgings and pleaded that 2500 Scots should cross to Ireland immediately even though the terms of the treaty were far from being settled.[47] Later that year, Clotworthy himself went to Ireland to command his regiment in the north, but by July it was reported that he and Monro were at odds.[48] The extent to which he had turned against the Scots in Ireland, however, only emerges from a document which, though undated, must have been written in 1644.

This document listed, under twenty-one headings, Clotworthy's 'disaffection' to the Scots 'both in England and Ireland'. It stated that Clotworthy and his officers held commissions from Leicester, who 'never meant well to the Irish service', and that Sir John and Lord Conway, the commander of the British settler forces in Ulster, had joined 'to cross and oppose' the Scots since their first arrival.[49] Subsequently, on his return to Westminster, when the king and the earl of Ormond arranged a cessation with the confederate Catholics in Ireland in September 1643, Clotworthy, it was charged, had pressed for the appointment of Lord Lisle, Leicester's son, as commander of all the British forces in Ulster, and had worked against those in England who wanted to make General Leslie captain general of all forces in Ireland opposing the cessation.[50] The charge continued that Clotworthy had told M.P.s that the Scots in Ulster 'did little service' there and that 'the work' could be done without them.[51]

To this end, he had moved in parliament that the Scottish army be reduced to 2000 men, a force 'which he and his party could master well enough'.[52] Significantly, not only was he alleged to have used his position on parliamentary committees to hinder supplies reaching the Scottish army, he was also accused of working, first with his father-in-law, Viscount Ranelagh, and after his death, with Ranelagh's son, in embezzling supplies intended for Ireland.[53] These charges may have been exaggerated, and we do not know what, if any, reply Sir John made to them, but the reference to Ranelagh and his son suggests that the pre-war alliance was still in effect. Moreover, the aim of the alliance had not changed. Clotworthy, it was reported, had said at one point 'that if the Scots had the command of the army in Ireland, they would conquer it and keep the kingdom to themselves', and had pressed in the committee of adventurers 'to plant the aforesaid part of Ulster by this rebellion only with the English adventurers . . . excluding the Scottish nation all together'.[54] If Thomas Wentworth, the old enemy, could have heard these opinions, he would have applauded. Three years after his death, Clotworthy and his friends had adopted his policy of keeping the Scots at bay.

The accusations against Clotworthy illustrate the multidimensional nature of the interaction between Scotland and Ireland during the 1640s. At one level there was conflict, essentially between the Irish and the Scots, inspired by Scottish strategic interests. These had been aroused, both by the self-consciousness consequent upon the covenanting movement, and by the threat to that self-consciousness posed by Wentworth's attempt to use an Irish Catholic army to suppress it. As the Scottish commissioners in London remarked in January 1642, a Scottish army had to be sent to Ireland 'to prevent the errection of a popish kingdom in so near a neighbourhood as may continually disturb our peace and purity . . .'[55]

At another level, the struggle for land, which had begun during the middle of the sixteenth century, continued. It was, after all, under Mary Tudor that legislation had been passed in Ireland proclaiming all Scots in Ireland to be outlaws, and it was only under James VI and I that this legislation was repealed. This territorial struggle, therefore, was a triangular one involving the English, the Irish and the Scots. Finally, there was the ideological struggle, which existed independently of the other two levels of competition (yet also interacted with them), and at the centre of this struggle lay the Solemn League and Covenant, approved in Scotland and by the English parliament in the autumn of 1643.

There was considerable delay in applying the Solemn League and

Covenant to Ireland, in large part because Scotland procrastinated about keeping her army there, but by April 1644 it had been decided to maintain in Ireland those regiments that had not already returned to Scotland, and to send supplies to other British forces that allied themselves with Scotland and the English parliament. On 4 April General Monro and his army at Carrickfergus signed the Covenant.[56] Within a week, the British forces in the Ards and Clandeboye had followed suit, although their commanders, Sir James and Lord Montgomery, declined to sign. By 28 April the population in Derry had defied its mayor and royalist governor and had adopted the Covenant, and by June, most other centres, with the exception of Lisburn and Newry, had demonstrated popular support for the Covenant even in the face of opposition from army commanders.[57] At Belfast, the anti-Covenanter commander was displaced by Monro's army, and men like Sir Audley Mervin, governor of Derry, and Lord Montgomery had agreed to sign by June as they accepted Covenanter control of most of Ulster as an accomplished fact.[58]

In looking at the Solemn League and Covenant, we have to recognise that its adherents in Ireland saw it from a perspective different from that of their counterparts in Scotland. To the Scots, one of its attractions was that it opened the way for the religious unity within the three kingdoms that they had desired, but been denied, during the negotiations leading to the treaty of London in 1641. Section I of the Solemn League and Covenant bound its adherents to 'the reformation of religion in the kingdoms of England and Ireland, in doctrine, worship, discipline and government, according to the word of God, and the example of the best reformed churches'; it also required those who signed it to 'endeavour to bring the Churches of God in the three kingdoms to the nearest conjunction and uniformity in religion . . .'[59] There can be little doubt that to most Scottish Covenanters this implied that the English and Irish Churches were to be built upon the Scottish model. In Ireland, however, the interest in the Solemn League and Covenant stemmed, not from a desire to see religious unity in the three kingdoms, but from a perception of the Covenant as a means of survival against the Irish. As I have tried to show elsewhere, the popular enthusiasm for the Solemn League and Covenant in Ulster among the British settlers, and the willingness of the populace as a whole to defy the established leaders when signing it, demonstrates the general conviction that only with the protection of the power of Scotland could the settlers remain in Ireland.[60] When it was thought that Monro might return to Scotland with his army, many of the settlers also decided to leave.[61] The Solemn League and Covenant was seen, therefore, primarily as a guarantee of security.

We gain a unique insight into how one Scottish settler in Ulster regarded the Solemn League and Covenant from an unpublished document among the Hastings manuscripts deposited in the Huntington Library of San Marino, California. This was probably acquired by John Bramhall, the Protestant bishop of Derry and friend of Wentworth, as it is among his papers. The document is undated, anonymous, and consists of one page only, but internal evidence reveals that it was written by a Scot in Ireland at the time that the Solemn League and Covenant was being considered for adoption there.[62] Although favourably disposed towards the Covenant, the author identified more with the Church of Ireland than with the Scottish Church and was probably a Scottish minister who had served in Ireland before the rebellion broke out.

The document is similar to others of the period in which various aspects of the Solemn League and Covenant were considered in the form of 'objections' and 'responses' to those objections.[63] In looking at the first article of the Covenant, for instance, the first objection was phrased as follows: 'Doe wee sweare by this article to the observation of the present practise of the church of Scotland in discipline and government?'[64] The answer was: 'No, but . . .'; and then it was explained that, as the Covenant applied to the civil as well (spelled 'asweil') as the ecclesiastical order, those who swore to the Covenant were bound 'to defend and maintaine the just Lawis and liberties one of another *against the common enemie*.'[65] Therefore, it was argued, if 'their [the Scots] church government[,] being established by Law amongst them', should be threatened by papists or prelates, 'we should assist' them, but it also followed that 'they in the Lyke case . . . are bound to maintaine and assist us'. The author then observed that this did not mean that 'we' are 'bound to the particular observation of that forme of government now practised in Scotland, or to any other form of government, untill an establishment be made by Lawful authoritie according to the word of god'. 'They', he went on to emphasise, 'are not to be a rule or standard for us to square our reformation by, or wee to them, but the word of god to us both.'[66]

The author made an interesting point when addressing the second article of the Covenant – that which dealt with the 'extirpation' of popery, prelacy and heresy. He argued that the Covenanters were not bound 'to destroy the personis of Prelatis or Papists as such', but only in as much as they plotted, combined or rose up 'against us by force'.

If such persons did not engage in these activities, 'we are bound', read the response, 'to labour for the Conversion, not destruction[,] of their personis.'[67] Finally, in dealing with the question of 'incendiaries and malignants', or article four of the Covenant, the same distinction was drawn between those who 'travel with desynes against the Publike' and those with no such design, against whom 'humanitie will teach us not to violate the bondis of Nature and friendship.' 'The wordis of the Covenant', he concluded, 'reflect not so much to men's personis as to their desynes.'[68]

This document may be unique in a second sense, in that the author may have been the only person to hold such views. No claim that this was a general interpretation of the Covenant in Ireland can be sustained. We see, nevertheless, a distinctly Irish Protestant perception of the Covenant, and a moderate, rational and humane one at that, comparable in principle (though obviously not in specifics) to at least some of the statements made by the confederate Catholics about religious issues.[69] In effect, it justified the adoption of the Covenant as a mechanism that assisted self-defence against what were seen as aggressive and offensive forces. It also recognised the necessity of calling upon Scottish resources to sustain this self-defence. At the same time, it asserted an Irish autonomy, or a right to establish local rules for the government of Church and State in Ireland, independent of Scotland. Thus we see the well-known phenomenon at work of the colonist asserting a measure of independence while, at the same time, relying heavily upon the mother country.

The most striking characteristic of Scottish-Irish relations during the final phase of the decade from 1638 to 1648 is the reversal of the aggressive-defensive roles of the two kingdoms. Monro's army was unable to prevent the Irish counter-expedition that provided Montrose with the core of his army. This expedition, led by Alasdair MacColla, whose motives were more clan-oriented than national, in some senses served the Irish in the same way as Monro's army in Ireland served Scotland. The series of strikes at the Covenanters' heartland by Montrose with his followers ensured that Monro would not receive the supplies he needed for an aggressive policy in Ireland.[70] The Irish military investment, therefore, ensured that the Scots would not become a major threat to the Kilkenny confederation, just as the Scottish investment in Monro's forces ensured that no major expedition could be launched from Ireland against the covenanting movement. Monro's failure to prevent the conjunction between Scottish royalists and the Scots-Irish clansmen does not invalidate this statement. Kilkenny and Edinburgh, moreover, treated their expeditionary forces in much the same way, supporting their initial thrust, and then neglecting, if not actually abandoning them. In the Scottish case, the most notable achievement of Monro's army between 1645 and 1648 was its survival despite its crushing defeat by Owen Roe O'Neill at Benburb in 1646.

These strategic and tactical similarities, however, conceal one fundamental difference between Scottish and Irish war aims. Behind the Scottish military expeditions lay an essentially 'unionist' policy for the three kingdoms. Irish war aims, for all their commitment to the three kingdoms, remained essentially 'separatist', if that term is understood in a seventeenth-century rather than a modern sense. Reference has already been made to the Scots' desire from 1641 to 1644 for unity of religion in the three kingdoms. 'Religion,' as they said, 'was the base and foundation of kingdoms and estates and strongest bond to tie the subjects to their prince in true loyalty.' It followed that there should be 'one confession of faith, one form of catechism, one directory for all parts . . . of public worship of God . . . in all the churches of his Majesty's dominions.'[71] 'All good means,' therefore, had to be 'used for the conversion of papists, and for the extinguishing of papistry in all his majesty's dominions.'[72]

By contrast, the Irish never expressed a desire to extend influence beyond the island of Ireland. One of the most extreme statements of Irish war aims emanated from Limerick, where one Catholic was reported to have stated that the Irish aim was 'to have a free state to themselves, as they had in Holland, and not to be tied unto any king or prince whatsoever.'[73] It was more common, however, for the Irish to demand 'the like freedom that the [king's] subjects in England have', and perhaps more significantly, 'all which Scotland hath, and commonly all kingdoms subject to any monarch.'[74] In other words, what they sought was internal political autonomy, the link between the three kingdoms being provided by the king and the king alone, which explains their desire to restore the king's prerogative. They sought freedom of religion for themselves, but they did not comment on religion beyond Ireland, nor did they ask for free trade between the kingdoms. The broad vision of the Scots led to an overextension of their resources so they attempted to fight on two, and after Montrose's appearance, on three, fronts at once. As a result, they failed to gain any significant benefit from the outcome of the struggle and became bitterly divided at home. The insular vision of the Irish, on the other hand, proved no more rewarding. They failed to send sufficient assistance either to Scotland or to England to prop up the monarchy, the one institution which might have been able to give them constitutional satisfaction within the context of the three kingdoms. Miscalculation in both Scotland and Ireland led ultimately to a common fate, a union imposed by England at the hands of an army led by Oliver Cromwell.

NOTES
1. D. Stevenson, *The Scottish revolution, 1637–44: the triumph of the covenanters* (Newton Abbot, 1973); *Revolution and counter-revolution in Scotland* (London, 1977), *Alasdair MacColla and the highland problem in the seventeenth century* (Edinburgh, 1980); *Scottish covenanters and Irish confederates: Scottish-Irish relations in the mid-seventeenth century* (Belfast, 1981).
2. *The earl of Strafforde's letters and dispatches*, ed. W. Knowler (London, 1739), II, 185, 195, 270; Wentworth to Northumberland, 15 April 1639, Sheffield City Library (S.C.L.), Strafford MS 10, pt b, p.69.
3. M. Perceval-Maxwell, *The Scottish migration to Ulster in reign of James I* (London, 1973), p.311.
4. Sir A. Mervin to Ormond, 25 April 1644, Bodl., Carte MS 10, fo. 409; J. Touchet, earl of Castlehaven, *The earl of Castlehaven's review: or his memoirs of his engagement and carriage in the Irish wars* (London, 1684), pp.81, 84. Raymond Gillespie has pointed out to me that if the Scots in Ulster numbered 8000 at the end of James's reign (Perceval-Maxwell, *Scottish migration*, p.311), an increase to 20000 by 1638 represents an increase of over eleven per cent per annum, which is abnormal for pre-industrial Europe. Some 10000 of those who took the Solemn League and Covenant in Ireland would have been Scots who arrived in 1642 as part of Munro's army. Some would have been English, but the majority were probably Scots who had settled in Ulster before 1641 or had been born there.
5. *Register of the privy council of Scotland, 1638–43* (Edinburgh, 1906), p.279.
6. British Library (B.L.), Harl. MS 2138, fos 176, 179v, 180, 188.
7. Fr Gonzalez to Fr Peregra, 15 Jan. 1639, Jesuit Archives, Dublin, MS A, no. 66. Translation, pp.224-6.
8. M. O'Dowd, 'Rebellion and war', typed MS, pp.6–7. I am grateful to Dr O'Dowd for permitting me to consult her typescript before publication; Perceval-Maxwell, *Scottish migration*, p.360; Depositons, T.C.D., 817, 170, 291v; T.C.D., 829, fo. 302; T.C.D., 823, fo. 169; T.C.D., 830, fos 1v, 4.
9. H. F. Kearney, *Strafford in Ireland, 1633–41* (Manchester, 1959), pp.85–103; Wentworth to Hamilton 10 April 1636, Scottish Record Office (S.R.O.), Hamilton MS GD 406/1/350; memo of

counties in Ireland to be planted, n.d., *ibid.*, 512; Wentworth to Laud, 7 Aug. 1638, *Strafford's letters*, II, 195.
10. *Calendar of state papers relating to Ireland, 1633-47*, p.152; Wentworth to Hamilton, 10 April 1636, S.R.O., Hamilton MS, GD 406/1/377; Lord Cromwell to Hamilton, 3 Aug. 1637, *ibid.*, 384; Hamilton to Cromwell, 1 Sept. 1637, *ibid.*, 387; Hamilton to Wentworth [*c.* 1637], *ibid.*, 8381.
11. T. W. Moody, *The Londonderry plantation 1609-41* (Belfast, 1939), pp.358, 394; C. V. Wedgwood, *Thomas Wentworth, first earl of Strafford, 1593-1641. A revaluation* (London, 1961), p.248; Instructions for farming Londonderry, S.R.O., Hamilton MS GD 406/1/501; Wentworth to Laud, 1 Mar. 1638, S.C.L., Strafford MS 7, fo. 70v.
12. *Cal. S. P. Ire., 1633-47*, p.181.
13. Wentworth to Laud, 3 Nov. 1638, S.C.L., Strafford MS 7, fo. 134; Antrim to Hamilton, 11 Jan. 1639, S.R.O., Hamilton MS, GD 406/1/652.
14. *Letters of Samuel Rutherford with biographical sketches of his correspondents*, ed. Andrew A. Bonar (Edinburgh, 1863), II, 254.
15. [Hamilton] to king, 15 June 1638, S.R.O., Hamilton MS GD 406/1/10775, 10488.
16. Wentworth to Laud, 10 April 1639, S.C.L., Strafford MS 7, fo. 182.
17. J. Livingstone, *A brief historical relation of the life of Mr John Livingstone*, ed. Thomas Houston (Edinburgh, 1848), pp.76, 83, 85, 87-8, 96-8; R. Baillie, *The letters and journals of Robert Baillie*, ed. D. Laing (Edinburgh, 1841), I, 64.
18. R. Loeber, 'Downing's and Winthrop's plantation in Ireland: the preamble to the New England plantation' typed MS. I am grateful to Dr Loeber for permitting me to consult his typescript before publication; M. F. Keeler, *The long parliament 1640-41, a biographical study of its members* (Philadelphia, 1954), p.136.
19. J. S. Reid, *History of the presbyterian church in Ireland* (Belfast, 1867), I, 230; M. Perceval-Maxwell, 'Protestant faction, the impeachment of Strafford and the origins of the Irish civil war', *Canadian Journal of History*, XVII (1982), 235; Moody, *Londonderry plantation*, pp.395, 446; *Cal. S. P. Ire., 1633-47*, pp.194-5.
20. *Diary of Sir Archibald Johnston of Wariston 1632-1639*, ed. G. M. Paul, Scot. Hist. Soc. 1st ser., LXI (Edinburgh, 1911), II, 351; *The journal of Sir Simonds D'Ewes*, ed. W. Notestein (New Haven, 1923), pp.13-14.
21. Antrim to Hamilton, 14 Jan. 1639, S.R.O., Hamilton MS GD 406/1/652.
22. Clandeboye to Wentworth, 23 Aug. 1639, *Strafford's letters*, II, 382-3; Borlase to Wentworth, 13 July 1639, S.C.L., Strafford

MS 19, pt b, no. 80; Chichester to Wentworth, 16 Aug. 1639, *ibid.*, no. 92.
23. Information against the lord lieutenant, 2 Dec. 1640, National Library of Scotland (N.L.S.), Adv. MS 34.2.9., fos 157–v.
24. Edward M. Furgol, 'The military and ministers as agents of presbyterian imperialism in England and Ireland, 1640–1648', John Dwyer, Roger A. Mason and Alexander Murdoch, eds, *New perspectives on the politics and culture of modern Scotland* (Edinburgh, 1985), pp.95–115.
25. John Nalson, *An impartial collection of the great affairs of state, from the beginning of the Scotch rebellion* (London, 1682), II, 686–8.
26. *Acts of the parliaments of Scotland*, V, 342.
27. *Ibid.*, p.343.
28. B.L., Harl. MS 163, fo. 209v.
29. *Acts parl. Scot.*, V, 337–43; M. Perceval-Maxwell, 'The Ulster rising of 1641, and the depositions', *Irish Historical Studies*, XXI (1978), 148–9.
30. J. T. Gilbert, *History of the confederation and the war in Ireland, 1641–1643* (Dublin, 1882), I, 15.
31. Depositions, T.C.D., 829, fos 304–v.
32. Patrick J. Corish, 'The rising of 1641 and the catholic confederacy, 1641–45', T. W. Moody, F. X. Martin, F. J. Byrne, eds., *A new history of Ireland* (Oxford, 1976), III, 290; Aiden Clarke, *The old English in Ireland* (Worcester and London, 1966), pp.159–60; Caroline M. Hibbard, *Charles I and the popish plot* (Chapel Hill, 1983), pp.211–14.
33. Conrad Russell, 'The British background to the Irish rebellion', *Historical Research*, LXI (1988), 179.
34. Sir James Balfour, *The historical works of Sir James Balfour* (Edinburgh, 1824), III, 119–20, 128–9.
35. *Ibid.*, p.125.
36. *Acts parl. Scot.*, V, 404–5; Stevenson, *Scottish covenanters*, p.44.
37. Stevenson, *Scottish covenanters*, pp.56–7; *Lords journals (L.J.)*, IV, 491–2.
38. Stevenson, *Scottish covenanters*, pp.69, 72.
39. Loudoun to Wariston, 5 Jan. 1642, N.L.S., Wodrow MS 66, No. 98.
40. Scot. coun. to commissioners, 5 Jan. 1642, S.R.O., PA 13/3, fo. 1v.
41. Scot coun. to commissioners, 15 Feb. 1642, *Ibid.*, fo. 12.
42. Stevenson, *Scottish covenanters*, p.61.
43. *Calendar of state papers Venetian, 1640–2*, p.267.
44. Stevenson, *Scottish covenanters*, pp.103–38.
45. *Ibid.*, pp.122, 132, 137, 140, 144.
46. M. Perceval-Maxwell, 'Protestant faction', pp.236–55.
47. Scot. commissioners to Scot. coun., 26 Jan. 1642, S.R.O., PA

13/3, fo. 5.
48. E. H., ed., *The history of the warr of Ireland from 1641 to 1653 by a British officer of the regiment of the Sir John Clotworthy* (Dublin, 1873), p.10; A. Borthwick to Wariston [July 1642], N.L.S., Wodrow, fol. MS 60, fo. 216v. This letter stated that Essex had just been appointed general for the parliament, an appointment which was made in July.
49. Sir John Clotworthy's disaffection to the Scots, both in England and Ireland [*c.* 1644], N.L.S., Wodrow fol. MS 65, fo. 198v.
50. *Ibid.*, fo. 198-v.
51. *Ibid.*, fo. 198.
52. *Ibid.*, fo. 198.
53. *Ibid.*, fo. 200.
54. *Ibid.*, fo. 200v.
55. Scot. commissioners to Scot. coun., 26 Jan. 1642, S.R.O., PA 13/3, fo. 5.
56. Stevenson, *Scottish covenanters*, p.160.
57. M. Perceval-Maxwell, 'The adoption of the Solemn League and Covenant by the Scots in Ulster', *Scotia*, II (1978), pp.7-10.
58. *Ibid.*, p.10; Stevenson, *Scottish covenanters*, p.161.
59. S. R. Gardiner, ed., *The constitutional documents of the puritan revolution 1625-1660* (Oxford, 1906), p.268.
60. M. Perceval-Maxwell, 'The adoption of the Solemn League and Covenant', pp.10-11.
61. *Ibid.*, p.7.
62. Huntington Lib., Hastings MS (H.L., HA) 15051. A modern hand in a note on the document states that it dates from about 1638. This is obviously an error. The document clearly refers to the Solemn League and Covenant and not to the National Covenant.
63. For another example of the same genre, though one expressing very different concerns, and from an English point of view, see Huntington Lib., EL 7731.
64. H.L., HA 15051.
65. *Ibid*. My emphasis.
66. *Ibid*.
67. *Ibid*.
68. *Ibid*.
69. Gilbert, *History*, II, 2-4.
70. Stevenson, *Alasdair MacColla, passim*; Stevenson, *Scottish covenanters*, pp.165-89.
71. The Scottish commissioners' desires concerning unity in religion . . . , N.L.S., 33.4.6, fos 142-3.
72. 'The Scottish desire that no papists be about his majesty or the prince', B.L., Stowe MS 187, fo. 53v.
73. Depositions, T.C.D., 829, fo. 310v.
74. Gilbert, *History*, I, 279, 289.

# INDEX

Abbott, George, archbishop of Canterbury, 7, 24n
Abercorn, earls of, *see* Hamilton
Aberdeen, 13, 14, 15, 47
Act of Classes, 139, 141
Act of revocation, 14, 113
Airlie, earls of, *see* Ogilvie
Alexander, Henry, 3rd earl of Stirling, 163-4, 186n
Alexander, William, 1st earl of Stirling, 157, 162-4, 177-8, 180-1, 186n
Altars, *see* communion tables
Althusius, Johannes, 49, 79-82
Ames, William, 49
Ancram, earls of, *see* Ker
Annandale, earls of, *see* Murray
Anstruther, Sir Robert, 171
Anstruther, Sir William of that ilk, 157, 171
Antrim, county, 197, 201
Antrim, earls of, *see* Macdonnell
Arbroath, Declaration of, 79
Ards, 204
Argyll, marquis and earls of, *see* Campbell
Armagh, county, 201
Arminianism, 34, 35, 38, 41, 50, 57
Arminius, Jacobus, 34
Armies: of the Bishops' Wars (1639-40), 145; Scots, in Ulster, 199-201; of the Solemn League and Covenant (1643-7), 141-2, 143-6, 147; of the Kingdom (1648), 140; of the Covenants (1649-51), 141-2; uniforms of, 145-6
Armour, 137, 144, 145-6

Articles, Committees of, 115
Artillery, 144-5
Arundel, earls of, *see* Howard
Atholl, earls of, *see* Murray
Augustine, St, 46
Ayr, 126

Baillie, Robert, 19, 68, 73, 90, 101, 186n
Balcanquhal, Walter, 9-10
Balfour, Sir William, 177, 186n
Balmerino, Lords, *see* Elphinstone
Balmerino Affair, 16
Banding, 6, 45
Banquetting House, 5
Barclay, William, 79
Barr, Robert, 195
*Basilikon Doron*, 52
Bedford, earls of, *see* Russell
Belfast, 204
Belhaven, lords, *see* Douglas
Bellenden, Adam, bishop of Dunblane, 3
Bellings, Richard, 198
Benburb, battle of, 207
Berwick, Pacification of, 95-6
Bible, 19, 74, 82
Bishops' wars, 20-1, 96-9, 113, 117
Boece, Hector, 72
Book of Canons (Scottish), 8, 14, 17, 33, 36, 55, 93, 110
Book of Common Order, 10
Book of Common Prayer (English), 3, 8, 10
Border, Anglo-Scottish, 106
Borthwick, Eleazor, 17
Bower, Walter, 72
Boyd, Robert, 47

# Index

Boyd, Zachary, 50
Boyle, Richard, earl of Cork, 201
Bramhall, John, bishop of Derry, 195, 205
Brechin, bishops of, *see* Lindsey
Brooke, Lords, *see* Greville
Bruce, Thomas, 1st earl of Elgin, 175
Buchan, earls of, *see* Erskine
Buchanan, George, 71, 72, 74, 79
Buckingham, dukes of, *see* Villiers
Bullinger, Henri, 70
Butler, James, earl (later 1st duke) of Ormonde, 202

Calderwood, David, 10, 90
Callendar, earls of, *see* Livingstone
Calvin, Jean, 47, 79
Calvinism, 34-8, 41, 48, 70, 76
Campbell, Archibald, Lord Lorne and 1st Marquis of Argyll, 16, 17, 81, 114, 120, 122, 125, 136, 140, 162, 169
Campbell, John, 1st earl of Loudoun, 16, 21, 83, 120, 123-4, 183, 200
Cannon, 137, 144-5, 148
Canons, Book of, 8, 14, 17, 33, 36, 55, 93, 110
Cant, Andrew, 17-18
Canterbury, archbishops of, *see* Abbott, Laud
Carmichael, James, 70
Carnwath, earls of, *see* Dalzell
Carlisle, earls of, *see* Hay
Carrickfergus, 194, 199, 204
Cartwright, Thomas, 49
Cary, Henry, earl of Falkland, 201
Cassilis, earls of, *see* Kennedy
Castlehaven, earls of, *see* Tuchet
Catholicism, Roman, 33, 35, 38-41, 52
Cecil, Robert, 1st earl of Salisbury, 4-7
Chain of Being, 71
Chairtres, John, 31
Charles I, 2-4, 5-7, 8-10, 12, 15, 17, 32, 34, 36, 39, 41, 74-80, 95-7, 100, 108-10, 126, 134-6, 155-83, 198-9, 202
Charles II, 2, 21, 114, 126, 161-2, 166, 170-1, 173
Church Courts (Scottish), 33
Clandeboye, 204

Classes, Act of, 126-7
Clotworthy, Sir John, 17, 98-100, 196-203
Coinage, 4, 73
Coleraine, 200
Commission on Teinds, 14
Committee of Both Kingdoms, 147
Committee of Estates, 138
Committees of War, 138-9
Communion Tables, 2, 9, 25n
Composite Supplication (Dec. 1637), 107
Connacht, 202; Plantation of, 195
Consecration (of Bishops), 7
Convention of estates, 92, 116, 199
Convocation (English), 9
Conway, Edward, 1st Lord, 202
Cork, earls of, *see* Boyle
Cork, county, 194
Coronations, 2-4, 22, 71, 114; coronation oaths, 3-4, 29n, 42
Coupar, William, 50
Court of High Commission, 33-5, 107, 110
Covenant, see National Covenant and Solemn League and Covenant
Cowper, Lords, *see* Elphinstone
Crane, Ryce, 52
Crawford, earls of, *see* Lindsay
Crichton, William, earl of Dumfries, 157, 175-6, 181
Cromwell, Oliver, 114, 126-7, 164, 172, 199, 208
Cross Petition, 5, 167
Cumbernauld Band, 15, 168-9, 176
Cunningham, William, earl of Glencairn, 7

Dalzell, Robert, 1st Lord Dalzell, 157, 171
Dalzell, Robert, 1st lord Carnwath, 170, 183
D'Ewes, Sir Simonds, 198
Denmark, Scottish contacts with, 101
Derry, bishops of, *see* Bramhall
Devereux, Robert, 2nd earl of Essex, 178
Dickson, David, 17, 48, 57
Dirleton, earls of, *see* Maxwell
Divine Right of Kings, 71, 109
Donegal, County, 194
Douglas, Robert, minister, 107, 114, 125

Douglas, Robert, Lord, 1st Lord Belhaven, 157, 164–5, 178, 182
Douglas, Robert, 7th earl of Morton, 161
Douglas, William, 6th earl of Morton, 157, 158, 161, 170, 179, 182–3
Douglas, William, 1st earl of Douglas, 158, 161
Down, county, 201
Down and Connor, 201
Down, diocese of, 195
Dumfries, earl of, *see* Crichton
Dunbar, battle of, 127, 141–2, 144–5
Dunblane, bishops of, *see* Bellenden
Dunkeld, bishops of, *see* Lindsay
Dunkeld, Lords, *see* Galloway
Dunfermline, earls of, *see* Seton
Duns Covenant (1556), 45
Durham, James, 48
Dysart, earls of, *see* Murray

Edgehill, battle of, 122
Edinburgh, 21, 68, 76, 114–17, 197; University of, 70
Elgin, earls of, *see* Bruce
Elphinstone, John, Lord Cowper, 16
Elphinstone, John, Lord Balmerino, 16, 77, 178
Engagers (1648), 107, 114, 125–6, 139–41, 143–5, 160–1, 169, 172, 174–5
England, Scottish relations with, 1, 92–5, 98–101
Episcopacy, Scottish, 17–19, 23, 33–6, 40, 71, 77, 90–1, 92, 94, 99, 107–9
Erskine, Alexander, 3rd earl of Kellie, 167, 174
Erskine, James, 1st earl of Buchan, 157, 174, 178
Erskine, John, 1st Lord Erskine, 174
Erskine, John, 2nd earl of Mar, 159, 161–2, 173–4
Erskine, John, 3rd earl of Mar, 157–8, 173–4, 182–3
Erskine, Thomas, 1st earl of Kellie, 166–7, 182–3, 189n
Erskine, Thomas, 2nd earl of Kellie, 166
Essex, earls of, *see* Devereux
Estates, Scottish, 118, 144
Eucharistic Doctrine, 33

Falkland, earls of, *see* Cary
Fast Days, 31
Federal Theology, 46–8, 52–5
Fiennes, Nathaniel, 100
Fiennes, William, Viscount Saye and Sele, 99–100, 202
Finn, 69
Five Articles of Perth, 7, 90–2, 108, 168, 172, 174, 176, 180
Forbes of Carse, John, 46, 50
Fortifications, 137, 146
Foxe, John, 52
France: armies of, 134, 136, 140; and the Covenanters, 95, 101; Wars of Religion in, 76

Galloway, James, 1st Lord Dunkeld, 172–3
Galloway, earls of, *see* Stewart
General Assemblies, 12, 13, 18, 33–4, 36, 42, 46, 52, 54, 56, 91, 94, 100, 108, 110, 114–15, 117, 120, 123, 160, 174, 185n
Gentlemen Pensioners, 4
Gibson, Sir Alexander, of Durie, 100
Gillespie, George, 18, 100
Glasgow, 82, 113, 114, 117
Glasgow, archbishops of, *see* Lindsay
Glencairn, earls of, *see* Cunningham
Gordon, George, 1st marquis of Huntly, 7, 24n
Gordon, George, 2nd marquis of Huntly, 158, 177
Gordon of Gordonstoun, Sir John, 155, 177
Graham, James, 5th earl and 1st marquis of Montrose, 20, 121, 126, 146–8, 156–8, 162, 168–9, 172, 174–5, 182, 206–7
Graham, William, 7th earl of Menteith, 157, 174
Grand Remonstrance, 13–14
Granvelle, Antoine Perrenot, Cardinal, 77
Great Seal of England, 7
Great Whore of Babylon, 19
Greville, Robert, 2nd Lord Brooke, 99–100
Guthrie, John, bishop of Moray, 3
Greyfriars Kirk, 69, 83

Haddington, earls of, *see* Hamilton
Haig, William, 98

# Index

Hamilton, Alexander, 136, 144–5
Hamilton, John, 48
Hamilton, James, 2nd earl of
  Abercorn, 157–60, 185n
Hamilton of Priestfield, Sir James, 175
Hamilton, James, 3rd Marquis and
  1st duke of Hamilton, 15–18,
  93–7, 122, 126, 140, 147, 157,
  159–61, 165, 179–83, 185n,
  193–7, 202
Hamilton, Thomas, 2nd earl of
  Haddington, 157–8, 175, 182
Hamilton, William, 1st earl of
  Lanark, 126, 160, 166
Hampton Court Conference, 8
Hay, George, 1st earl of Kinnoul,
  157, 161, 170
Hay, George, 2nd earl of Kinnoul,
  161, 170, 178, 182
Hay, George, 3rd earl of Kinnoul, 170
Hay, James, 1st earl of Carlisle, 170
Hay, William, 4th earl of Kinnoul,
  170
Heidelberg Confession, 47
Henderson, Alexander, 17, 38, 53,
  54, 73, 77, 81, 83, 107, 113
Henderson, Sir Francis, 172
Henderson, John, 171
Henrietta-Maria, Queen, 39
Henry, Prince, 163–5, 173
Hepburn, Sir Adam, 120, 131
Holland, earls of, see Rich
Holyroodhouse, 2
Hooper, John, 46
Hooker, Richard, 18
Howard, Theophilus, 14th earl of
  Suffolk, 3
Howard, Thomas, earl of Arundel,
  202
Howie, Robert, 47
Huguenots, 109
Huntly, marquisses of, see Gordon

Incendiaries, 116
Ireland, Irish links with, 6, 8, 15–17,
  21, 93–4, 121–3, 194–208
Iranaeus, 46
Irish Rebellion, 20, 140, 194,
  198–201

James IV, King, 2
James VI, King, 4–5, 7–8, 10, 12,
  13, 15, 34, 38, 52, 70, 71–2, 74,
  78, 90–3, 115, 155–6, 165–6,
  168–9, 171, 173, 175, 176, 178,
  202
Johnston of Wariston, Sir Archibald,
  37–8, 49, 56, 68, 75–6, 81, 83,
  96–7, 98–103, 120, 131, 178,
  182, 200
Jones, Roger, 1st Viscount Ranelagh,
  201–2

Kellie, earls of, see Erskine
Kennedy, John, earl of Cassilis, 16, 56
Ker, Robert, 1st earl of Roxburghe,
  157, 163, 181–2
Ker, Robert, 1st earl of Ancram, 157,
  164, 168, 181, 183, 186n
Ker, William, 1st earl of Lothian, 31,
  157–8, 164, 179, 181, 186n
King's Covenant, 108, 167–8, 170,
  177
Kilkenny, Confederation of, 206
Kinnoul, earls of, see Hay
Kintyre, 196
Knox, John, 45, 73, 109

Lanark, earls of, see Hamilton
Lances, 144
Laud, William, archbishop of
  Canterbury, 8, 13, 16, 22n, 35,
  39, 77, 93, 97–8, 180, 194–5
Legends, Gaelic, 69
Leicester, earls of, see Sidney
Leinster, 20
Lennox, dukes of, see Stewart
Leslie, Alexander, earl of Leven, 120,
  136, 138, 140–1, 143–4
Leslie, David, 141–2, 143, 145, 147,
  174
Leslie, John, 6th earl of Rothes, 16,
  37, 68, 77, 83, 100, 155, 178,
  183
Levellers, 12
Leven, earls of, see Leslie
Limerick, 194, 199, 207
Lindsey, Alexander, bishop of
  Dunkeld, 3
Lindsay, David, bishop of Brechin, 3
Lindsay, Ludovick, 16th earl of
  Crawford, 158, 177, 189n
Lindsay, Patrick, archbishop of
  Glasgow, 3, 23n
Linlithgow, earls of, see Livingstone
Lisburn, 204

Lisle, Viscounts, *see* Sidney
Lithgow, William, 73, 74
Livingstone, James, 1st earl of
  Callendar, 157–8, 176–7, 181–2
Livingstone, John, 1st Lord
  Newburgh, 173–4, 178, 181, 196
Lockhart, Sir James, 177–8
Loftus, Sir Adam, 201
London, 117, 195–7; treaty of, 118, 198, 204
Londonderry, 195–204
Long Parliament, 95, 100, 117, 123
Longford, County, 194
Lords of the Congregation, 10, 46
Lords of Erection, 16
Lorne, Lords, *see* Campbell
Lothian, earls of, *see* Ker

Maccolla, Alasdiair, 206
Macdonnell, Randal, 2nd earl of
  Antrim, 20, 93, 127, 195–9
Magna Carta, 19
Major, John, 72
Mar, earls of, *see* Erskine
Marston Moor, battle of, 144
Mary of Guise, 46
Mary Queen of Scots, 72
Mass, Roman, 17
Maule, Patrick, 1st earl of Panmure, 165–6, 180, 182
Mauchline Moor, battle of, 126
Maxwell, James, 1st earl of Dirleton, 165, 180, 181, 187n
Maxwell, John, bishop of Ross, 3, 166
Maxwell of Pollok, Sir George, 36, 48
Maxwell, Robert, 1st earl of Nithsdale, 157, 166, 175, 180, 181, 182
Mayo, County, 194
Melvillianism, 8, 36, 40, 71, 73, 108
Menteith, earls of, *see* Graham
Mercenaries, Scottish, 136–7
Meroz, 127
Mervin, Sir Audley, 204
Migration to Ulster, Scots, 194
Military Revolution in Scotland, 124–5, 137–8, 141, 148
Millenarianism, 51–4
Monck, George, 194
Monro, Robert, 204–6
Montague, Richard, bishop of
  Chichester and Norwich, 35

Montgomery, Robert Viscount, 204
Montrose, marquisses of, *see* Graham
Moray, bishops of, *see* Guthrie
Mornay, Philippe Duplessis, 71–2
Morton, earls of, *see* Douglas
Murray of Stanhope, Sir David, 172
Murray, James, 2nd earl of
  Annandale, 167, 187n
Murray, James, 4th earl of
  Tullibardine, 169
Murray, John, 1st earl of Atholl, 157
Murray, John, 1st earl of Annandale, 157, 167–8, 169, 178, 180–1, 187n
Murray, Mungo, 2nd viscount
  Stormont, 157–8, 169, 182
Murray, Patrick, 3rd earl of
  Tullibardine, 157, 168–9, 178, 182
Murray, Will(iam), 1st earl of Dysart, 161–2, 168, 178, 180, 182, 185n
Muskets, 137, 143, 145

Napier, Archibald, 1st lord Napier, 157–8, 168, 177, 180
Napier, Archibald, 2nd lord Napier, 168
Napier of Merchiston, John, 51
National Covenant:
  ambiguities of, 90
  appeal to England, 16–18, 96–101
  as a band, 42–5, 90
  and civil disobedience, 54–7, 73–4
  Dutch Revolt as model for, 77–8
  and foreign support, 100
  interpretations of, 11–14, 38–45, 77–81, 91–3, 107–13
  making of, 90
  military defence of, 17, 20–1, 95, 134–48
  and the Millenium, 52–4
  opposition to, 14–16, 159–78
  origins of, 7–8, 32–7, 45–9, 75, 91, 107–8
  and previous Covenants, 12, 45–9, 70–1
  political organization in defence of, 113–20
  popular reaction to, 31–3, 54, 58–9, 68
  propaganda for, 94, 96–9
  and resistance theory, 70–5
  Scots at Court and, 159–78

# Index

signing of, 1, 31, 37-8, 68-9, 91
and union of the kingdoms, 6, 92-4
National Petition (20 Sept. 1637), 107
National Supplication (17 Oct. 1637), 107
Negative Confession (1581), 11, 12, 38-9, 70, 76, 90, 94, 108
Netherlands, Scottish links with, 74-5, 97-9, 101, 109, 134, 136-7, 207
Netherlands, Revolt of the, 76-9
Netherlands, armies of, 136, 142-3
Newburgh, earls of, *see* Livingstone
Newburn, 196
Newcastle, 197-8
Newry, 204
Nithsdale, earls of, *see* Maxwell

Oaths, Scottish, of 1639, 95
Ogilvie, James, 1st earl of Airlie, 158, 177
Olevanius, Casoar, 46-7
O'Neill, Owen Roe, 207
Ormond, earls of, *see* Butler

Pamphleteering, 38
Panmure, earls of, *see* Maule
Paraeus, David, 46-7
Parker, Robert, 49
Parliament (Scottish), 12-13, 36, 49, 92, 97, 102, 115, 119, 138, 191n
Parsons, Sir William, 205
Penal statutes, 40
Perth, *see* Five Articles of
Petitions (1637), 32, 37, 38, 44, 55; of English peers, 99, 102
Phillip II, king, 77
Pikes, 137, 143, 145
Pistols, 137, 144, 145
Plotters (1641), 116, 121
Portpatrick, 194
Prayer Book (1637), 10, 13, 14, 16, 17, 32, 35, 37, 44, 55, 90, 93, 95, 98, 107, 110, 166, 168; riots over, 44
Prelacy, 15
Prerogative, royal, 42
Presbyterianism, 8, 9, 12, 15, 18, 33, 36, 37, 40, 55, 56, 113, 114, 123
Preston, battle of, 126
Privy Council, 5, 7, 9, 22, 122, 134, 135, 148
Protestors, 127

Psalm book, 33
Pym, John, 190

Quartering, 139

Rabelais, Francois, 77
Rait, William, 58
Ranelagh, Viscounts, *see* Jones
Raphoe, Roman Catholic bishops of, 194
Reformation, Scots appeal to, 93
Regicide, 21
Resolutioners, 127
Rich, Robert, earl of Holland, 3, 178, 202
Ripon, 117
Rollock, Henry, 53
Rollock, Robert, 47, 50-1, 53, 70
Roscommon, County, 194
Ross, bishops of, *see* Maxwell
Rothes, earls of, *see* Leslie
Roxburghe, earls of, *see* Ker
Row, John, 9
Rowe, James, 57
Rubens, Peter-Paul, 5
Rump Parliament, 22
Rushworth, John, 22n
Russell, William, earl of Bedford, 202
Rutherford, Samuel, 17, 34, 52, 81, 100, 107, 113, 116, 195-6, 202

St Andrews, archbishops of, *see* Spottiswoode
Salisbury, earls of, *see* Cecil
Saye and Sele, Viscounts, *see* Fiennes
Scone, coronations at, 2
Scot of Harden, Sir William, 49
Scotichronicon, 72
Seton, Charles, 2nd earl of Dunfermline, 74, 157-8, 174-5
Ship Money, 99
Sidney, Philip, Lord Lisle, 202
Sidney, Robert, earl of Leicester, 200, 202
Sligo, county, 194
Smart, Peter, 96
Solemn League and Covenant, 21, 73, 114, 123, 124, 193, 194, 203-5
Spain, the Covenanters and, 95
Spalding, John, 3, 13, 14, 16, 17, 68
Spottiswoode, John, archbishop of St Andrews, 3, 9, 24n, 75, 172, 191n

Spottiswoode, Sir John, 172
Star Chamber, 5
Stewart, Alexander, 1st earl of Galloway, 157, 178, 182
Stewart, Esme, 70
Stewart, James, 4th duke of Lennox, 156-7, 160, 179, 182-3
Stewart, John, 1st earl of Traquair, 16, 94-5, 121, 157, 172-3, 182-3
Stewart, Sir Robert, 194
Stewart, Sir William, 172
Stirling, coronation at, 2
Stirling, earls of, *see* Alexander
Stormont, viscounts, *see* Murray
Strafford, earls of, *see* Wentworth
Strangford lough, 195
Suffolks, earls of, *see* Howard
Supplication and Complaint, 14
Supremacy, Royal, 92
Sweden, Scottish links with, 97, 117, 134, 138-9, 144
army of, 136-7, 138, 140-1, 142-5, 148
Swords, 137, 143, 145

Tables, The, 91, 107, 110, 113, 115, 117-18, 138
Teinds, 14, 16
Thirty Years War, 39, 52
Tower of London, prisoners in, 16
Traquair, earls of, *see* Stewart
Treaty of London, *see* London
Tuchet, James, earl of Castlehaven, 194

Tudor, Mary, 203
Tullibardine, earls of, *see* Murray

Ulster, Scots in, 20, 123, 140-6, 194
Union of the Crowns, 1, 4, 73, 79, 91, 96
Unionism, in the 17th century, 4-6, 8, 41, 102, 123
Union, Act of (1707), 123
Urquhart, Sir Thomas, 77, 186n
Ursinus, Zacharius, 46

Valesius, Thomas, 30
Vane, Sir Henry, 202
Vanlore, Sir Peter, 186n
Villiers, George, duke of Buckingham, 156, 159-61, 164, 167, 170, 175-6
*Vindiciae contra Tyrannos*, 71

War of Three Kingdoms, 20
Wentworth, Thomas, earl of Strafford, 93-5, 193-205
Western Association, 140-2
Wexford, county, 194
Whiggamore raid, 126, 138, 140
Windebanke, Sir Francis, 95
Worcester, battle of, 128

Yeomen of the Guard, 4

Zwingli, Ulrich, 70